Lester
Pearson
and the
American
Dilemma

Also by   *Lester Pearson and the Dream of Unity*
PETER STURSBERG *Diefenbaker: Leadership Lost*
                 Diefenbaker: Leadership Gained
                 Mister Broadcasting
                 Those Were the Days
                 Agreement in Principle
                 Journey Into Victory

PETER STURSBERG

Lester Pearson and the American Dilemma

DOUBLEDAY CANADA LIMITED
Toronto, Ontario
DOUBLEDAY & COMPANY, INC.
Garden City, New York
1980

ISBN: 0-385-13479-7
Library of Congress Catalog Card No. 79-7716

Copyright © 1980 by Peter Stursberg
All rights reserved

Printed and bound in Canada by T. H. Best Company Limited
Book design by Robert Garbutt

First Edition

Preface

        THIS IS THE SECOND volume of my oral or living history study of Lester B. Pearson, the only Canadian to win the Nobel Peace Prize. It deals with his career in international affairs, first as diplomat, then as external affairs minister and prime minister, and, as the title suggests, is concerned with the problem of Canadian–American relations while paying full attention to his work at the United Nations and in peace-keeping generally. The first volume, *Lester Pearson and the Dream of Unity*, concentrated on national affairs and was about Pearson as politician and prime minister and his efforts to keep Quebec in confederation. The publication of *Lester Pearson and the American Dilemma* completes my oral or living history examination of the prime ministers of the tenth decade of Canadian confederation. The Pearson books were preceded by two volumes on John G. Diefenbaker, the only Conservative prime minister of Canada in more than forty years, *Diefenbaker Leadership Gained 1956-62* and *Diefenbaker Leadership Lost 1962-67*.

   Lester Pearson and the American Dilemma is different from the three other books of this documentary series in that the latter depended upon interviews with politicians or people in the political process while this volume relies mainly on the memories of diplomats. I must say that I found them to be as frank and forthcoming as the politicians, which is yet another proof that people are more at ease when speaking and recording their views than when writing. Quite obviously, diplomats are just as much a part of the electronic era as the rest of us, and, presumably, spend as much time on the telephone as we do. Since this book is about international affairs, I went abroad for some of the interviews, and I must thank such statesmen as Dean Rusk, Lord Home of the Hirsel, Averell Harriman, Malcolm Macdonald, and Henry Cabot Lodge for giving me so much of their time to talk about Pearson and Canadian foreign policy, and for not putting any conditions on their interviews. In fact, Dean Rusk, who told me that he was not writing his memoirs, did not even ask to see the transcript.

I interviewed most of Mr. Pearson's associates in the Department of External Affairs. Although both Hume Wrong and Norman Robertson, who had been so close to him in the early days, had died some time before I began this project, I believe that the recollections of Paul Martin, H. F. "Temp" Feaver, Escott Reid, John Holmes, George Ignatieff, Arnold Smith and Geoffrey Pearson, to mention but a few, provide the fullest possible re-creation of Canada's greatest diplomat and the policies he espoused.

Only one person really turned me down, and he was Pierre Elliott Trudeau. I wanted to interview him because when he became prime minister, he attempted to reverse the pro-Western foreign policy that had been established by Mike Pearson, and lead Canada down a neutralist course. Some three months after I made the request, and after I had submitted a typewritten list of questions, a Mr. McDonald from the prime minister's office rang me to say that Mr. Trudeau would not grant the interview: he was too busy. I was able to fill out the details of this essay into non-alignment by interviewing Mitchell Sharp, who was Trudeau's foreign minister; Paul Hellyer, who was in the Cabinet at the time; and Léo Cadieux who led the fight against the scuttling of our NATO commitments.

All of the interviews for this book and the other Pearson and Diefenbaker books are deposited in the Public Archives of Canada and will be opened for general research in 1981. Full transcripts had to be made, and I am grateful to the Parliamentary Library in Ottawa for undertaking this onerous task. I have had the greatest cooperation and assistance from the Public Archives and the

Parliamentary Library: both Dr. W. I. Smith, the Dominion Archivist, and Erik Spicer, the Parliamentary Librarian, have been strong supporters of this living history project. I want to thank Ernest J. Dick and Jacques Gagné of the historical sound recording section for their help, and J.H. "Cy" Taylor for checking the manuscript. Most of the photographs in this book came from the comprehensive Duncan Cameron collection in the Public Archives.

Finally, since the challenge of this book is in the editing, to convert the spoken word into the written word, I am greatly indebted to my editor at Doubleday, Betty Jane Corson. Once again, I wish to say how much I owe to my wife, Jessamy, for her patience and understanding.

Peter Stursberg
Vancouver, B. C.
November 1979

Prologue

AS A SON OF THE MANSE, Lester Pearson could be said to have been born into the establishment of turn-of-the-century Canada, which was still emerging from colonial status to nationhood. His father, the Reverend Edwin Arthur Pearson, was a Methodist minister and an influential figure in the countryside and small towns around Toronto where he conducted his ministry. When he was given an honorary doctorate of divinity by Victoria College in 1927, the tribute accompanying the award described him as being "in very many respects the ideal Christian minister." He had the largest church in Peterborough and the Pearson family were looked upon as social leaders in the community; young Lester was remembered as a friendly boy who was always ready and willing to join in any games or sports. Although he was only twelve years old, he entered the town's annual ten-mile road race and showed his stamina and determination by finishing the course.

The future Nobel Peace Prize winner and prime minister was the second of the parson's three sons: his birthday was April 23, 1897; his birthplace, Newtonbrook, one of the small towns that have been swallowed up by metropolitan Toronto. He was named Lester Bowles Pearson after his mother, Annie Sarah Bowles, and his maternal grandmother, Jane Lester. It was during World War One when he joined the Royal Flying Corps that he acquired the nickname "Mike" from his commanding officer, who did not consider Lester to be a fitting name for a would-be fighter pilot. His immediate family and those who knew him before the war always called him "Lester" or "Les."

By his own account, Lester Pearson had a happy, secure childhood. The parsonage, which was usually a big brick house with a large yard, "was the centre of our life, growth and training," he wrote in his memoirs. "The air was pure and the skies clear and blue. We did our own work and made our own fun, together. The pace of life was less hurried, and we lived more closely with nature." Every three years or so, there was a move to a new parish, which meant new surroundings and new circumstances, but, fortunately for him, he was able to make friends easily, and the Ontario school system was very much the same wherever they lived.

For the parson's son, regular and repeated attendance at church was expected, four times on Sundays and usually once again during the week, which "became at times almost oppressive" and, Pearson indicated, did not make for very faithful attendance in later life. However, it did provide him with an extensive knowledge of the Bible; he could quote passages from both the Old and the New Testaments, and when the question of Palestine came up at the United Nations, he found that he was dealing with a place that was familiar. In fact, he probably knew more about the geography of the Holy Land than he did of his native Ontario— from Dan to Beersheba, through all the land of Israel. And there was a lot said at Sunday school about the historic home of the Jews but nothing about the Arab inhabitants.

His father was the kind of clergyman who could be sincerely described as "a man of peace"; he was greatly concerned over the arms race in Europe and warned his congregation about the evils of rapacious nationalism. These sermons must have impressed his son, sitting below the pulpit, and they were to be confirmed by his own experience as a teen-aged soldier in World War One. "The children of the Methodist parsonage had to set an example," Pearson wrote in his memoirs, and there was no doubt that, as a result of this upbringing, he acquired the Protestant work ethic and a highly developed sense of duty. At the same time, his lackadaisical attitude, the seeming absence of any ambition, may have been due to the religious teaching and the conviction of his parents that such things as the future and a career should be left in the hands of the Lord.

Then, there was the traumatic effect of the Great War. In 1915, when he had just turned eighteen, Lester Pearson volunteered and was shipped overseas almost immediately to serve with the army medical corps at Salonica. It was a dismal, dreary front, and there was mounting frustration over the fact that the Allies could not advance but would not withdraw, and, finally, after almost two years of this, Pearson got his father to pull some strings and have him transferred to England. There, he got his commission and was in training to be a flyer when he was involved in a traffic accident and was invalided home.

It was an experience that he never forgot. John Holmes, who was one of his principal aides when he was external affairs minister, remembered a dinner party in London just a year or so before he died. Mike had just been to see the film "Oh, What a Lovely War," and he was full of it and obviously was in sympathy with the presentation, Holmes said. There was an outpouring of reminiscences about Salonica, about what a ghastly campaign it had been, all the bungling that had gone on, and about how the warm clothing that was supposed to have been sent to Salonica went to Gallipoli.

Pearson took his officer training course at Oxford, and it was the best four months of his war service. It was something that he had always dreamed of, to live at an Oxford college. When he returned to Canada and was demobilized and had graduated from the University of Toronto, he was determined to return to Oxford as a student and was able to do so by winning a Massey Foundation Fellowship. His tutor at St. John's College was W. C. Costin, who was also the tutor, at different times, of Michael Stewart, who became British foreign secretary, and Dean Rusk, the American secretary of state from 1961–69.

When Mike applied to join the fledgling Department of External Affairs in Ottawa, Vincent Massey, who had been his professor at the University of Toronto and was to become the first Canadian governor-general, wrote a "private and confidential" letter to Dr. O. D. Skelton, the under-secretary of the department. In it, he said of Pearson that "there is something curiously loose jointed and sloppy about his mental make-up which, as a matter of fact, is reflected in some measure in his physical bearing." However, his other qualities might offset this deficit. While Dr. Skelton agreed wholeheartedly with Mr. Massey, saying that he had "exactly hit the nail on the head," he nevertheless reversed his comment and wrote, "There is something curiously loose jointed in his physical bearing and perhaps to a lesser extent in his mental make-up."

Of course, what Dr. Skelton was describing were the relaxed manners of an athlete, and Lester Pearson was a keen sportsman, playing hockey and football at the University of Toronto, hockey and lacrosse at Oxford, and even semi-pro baseball one summer in Guelph, Ontario. It was his prowess as an athlete that produced his superb sense of timing, which stood him in good stead in diplomacy and politics. John Holmes remarked on it, and so did another associate, Escott Reid, who said that he had this "uncanny feeling for the precise moment"; Holmes, who was referring to his activities at the United Nations, spoke of him as a great tactician who was "a born athlete" and "a brilliant quarterback."

Lester Pearson was a classical example of an old-fashioned liberal, according to Douglas Fisher, the political commentator and former member of Parliament, who was not a great admirer of his. Pearson, he said, was the product of the University of Toronto's history school approach, and Fisher had taken the same course, although much later. There was a great deal of "on the one hand" and "on the other hand," and the emphasis was on careful reading of sources and assembling the key features together in a running narrative. There were no long, deductive leaps forward, and not much involvement in theory. Pearson was the high priest of this cool and cautious analysis; he had not only studied it but had actually taught it.

Above all, Lester B. Pearson was a member of the elite, which, in Canada, was an elite not so much of money but of education and upbringing; he had been brought up in the parsonage and in the Methodist Church, he had done his duty in the war, he had been to the Universities of Toronto and Oxford, and he symbolized what everyone regarded as the ideal Canadian. Thus, he would be perfectly suited for diplomacy, which was an elitist occupation if there ever was one.

Contents

The Cast

Howard Green	*Canadian External Affairs Minister (1959-63)*
Paul Martin	*Canadian External Affairs Minister (1963-68)*
Mitchell Sharp	*Canadian Finance Minister (1965-68)*
	External Affairs Minister (1968-74)
Dean Rusk	*U. S. Secretary of State (1961-69)*
William P. Bundy	*U. S. Assistant Secretary of State (1964-69)*
Alex Douglas-Home	*British Commonwealth Secretary (1955-60)*
(Lord Home)	*Foreign Secretary (1960-63) Prime Minister (1963-64)*
Malcolm MacDonald	*British statesman*
Walter Gordon	*Canadian Finance Minister (1963-65)*
	President of Privy Council (1967-68)
Louis Rasminsky	*Governor of Bank of Canada (1961-73)*
William Clark	*British journalist and official*
	Vice-President of World Bank
Gen. E. L. M. Burns	*Canadian disarmament negotiator*
	Commander of UNEF (1956-59)
Arnold Smith	*Canadian diplomat*
	Secretary-General of Commonwealth (1965-75)
Geoffrey Pearson	*Canadian diplomat*
	Son of L. B. Pearson

Charles Ritchie	*Canadian diplomat*
	Ambassador to United States (1962-66)
Averell Harriman	*U. S. diplomat*
John Holmes	*Canadian diplomat*
Escott Reid	*Canadian diplomat*
George Ignatieff	*Canadian diplomat*
Henry Cabot Lodge	*U. S. diplomat*
Chester Ronning	*Canadian diplomat*
	Envoy to China (1945-51)
Max Wershof	*Canadian diplomat*
Ernest Côté	*Canadian diplomat and official*
	Columbia River Treaty negotiator
Paul Hellyer	*Canadian Minister of National Defence*
	(1963-67)
Léo Cadieux	*Canadian Minister of National Defence*
	(1967-70)

ALSO
H.F. "Temp" Feaver, Jean Fournier, John Matheson,
Richard O'Hagan, J.W. Pickersgill, Sidney Pierce,
Mel Watkins, Lubor Zink.

Lester
Pearson
and the
American
Dilemma

I In at the Beginning

IN THE SUMMER of 1926 Lester B. Pearson came to Ottawa to do research in the Public Archives of Canada on the United Empire Loyalists, about whom he intended to write a book (a lot of material was collected but the book was never written). While there, he visited Parliament and, on more than one June evening, sat in the gallery of the House of Commons, fascinated by the debate raging below that was to lead to the 1926 general election. He was also fortunate enough to meet some of the important people in the capital, including Dr. O.D. Skelton, who had just been appointed under-secretary of state for external affairs. Apparently the young history professor from the University of Toronto made an impression, for Dr. Skelton wrote to him the following year, telling him of examinations that his department was holding and suggesting that he should be a candidate. Although Pearson said that he felt no urge to leave academic life, he nevertheless decided to fill out the forms when they arrived, which they did in June 1928. By August of that year he was launched on his diplomatic career.

Mike Pearson could not have come to Ottawa, nor met the people he did, at a better time, but, as his son Geoffrey was to say, his timing was always good: Mike never seemed to plan his career but left it to chance or fate, although when the opportunities occurred, he was ready or made himself available. Dr. Skelton was looking for bright young university men to staff the foreign service that he was setting up and to become the future ambassadors and high commissioners of Canada. The colonial era

3

had ended; actually, it came to a close with World War One and Prime Minister Sir Robert Borden's insistence on Canada signing the peace treaty and having independent membership in the League of Nations. Even before the war, Earl Grey, who had recently retired as governor-general, had advocated that a separate ministry or agency be split off from the Colonial Office to look after Canada, Australia, and the other self-governing parts of the British Empire. It was not until 1926 that the Dominions Office was set up and the constitutional framework created in Westminster for the emerging Commonwealth. That was the year Sir Joseph Pope died: he was the first deputy minister of external affairs, and he would have scarcely envisaged such a change, nor appreciated it.

The Department of External Affairs was Sir Joseph Pope's creation. It was he who had argued that there should be an extension of the secretary of state's office to handle all the dispatches and messages from the Imperial government, and that it should be a separate entity and come under the aegis of the prime minister. He modeled the department, which came into being on June 1, 1909, after the Australian Department of External Affairs. The self-governing dominions were affected by the same problem—a breakdown in communication with Westminster—as their administrations became more complex. It was necessary to have a clearing house for the correspondence that flowed through the governor-general to and from the Colonial Office; that was all the department was, at first.

Sir Joseph Pope, who had been secretary to Sir John A. Macdonald, Canada's first prime minister, would look askance at any suggestion that there should be Canadian representation abroad or an independent foreign policy. A product of the Empire, he was reluctant to interfere with the long-established tradition of British responsibility for the country's external relations. However, a Canadian advisory office had to be established to service Canada's membership in the League of Nations, and a commissioner-general's office was opened in Paris. The rush of postwar events was pushing Sir Joseph against his will into the twentieth century. However, while he could not do much about the expansion abroad, he did keep the growth of the department at home to a minimum. When Dr. Skelton took over, the Ottawa staff consisted of three officers. There were not many more when Lester Pearson joined; he had taken the examination for first secretary and come first, so that he started with a fairly high rank, just below that of Jean Desy, the newly appointed counselor of the department.

Accommodation was cramped in the East Block of the Parliament

Buildings. Everyone wanted to be there because the prime minister had his office there and the Cabinet met in the Privy Council Chamber on the second floor. Pearson had to share a room in the attic with two other newly recruited officers. The East Block was a Victorian Gothic building with spires and crenellated roof, and while the offices on the main floor were spacious enough and well furnished, those on the third floor (the attic) were under the roof and had sloping ceilings and old wooden desks. Dr. Skelton's quarters were on the main floor and, according to an eyewitness account, his desk, couch, and chairs were piled high with files, which may not have been due as much to his untidy working habits as to the fact that the department had very little storage space. In fact, as late as 1941, Norman Robertson, who succeeded Dr. Skelton as under-secretary on the latter's death, was complaining about the lack of accommodation; he said, in a memo to the prime minister, "We have five third secretaries working in a single room immediately below the [Privy] Council chamber," and, "The question of bringing in additional temporary assistance from outside or retaining somebody like Colonel [Georges] Vanier for service in the department may turn, at present, on the fact that we have no room in the place for a single additional man."

During 1929 Pearson was able to escape from the attic of the East Block for a brief period and spend a couple of months in Washington on loan to the Canadian Embassy there. In 1930 H. F. "Temp" Feaver, who had just got his master's degree in international law at Harvard, joined the department as a third secretary and was allotted a desk in Pearson's office. Temp (a schoolboy nickname given him because of losing his temper) recalled that the cluttered working conditions did not slow Mike down.

H. F. FEAVER

[His desk] was like my own, not as tidy as it should be, but certainly his mind was tremendously active. He had a great imagination and he was always ready to query procedures and processes. For example, if somebody said to him, "Well this is the way it's always done," Mike says, "Well, just because it's always done that way doesn't mean to say it is the right way. Let's examine it." He had a very inquiring mind and I think that contributed tremendously to his eventual great success in his career.

By the time Charles Ritchie joined the department at the end of August 1934, Lester Pearson had graduated from the attic of the East Block. He had come to the attention of Prime Minister R. B. Bennett, who appointed him secretary of the Price Spreads Committee of the House of Commons. He continued as such when the committee was raised to the status of a royal commission and did such a good job that he was awarded the O.B.E., on Mr. Bennett's recommendation, as well as a special honorarium of one thousand dollars by Parliament. Ritchie, a Nova Scotian like Temp Feaver, had been educated at Oxford, Harvard, and the Ecole des Sciences Politiques in Paris; he had done some school-teaching but was back at Harvard on a fellowship when he took the external affairs exam.

CHARLES RITCHIE

I was in an attic in the East Block with sloping ceilings—the window was about the level of your knees—which I shared with Temp Feaver and Alfred Rive. We had every kind of odd job from doing decoding of a very primitive kind, passport work, newspaper cuttings, crank letters—anything and everything. There was no plan, no education for young people entering the department. Nothing was planned. In fact, I might almost say there was no administration in the department. Dr. Skelton never gave it a thought. When I think of the departments now, including our own, with tremendous emphasis placed on administration, I wonder how we muddled through. There was a lady called Miss McCloskey, a powerful personality she was too, and she really ran the administration of the department with two girls.

In December 1937 Max Wershof joined the department. Although he would deny that he was an infant prodigy, Wershof was certainly an early achiever. He finished high school in Edmonton at the age of thirteen and got his B.A. in the University of Alberta at eighteen and his law degree at twenty-one. When Bible Bill Aberhart came to power, young Wershof shook the dust of the prairies off his feet and returned to his native town of Ottawa, where he practiced law for a few years before joining External Affairs (by means of the competitive exams). He shared an office in the attic of the East Block with another new recruit, Jean Chapdelaine.

MAX WERSHOF

There were no divisions of the department when I first came in and indeed for several years after because the number of officers was so small that there was no reason to have divisions. Now that was a wonderful thing for a young officer because people like Chapdelaine and myself, we worked for everybody. I mean every senior officer could and did assign work to us and neither they nor I worried about whether I was being given too many jobs simultaneously by different officers. We were just delighted to be noticed and to be considered worthy of having jobs assigned to us. I used to get all kinds of jobs directly from Dr. Skelton and from Laurent Beaudry, who was called assistant under-secretary, from John Read, who was the legal adviser. As time went on, I did more and more for John Read, I suppose because I was a lawyer. Everybody gave me jobs, and if that resulted in my working in the evenings and on weekends, I was just delighted to be used in that way.

Oscar Douglas Skelton had had a brilliant career as a professor of political science at Queen's University (the favored school of the Canadian Liberal Establishment) in Kingston, Ontario, before taking on the task of organizing Canada's foreign service. He had an international reputation as an economist and writer. One of his books, entitled Socialism: A Critical Analysis, *which was a result of his graduate studies at the University of Chicago, was published in 1916 and won immediate favor. It was translated into several languages, including Russian, and, according to K. P. Kirkwood, who did an exhaustive study of the Department of External Affairs, both G. D. H. Cole and Lenin described it as the best serious criticism of socialism written up to that time.*[1]

---

[1]Apparently, Lenin was so impressed with Skelton's work that he ordered a copy to be placed in his tomb. Kirkwood claimed that, according to press reports, the book was in the mausoleum in Red Square, Moscow, up to 1941 (the time of the Nazi invasion of the USSR). However, a recent inquiry at the Canadian Embassy in the Russian capital elicited the information that no trace of the book could be found in Lenin's known library holdings. Furthermore, it was said that Lenin in his tomb "had no visible company, books or otherwise" now (1979). As there is a constant rewriting of history in the Soviet Union, there is probably no way of checking the accuracy of the Kirkwood report.

In 1922 Dr. Skelton spoke to the Canadian Club in Toronto on "Canada and Foreign Policy." He argued strongly against the concept of a unified foreign policy for the whole Empire, and said that there must be recognition of what he called "severalty and distinctive national standing." He asserted that "each part of the British Empire has its own problems and must make its own policy," and gave as an example the St. Lawrence Waterway. Dr. Skelton said that it would not be logical for Britain, Australia, and South Africa to be involved in the settlement of such an issue, and yet that was what the proponents of a unified Empire policy seemed to want. This forthright plea for an independent Canadian foreign policy (within certain limits) did not sit well with the Loyalist members of the Canadian Club in Toronto, and had no attraction for Sir Joseph Pope, then under-secretary of state for external affairs.

It may have been because of this speech that Dr. Skelton was appointed adviser to Prime Minister Mackenzie King at the Imperial Conference in London in 1923, and adviser to the Canadian delegation in Geneva the following year, although there are observers who suggest that Dr. Skelton's biography of Sir Wilfrid Laurier, the great Liberal leader, may have had a greater claim on the Liberal government of the day. At any rate, these advisory appointments were the first steps to his joining the Department of External Affairs, first as counselor and then as under-secretary, succeeding Sir Joseph who retired in 1925.

Dr. Skelton was faced with a formidable task: he had to begin at the beginning since the small department that he had taken over was concerned with maintaining the ties of Empire and little else. There were a corporal's guard of Canadians abroad, in offices in Geneva, Paris, and London, but he would have to have many more if he were to provide Ottawa with the reporting and assessment of international affairs that was so essential to the formation of an independent foreign policy. Up to then, the Canadian government had been dependent on British intelligence, which did not always take into consideration the requirements of the dominions. Although Dr. Skelton was a dedicated nationalist, he was a cautious reformer who believed in advancing deliberately but slowly. Furthermore, the Thirties were hardly the time for any rapid expansion, and he was under constant constraint by both the prime ministers he served. R. B. Bennett asked him to stay on as his adviser, which was a singular tribute to Dr. Skelton's knowledge and understanding of international affairs, but the Conservative prime minister kept the department's *growth to a minimum. While Mackenzie King was anxious to have representation abroad, he was faced with an economy-minded Parliament and could not have moved more quickly if he had wanted to—and there is evidence that he did not want to, as he was said to have complained privately to the American envoy (Pierrepont Moffat) that Pearson and Robertson "wished to go too fast" in the direction of diplomatic expansion.*

To help him create a Canadian foreign service and a Canadian foreign policy, Dr. Skelton chose academics like himself, professors and scholars, the very well educated who had been to Oxford and Harvard and Paris. These were the so-called "Skelton boys," and, of course, Lester Pearson was one of the first of them; they were the same sort of nationalists as the under-secretary was, and they gave the department the feeling of excitement and of soaring expectation. They were the brightest and best and there was a touch of arrogance about them because they felt that they had joined the "elite" department of the government. The atmosphere in their cluttered attic offices was that of a faculty club; in fact, later recruits were to speak of the "University of the East Block."

CHARLES RITCHIE

There was a group of very remarkable men in the department: Mike, Norman Robertson, Hume Wrong, and others. It had a very special atmosphere of its own. To me it was an education really, an education in public service. That sounds rather pompous and yet they were very unpompous people. They had a great dislike of pretension and particularly diplomatic pretension. Ours was to be a different kind of service—more ordinary Canadian without fuss and protocol and all that kind of thing. I remember Norman saying to me at the very beginning, "Never enter in your passport 'Diplomat'; always put 'Civil Servant.' We are not trying to be anything special." That was the tone. Self-advertisement of any kind was looked down upon and regarded with such amused contempt that any person in the department who had any tendency in that way, in that circle of the department, became a joke figure. That was the tone of the department, immensely stimulating intellectually, rather academic. They were all academics.

H. F. FEAVER

It was really tremendously exciting. Were we too idealistic? Perhaps so. We really felt we had a special mission for Canada, and the world. Mike, whose influence was very strong, didn't believe in a narrow Canadian nationalism; it was part of a world effort. Of course, we worked on Saturday mornings, that was part of the routine, but we would go back to work on Sundays, happy to think that we were perhaps contributing something to achieve the objectives of the department as a whole.

In 1944 Jean Fournier entered the foreign service—he was the first of the World War Two veterans who were taken on to man the new embassies and high commissions that were being opened.

JEAN FOURNIER

We were joining a new department when the reputation of Canada in the world was quite extraordinary, and we were riding on the crest of a fantastic wave. We were proud of ourselves, having just come back from overseas, and we were right at the very beginning of a service and to have the pleasure and great satisfaction of working with people like Norman Robertson, Hume Wrong, John Read, and Arnold Heeney—you couldn't ask for more.

There was what we called the East Block University, which brought together all the known veterans who'd just joined the department, and we were given lectures, some of them took the form of beer and sandwiches at night in the homes of some of the under-secretaries. On one of those occasions, Mr. Pearson was visiting Ottawa and we spent the evening listening to him. It was an amusing ending in that he said to us, "Well, you're all going to become ambassadors or high commissioners someday; now where would you individually like to be?" This took us a little bit by surprise. I was the last to have to answer that question and I said that I would like to be the first high commissioner in Edinburgh. I had spent most of my leaves in Scotland during the war.

There was no requirement for French in the early examinations for the Department of External Affairs, which was "surprising," as Lester Pearson said in his memoirs, since French was "the traditional language of diplomacy and of thirty per cent of all Canadians." Furthermore, the newly recruited officers were not asked to learn French. Temp Feaver said that he studied the language regularly at the Institute Jean D'Arc in Ottawa; he had not been encouraged to do so by Dr. Skelton but did it instinctively. It was all part of the Canadian situation at the time. No one was concerned with bilingualism; English was the language of the federal government and of the country as a whole, and while French might have been the language of diplomacy in the Thirties (although there were signs of its being surpassed), the department's main dealings were with the English-speaking world.

CHARLES RITCHIE

I had the advantage myself of speaking a bit of French, and there was a very distinguished and charming French Canadian, [Laurent] Beaudry, who was on my examining board when I came into the department and I did speak to him in French then. But, of course, it was not used in the department; nor did most of the men [the top officials] speak French—although they could read it and understand it, they didn't speak it. The French element in the department was very restricted in input and influence in terms of what it became later. There were some able and distinguished French Canadians who were serving abroad. They didn't come home much; they didn't much want to come home because it was really an Anglo–Saxon affair and I don't think they felt very at home in the department although there was no conscious effort to exclude them. That was the way things were in those days.

Laurent Beaudry became Dr. Skelton's deputy, which was a recognition of the French fact in Canada; later he was made associate undersecretary when that position was created in 1947. Nevertheless, there was an overwhelming predominance of English-speaking Canadians in the service, especially in Ottawa, although the Kirkwood study of External Affairs claims that the department was not "perhaps unduly discriminatory" and "maintained a careful balance, proportional to the employed population of Canada as a whole." Certainly, there were many more French Canadians among the officers in External Affairs than in similar positions in any other department of the federal government. Louis St. Laurent did encourage such persons as Louis Audette to enter the service, but that was before Mr. St. Laurent was made secretary of state: he was the first minister of external affairs, as prior to his appointment in September 1946 the portfolio was always held by the prime minister. When he was minister, he showed no partiality for Francophones and did nothing to increase the use of French. Another French Canadian veteran to join the department after the war was Ernest Côté, who was born in Edmonton and grew up in Alberta so that he was fluently bilingual.

The working language of the department remained exclusively English; correspondence with other departments had to be carried on in English, and, as the Kirkwood study pointed out, much of the external correspondence was in English "because of Canada's most intimate external relations with the United States, the United Kingdom and the Commonwealth countries."

JEAN FOURNIER

The first time I used written French that I can remember was when Mr. Paul Martin became the secretary of state for external affairs in 1963, a few months before I left Ottawa. We were asked to write a political analysis of John the Twenty-Third's *Pacem in Terris* Encyclical and that was done in my division. I was head of the European Division then, and it was done entirely in French and it came back two weeks later with notes in the margins in the handwriting of Mr. Martin.

As might be expected, the French Canadians who joined the foreign service in the early days were completely bilingual, and so they had no difficulty working in English. However, the later recruits who were not as fluent did suffer—and Louis Audette could understand this, although he himself was just as much at ease in English as in French. "If you are working in a language which is not yours, which you don't speak with full freedom," he said, "fatigue becomes a major factor." They were tired at the end of the day.

While the French Canadians never felt alienated in the department and were integrated in its work, there was one thing missing in their otherwise friendly relations with their English Canadian colleagues and that was that they could not share their jokes—there was no way of translating them. Every now and then, a group of Francophone officers would get together to speak French and gossip.

ERNEST CÔTÉ

One of us would phone several of the others, maybe a group of eight or ten, and say, "How about meeting on Wednesday for lunch and let's go '*au Canada*.'" So we'd take the tram from the Château Laurier and cross over to Hull and have lunch with Madame Burger. And there recount to one another, regale one another with all manner of French Canadian jokes or current events in Quebec and the rest of events that we would hear about. Then we'd walk back across the interprovincial bridge—in those days, you know, you could account for quite readily an hour and a half for lunch, an hour and three-quarters, on these occasions. We'd come back, revived both mentally and spiritually and physically from these meetings. It's only a good deal later—I should judge about in the mid-Fifties—that one found an increasing number of Anglophones in the department who were proficient in French and who could understand some of the jokes that were going on, people like Jake Warren, who spoke quite fluent French, and several others.

While the French Canadians did not feel completely at home in the English language milieu of the department, and of Ottawa, there was no resentment. It was accepted. They regarded themselves as nationalists, French Canadian nationalists, who looked on Quebec as their homeland, but were not narrowly provincial, nor separatists; they wanted to retain their identity but as citizens with equal rights in the country as a whole. Jean Fournier was no exception, despite the fact that he was to leave the federal civil service to work for the Quebec government and eventually become its representative in London as agent general. Dr. Skelton and, after him, Norman Robertson and Lester Pearson were anxious that the Quebec or French Canadian point of view be taken into account in the formulation of foreign policy, and they came to rely on their French Canadian colleagues to inform them about this.

JEAN FOURNIER

In some of our memoranda we would say for internal, political reasons, we think that you should take such and such into account. There was a question at one stage whether Air Canada should equip itself with La Caravelle for short-distance flights within Canada. We thought that Quebec's position should be made known, that Quebec strongly recommended La Caravelle. That was the European Division. But there were a lot of other divisions involved in the question, which had technical considerations, financial considerations, and so on. That's an example of a relatively small thing.

There were other questions, too, when we were determining what our policy should be toward France and Europe and so on, where the Quebec point of view was to be taken into account. But it wasn't very easy to always know what the Quebec point of view was. You couldn't ask the government; the Quebec government didn't deal with foreign affairs. You had to guess it by reading what was said in editorials across Quebec, because there were rarely statements on foreign policy emanating from French Canadian speakers in Quebec.

After joining External Affairs in 1928, Lester Pearson spent some seven years in Ottawa before getting his first posting abroad. The department remained small in its cluttered quarters in the East Block; there was little hope for expansion or advancement in the Thirties. However, Pearson did do some traveling during this period; he was sent to various international conferences and meetings of the League of Nations. In fact, Lou Rasminsky, who was to become governor of the Bank of Canada, recalled that the first time he met Mike Pearson was when he came to Geneva in connection with a disarmament conference in 1932. Rasminsky had just joined the League as an economist; he supposed that he had the same impression of Pearson as everyone else: that he was great company, that he was basically outgoing, and that he was extremely able and on his way to greater things. These assignments abroad were an important part of Pearson's education as a diplomat, and while, at this time, he may have had all kinds of challenging ideas, there was a certain amount of confusion in his thinking about international affairs. While still a professor, he gave a speech on the Locarno Peace Treaty that got contradictory headlines in the Toronto newspapers: "Must Rely on British

Navy to Avoid War," one paper said, while another said, "Must Break Away from British Empire to Avoid War."

There was no doubt that Pearson agreed with Dr. Skelton in his desire to shake off British dominance and to have an independent foreign policy, and it is likely that Dr. Skelton sounded him out when he met him in 1926 which may be the reason why he was so keen on having Pearson take the examinations and join the department. Geoffrey Pearson said that his father came out of World War One a nationalist and fretted during the Thirties about British control of Canadian foreign policy. Later he was to fret over American and British decisions taken without consultations with Canada during World War Two. Pearson would have agreed with the stand taken by his good friend, Walter Gordon, who was to become his finance minister in 1963.

WALTER GORDON

In the 1930s, like most of the people of my age, I was all in favor of breaking loose from Britain. I didn't like our colonial status at that time. As you know, Mr. King was all for breaking the ties with Britain, which I was in favor of, but, of course, then he proceeded to allow even tighter ties to bind us to the United States in a colonial or satellite state.

GEOFFREY PEARSON

He is remembered as an internationalist, but you can't be an internationalist without first being a nationalist. You cannot be someone who understands international politics without representing a country which has a need for international cooperation. You could say that great powers like the Americans and the Russians are nationalist because they don't need international cooperation. We have always needed it, but in order to get it we had to have some nationalist base; otherwise people didn't take us seriously. So he was a nationalist about things like the flag and about status, Canada's status; he was an internationalist when it came to participation in international conferences and treaties and so on.

Mike Pearson's attitude toward Britain was ambivalent. William Clark, the British journalist who was Prime Minister Eden's press secretary at the time of Suez and who knew Pearson well, said that he had a "certain reverence" for the old country. And there was no doubt about his high regard for Oxford University, where he had such a glorious time in the early Twenties. He wanted his son to have the same experience, and Geoffrey did go to Oxford but he did not appreciate it the way his father had, and could not really understand why his father had liked it so much. While Clark spoke of Pearson's reverence, he did say that Pearson had made it clear that Canada was more bound up with Washington than with London.

In 1932 the Imperial Economic Conference was held in Ottawa. Lester Pearson was appointed assistant to Dr. R. J. Mannion, the minister in charge of press and information. However, Dr. Mannion knew very little about what was going on since Prime Minister Bennett kept most of the information to himself; so he turned over the duties of looking after the press to his assistant, Mike Pearson, who knew even less. However, Pearson had a friend, Malcolm MacDonald, the son of Ramsay Mac-Donald, the British prime minister, who was a member of the British delegation and was well briefed and ready to pass on his knowledge to his Canadian counterpart. Temp Feaver, who was assigned to the conference secretariat in a junior capacity, recalled that there was a moment when it looked as if the meeting might break up in considerable disarray because of the hard line that Prime Minister Bennett took, but eventually matters were settled. In the circumstances, it was not an easy task, for Pearson to be the press officer for the host country, and it proved a test of his diplomatic skills. The British were shocked at Bennett's behavior.

MALCOLM MACDONALD

I think that is true. Not only was Stanley Baldwin upset, but so was Neville Chamberlain, and as chancellor of the exchequer, he was the main negotiator for us at this economic conference. The British delegation was made up chiefly of Conservatives, and they expected to find in Bennett a colleague in the cause of Imperial preferences, which would be mutually beneficial to Britain and to the overseas community. They were disappointed that Bennett should be in favor of Imperial preferences all right, but to the advantage of Canada and to hell with Britain—I mean to hell with Britain's economic interests. No doubt that's an exaggeration, but they were disappointed and he was really very tough—I knew Bennett well and I was very fond of Bennett.

When the last crisis was resolved and the conference was over, Malcolm MacDonald complained rather bitterly to Mike Pearson about Prime Minister Bennett's policies and tactics, especially about the latter, and assured him that another conference like this would end the Empire. To this, Pearson made the wry comment, in his memoirs, that the British obviously preferred to play on their own grounds where the rules and atmosphere were that of cricket rather than baseball. And it was to be many years before another Empire or Commonwealth conference was to be held far from the comforting shadows of Westminster.

Actually, Lester Pearson admired the way that Mr. Bennett had suppressed his Empire loyalties to fight for Canadian interests at the Ottawa conference. He owed a lot to the prime minister, who had not only sent him to various international conferences but appointed him to two royal commissions and got him the award of the O.B.E. Although Pearson was to make light of the Order of the British Empire, it was a tribute to the valuable work he had done as secretary of the Price Spreads Committee. Finally, Prime Minister Bennett approved of his first posting abroad, to Canada House in London; it was one of Bennett's last official acts.

2 *First Posting Abroad*

ALTHOUGH HE HAD *been posted to London, Lester Pearson was still in Ottawa when the Special Assembly of the League of Nations was called to consider Fascist Italy's invasion of Ethiopia. It was hurriedly decided that he should attend this meeting, which was to begin October 9, 1935, before taking up his duties in Canada House. He had to leave immediately, and his sudden departure meant that his wife Maryon had to pack up and make all the arrangements for moving the family. Pearson was secretary and adviser to the Canadian delegation, which was headed by Howard Ferguson, the Canadian high commissioner in London, and included Dr. W. A. Riddell, the permanent representative of Canada in Geneva.*

This emergency session of the League of Nations made a lasting impression on Mike Pearson. There were moments of high drama in the Palais des Nations, of hope and exhilaration, of frustration and disillusionment. For the first time Canada played an important role on the international stage, but Dr. Riddell's initiative, which had been well received, was repudiated because of the confusion at home over an election and change of government. In the end the League failed—Mussolini was triumphant and Ethiopia conquered—but Pearson never lost his faith in international organization. In his memoirs he wrote that the Italo-Ethiopian dispute confirmed his conviction, which had been developing since he began teaching history, that only by collective action could peace and security be assured in the world. Paul Martin, who had known

18

Pearson from college days and was to become his external affairs minister, attended a later session of the League and remembered Mike's attachment to the world body.[1]

PAUL MARTIN

I stayed with him on my way to Geneva. And I remember him saying to me, "Oh my gosh, I envy you going to the League of Nations as a delegate." He had been there, I think, the year before at some committee meeting as an official, but he told me, "I really envy you very much."

It was in a tense atmosphere that the League of Nations met on October 9, 1935: Howard Ferguson made a firm statement, saying that Canada was willing to join with other nations "in considering how by unanimous action peace can be maintained." On the morning that the Special Assembly was to decide on the question of aggression, Mr. Ferguson received a telegram from Prime Minister Bennett in Ottawa instructing him to refrain from voting since Parliament was dissolved and a new one was to be elected the following Monday. There was consternation in the Canadian delegation, but Pearson was able to persuade Mr. Ferguson that he should immediately get in touch with Mr. Bennett, which he did (his transatlantic telephone call was the first ever made by the Canadian office in Geneva to Canada). When Mr. Ferguson explained the situation, the prime minister agreed to rescind the order and leave it to his judgment. Canada joined all the other members of the League, except Italy, Austria, and Hungary, in voting to condemn the Fascist government for aggression against Ethiopia.

There was some argument whether Canada should be a member of the sanctions committee—Dr. Skelton was against this but R. B. Bennett remained prime minister until October 23 despite the fact that his government had been defeated in the election, and Mr. Bennett's position was that Canada should discharge its obligations under the covenant. Dr. Riddell, who took Mr. Ferguson's place as head of the Canadian delegation, was disturbed that the proposed sanctions did not include oil, and suggested that this should be added to the list. However, he did nothing

---

[1]Paul Martin was one of the few delegates to the League of Nations who became a delegate to the United Nations. War and politics had done for the rest.

about it until he received information that the new Liberal government agreed to economic sanctions but opposed any military sanctions. He therefore proposed an amendment, but before proceeding further he sent two urgent telegrams to Ottawa describing his action. When he received no reply by November 2, he moved the amendment, which received the unanimous approval and commendation of the sanctions committee. As might be expected, the Fascists were furious and asserted that oil sanctions meant war. This was the sort of reaction that was bound to affect such timid internationalists as Dr. Skelton and Mackenzie King, who were fearful of any foreign entanglements. However, it was not till December 2 that the Canadian government repudiated Dr. Riddell's initiative and disavowed the so-called "Canadian proposal" for oil sanctions.[2]

On February 11, 1936, Prime Minister Mackenzie King said in the Canadian House of Commons: "I am not at all sure that when the whole story comes to be told, that but for the action of the government of Canada in this particular matter [repudiating the oil sanctions] at that particular time, the whole of Europe might have been aflame today." Mike Pearson quoted this excerpt from Hansard in his memoirs and commented: "My own view is that the failure in 1935 of the members of the League of Nations, including Canada, to stand up to a single aggressor, had much to do with the world war in 1939."

PAUL MARTIN

All I knew was that Howard Ferguson had gone to that Assembly at the instance of Mr. Bennett, the prime minister, and the delegation's work was interrupted by the results of the election. Mr. Ferguson quite sincerely had taken the responsibility to back

[2]In a letter dated August 14, 1936, Prime Minister Mackenzie King wrote to Carl Goldenberg about an article he had written in the *Fortnightly* review. While praising it as well balanced and correct, Mr. King felt that the author had overemphasized "isolationist sentiment" as being the reason for "the recent repudiation of Canada's delegate to the League Assembly." The prime minister went on to say: "It was not as a delegate to the Assembly that Riddell acted in putting forward the suggestion of oil sanctions. He was simply serving as a member of a Committee which had been set up at the instance of the Council of the League to explore opinion, et cetera. He acted wholly without authority in putting forward the proposal he did, and a repudiation of him or of the proposal was due to that cause. There was, of course, the belief that an action of the kind, if applied, might result in war. Apart altogether from any isolationist sentiment, Canada would not have wished, directly or indirectly, to contribute to such an appalling disaster. Our foreign policy is one which, at every turn, aims at peace."

up Dr. Riddell and his suggestions for the imposition of oil sanctions, and that policy was repudiated when Mackenzie King came into office. And there is a series of communications between Dr. Skelton and Riddell on that question, which I think confirms that they had gone beyond their real authority.

I must say, at the time I felt somewhat sympathetic to the position taken by Dr. Riddell. I didn't know all the workings, I didn't know whether instructions had been received or not; but I was a strong believer in the League of Nations. And I'm now confirmed in reading a book by a Canadian, Aster, on Anthony Eden that those oil sanctions might have worked. Eden had proposed to Dr. Riddell that he should make the suggestion of oil sanctions because he felt that if he [Eden] were to do it it wouldn't carry as well as a country less implicated in the whole situation than Britain. In any event, that was the beginning of my parliamentary interest in foreign policy, that whole issue.

Mr. King had made great reservations on Article 10, on Article 16 of the covenant of the League. I didn't agree with those reservations, either as a student or as a young practicing lawyer or as a young MP. I felt that we had placed too many restrictions, reservations, on our positions and that one of the reasons why the League proved to be ineffective was because so many countries did the same. Mr. King I don't think ever really believed in the League of Nations as Pearson did, as I did, as Mr. St. Laurent did.

Lester Pearson was not in Geneva during the exciting days when Dr. Riddell occupied center stage and the Canadian proposal for oil sanctions was the focus of international interest and attention; he had gone to London where he was soon to be joined by his family and spend some time looking around for a house and settling in. However, when Dr. Riddell left Geneva, after the repudiation of his initiative by the new government of Prime Minister Mackenzie King, Pearson was appointed to take his place on the sanctions committee of the League of Nations. There was not much to do: it was largely a watching brief since the powers that be in Ottawa did not want to become involved in any of the committee's work.

In London, Pearson's main job was as a liaison officer with Whitehall; he kept in close touch with the Foreign Office and the Dominions Office and helped to prepare the reports and dispatches for Ottawa which, he complained, were often ignored. He had been appointed counselor at

Canada House and was next in rank to that of the official secretary,
Georges Vanier, and the high commissioner, Vincent Massey (with the
change of government, Massey had succeeded Howard Ferguson). The
most dramatic event in the first year or so of his posting abroad was the
abdication crisis of December 1936—and Pearson found that his friend
and helpmate of the Empire Economic Conference in Ottawa, Malcolm
MacDonald, was in the key position of dominions secretary in the British
government.

MALCOLM MACDONALD

Of course all the dominions were very much concerned, and I kept not just Mike but Vincent Massey informed. There were two or three meetings every day, in my office, of all the dominion high commissioners so that they could supplement telegrams which I kept sending to the prime ministers overseas, giving them the latest information, giving them our latest British Cabinet view of it, and asking their views as to what the next step should be in return.

The amazing thing was that from the beginning to the end of the crisis, although the prime ministers [were from] the six independent nations in the Commonwealth, including Britain of course—some Conservatives, some Liberals, one Socialist, some Roman Catholics, others Methodists, others the Reform Dutch Church; some of them monarchists and two of them republicans, de Valera and General Hertzog in South Africa—they spontaneously agreed on what alternatives were possible and what other alternatives were unacceptable. Mackenzie King and the Canadian Cabinet agreed with the step-by-step process, and absolutely spontaneously.

If I may say so, the only disagreement occurred on the first day on a certain issue. I sent the first telegram to all the prime ministers saying that the crisis had begun, that there was confidential talk between Baldwin and the king, and saying what the king's reactions were and so on, and what Baldwin thought were the two or three possible alternatives and one or two impossible alternatives. One of the impossible alternatives was that the king should marry Mrs. Simpson and she should be queen; he said that was impossible in the British population's eyes, and secondly it was impossible that he should marry Mrs. Simpson in a morganatic way.

I got telegrams back from all the prime ministers except one agreeing with the British government's view and spontaneously. One reply came from the Socialist Prime Minister [Michael Joseph Savage] of New Zealand saying, "I do not agree that it's impossible for the king to marry Mrs. Simpson. He can marry her and he can stay on the throne." I forget whether he said that she could be queen or whether it should be a morganatic marriage. But he said, "She's a commoner; what's wrong with that? This is modern times."

This was slightly embarrassing because I hadn't said anything about Mrs. Simpson in the telegram. But by a good chance the minister of finance [Walter Nash] of New Zealand happened to be in London at the time on financial negotiations. He became a very good Labour prime minister. He was a friend of mine from the 1924 years when I had been to New Zealand to debate for the Oxford University and he was the secretary of the Labour Party. I asked him to come and have a talk. I told him this situation and he said, "Leave this to me. I have just come through the United States of America and, of course, unlike your press the newspapers there are full of stories of Edward VIII and Mrs. Simpson, and I've read about her marriage history and so on. I'll tell my prime minister just the facts of her past married life, and I'll advise that we agree that the king can marry her, of course, if he wants to, but in so doing he should abdicate."

He sent a telegram to the New Zealand high commissioner and a few hours later he rang me up and said, "Malcolm, can I come and see you?" He came and he said, "Here's the answer; he agrees."

As a Cabinet minister, Malcolm MacDonald was probably Mike Pearson's best contact in London; they had lunch together now and then, and they would discuss the European situation, the weakness of the League of Nations, the Spanish Civil War, and the growing Nazi menace, and worry about what was happening to the world. During his time at Canada House, Pearson met many of the up-and-coming young people of Britain, including Alex Douglas-Home who was parliamentary private secretary to Neville Chamberlain when he became prime minister in 1937 and who was to be commonwealth secretary at the time of the Suez Crisis and later prime minister of Britain when Lester Pearson was prime minister of Canada.

In those days there was a tendency for Canadians either to be swallowed up whole in London, to lose their accent and become more British than the British, or to become aggressively Canadian and North American and anti-British in order to assert their identity. Somehow Pearson was able to avoid both extremes: he wore the short black coat, striped trousers, and Homburg hat, which was almost standard diplomatic dress then, and carried a furled umbrella, and, as he himself said, "Anyone watching me enter my club, The Travellers, would have thought that I was the patterned product of Eton, Oxford, and the Foreign Office, unless he heard me speak." Mike retained his Canadian accent and remained very much a Canadian at the Court of St. James, and not a colonial copy of an upper-class Englishman. Malcolm MacDonald recognized this dualism in commenting on Pearson's attitude toward Britain, and so did Charles Ritchie, who had come over to be executive assistant to High Commissioner Massey.

MALCOLM MACDONALD

Mike was always an extremely good Canadian, a Canadian first, as well as an internationalist. He wasn't one of the old school. But Mike also had a very friendly feeling toward Britain and the British because of Oxford and various other things— affections which the Canadians and the British shared, affections which Mackenzie King, for instance, shared. But Mike, less sensitively so, nevertheless firmly, never wanted Britain to interfere as in old colonial times with Canada's right to make its own decision in international policy as well as national policy. But I think there was a very happy family attitude between the patriotic Canadian and the friendly person who had some regard for Britain.

CHARLES RITCHIE

This was one of the differences between Pearson and Mr. Massey. Mr. Massey was 100 percent Chamberlain and Mike wasn't. Mike was a very realistic friend of Britain and the British, very Canadian, very unlikely to be taken in by the charms of the social life which the British in those days were very good at laying on and to which Mr. Massey was rather susceptible; but Mike was a steady friend of Britain. He got very impatient with the British, with their slowness. He often found that it was necessary to put pretty cogently the Canadian position. I always felt that he was deeply at home in London, more really than in any other place outside Canada.

Of the high commissioner, Lester Pearson said that he was a skilled professional diplomat and an understanding and considerate chief who was more at ease in the stately homes of England than at a meeting of Canadian businessmen or tourists. Mr. and Mrs. Massey were personal friends of the Royal Family, and Pearson wrote that "Mr. Massey seemed to know every duke by his first name." The Canadian students in Britain at the time seemed to sense this, but what these youths, who were mostly idealists and radicals, resented was the way that Canada House supported Prime Minister Chamberlain through thick and thin. In this, the high commissioner was merely reflecting the attitude of the Canadian government, and particularly the growing isolationism of Mackenzie King, whose view was that it was best for Canada to stay out of the whole European mess. Although the students found that Mr. Massey was kind and helpful, they did not relate to him in the way they did to Lester Pearson, who was sympathetically disposed to what they believed. One of these students was a Rhodes scholar, Arnold Smith, who was to become the first secretary-general of the Commonwealth.[3]

[3]After getting his BCL at Oxford in 1938, Arnold Smith married and took his bride to Tallinn (Reval), Estonia, where he had found a job as editor of an English language newspaper. In August 1939 he received a telegram from Lord Halifax asking him to join the British Legation in Tallinn, which he did on a part-time basis. When war broke out, the twenty-four-year-old Canadian became a special envoy of the Estonians; he was sent on a mission to persuade the Finns to join the Estonians in resisting the Russians. It was his first diplomatic assignment and unsuccessful. At the time that Paris fell, the Soviet Union took the Baltic States, and Smith watched masses of Red Army troops descending on Tallinn in the first-ever parachute attack. It was not until September 1940 that he and his wife were evacuated through Leningrad, across Russia, to Istanbul; he was then ordered to Cairo where he worked for the British government in psychological warfare. A couple of years later, while still in Cairo, he was recruited by the Canadian government and sent to Kuibyshev, the temporary wartime capital of the Soviet Union.

ARNOLD SMITH

I recall feeling that he was on the side of the angels. He was against appeasement. He was against isolationism; he saw the danger of Hitler and I felt that he agreed that the best hope of avoiding a war would be to stand up firmly to Hitler, and appeasing him was the best way of heading into a war on the worst terms. I didn't at that time see things he wrote to Ottawa, you know. This was lunch conversation, dinner conversation. But he always seemed to me to see things pretty whole and straight and be very frank. He was also very practical. He had a feel, I think, for what is possible and what isn't possible, and you sensed this. I think he was a superb diplomat.

Then came the Munich Crisis, which reached its climax at the end of September 1938; it followed on the Anschluss, the annexation of Austria, which was such an awesome demonstration of German will and power in face of the disarray and weakness in France and Western Europe. The unemployed were put to work digging trenches in the London parks by day and under floodlights at night; they piled sandbags under the ground-floor windows of the government buildings in Whitehall. Anti-aircraft guns were unlimbered around the Houses of Parliament but the newspapers claimed that one of them was of 1916 vintage and had not been fired in more than twenty years. However, what really brought the crisis home was when the government began shoveling out gas masks. It was obvious to Mike Pearson and other observers that Britain was totally unprepared for war, and it was therefore with a collective sigh of relief that the populace heard about Neville Chamberlain returning from Munich with "peace in our time."

MALCOLM MACDONALD

We in Britain, in our Cabinet, were considering whether Britain should go to war or try to carry on in the light of that issue [Munich Crisis]. As dominion secretary I was in touch almost every hour of every day and every minute with the dominion prime ministers, telling them what the latest news in Europe was and what the British Cabinet's attitude was. In addition to sending all these telegrams—of course copies went to the Canadian High

Commission and Australian High Commission and others—I had meetings sometimes once, sometimes twice, and sometimes three times a day with the high commissioners in London to give them supplementary information. Very often it was Vincent Massey who was there, but now and then Mike came when Vincent was away. Mike was absolutely in touch with the whole thing. He and I kept in communication. Now that was 1938, the Munich Crisis. And again there was complete agreement between all the Dominion governments and the British government.

The euphoria over the Munich agreement did not last long, and soon there was self-doubt, self-reproach, and recrimination. It was becoming evident that all that Chamberlain had achieved in his personal diplomacy—and this was one of the first examples of meetings at the summit which were to become so popular with the increasing ease and speed of travel—was to gain time at the expense of Czechoslovakia. Most of the Canadian students were opposed to the policy of appeasement, and one of them, another Rhodes scholar, George Ignatieff,[4] expressed his anti-appeasement views pretty frankly, as he said, to Mike Pearson, and, although he realized that Pearson could not detach himself from the official government position, he nevertheless felt that there was an understanding there and that he was really on their side.

Shortly after the Munich agreement, Pearson arranged for a meeting of some fifty to sixty of the Canadian students at Vincent Massey's residence in Hyde Park Garden. He acted as moderator, and, as Ignatieff said, drew the students out, but did not take any position. Mr. Massey just listened.

[4]George Ignatieff was born in St. Petersburg on December 16, 1913, the son of Count Paul Ignatieff and Princess Natalie Mestchersky. His father was minister of education and public instruction in the tsar's wartime government and narrowly escaped being executed by the Communists. The family escaped from Russia during the civil war in 1920. His grandfather, Count Nicholas Pavlovich Ignatieff, was in China in 1860 when an Anglo-French force burned the Summer Palace near Peking; he was able to negotiate the withdrawal of this force and the man he dealt with was Lord Elgin, who had been governor-general of Canada between 1847 and 1854. However, the young Count Ignatieff—he was twenty-eight years old at the time—is best remembered for having drawn the boundaries between China and Russia along the Usuri and Amur rivers. After these labors he rode home, leaving Peking in November and arriving in St. Petersburg the following February, which must be the longest horseback ride in history.

GEORGE IGNATIEFF

We were invited to state our views (a) on what should be Canada's attitude to the question of the immediate relationships with Nazi Germany and Fascist Italy and (b) what should be, in our view, Canada's position in the event of war. There was a very free-for-all discussion. My view was that there should be a rearmament program and there shouldn't be this hands-off policy toward Spain, the Republican government in Spain, and that I do remember arguing.... I remember saying this, that those of us who may take this hands-off policy and believe that we can be separated from the tremendous confrontation between totalitarian fascism and the democracists because of distance will be paying with our lives. Britain and France would be brought in and I felt then very strongly that the growing impetus of, and momentum of, Fascist and Nazi aggression and success in aggression would end in a war. And that the only hope of keeping the peace was to have a collective security front.

Now Mike, I think his ethics were very much involved and I think that he felt that it was perhaps a wicked thing to accept the rule of force and to sell the League of Nations and all the concept of collective security down the river. The other thing was that Mike saw earlier than perhaps some of his colleagues in the Canadian government that the policy of appeasement wasn't even accompanied with buying time to strengthen democracies. He was more aware perhaps than some others that there wasn't a sufficiently concerted and effective program of rearmament and mobilization. He as well as some of us were also concerned about the way in which the rift between Soviet Russia and Western democracies took place over the nonresistance to the take-over in Czechoslovakia.

In recalling the past, George Ignatieff was the only one of those I interviewed who put down the Spanish Civil War as an important factor in the late Thirties. Lester Pearson made no mention of it in his memoirs. Perhaps, in the passage of time, it was forgotten or people just did not want to remember, because the Spanish Civil War was a soul-shattering experience for anyone who lived through those troubled times, especially for the young and the young middle-aged like Pearson, who was in his early forties then. As Ignatieff said, the Canadian students at that meeting

*in Mr. Massey's London residence were upset over the hands-off policy —
or the "nonintervention policy," as it was called—because they knew that
its only effect was to deny supplies of war materials and even food to the
legitimate republican government of Spain while Franco and his rebels got
all the armaments and munitions and men they needed from Hitler and
Mussolini. The best that could be said of this policy was that the British
and French governments had instituted it because they were afraid, which
made them appear contemptible. However, many young people believed
that the nonintervention policy was meant to destroy the Spanish loyalists, that those in power in London and Paris were on the side of the
Nazi Germans and Italian Fascists, and were hoping that, after Spain,
they would attack the Soviet Union and extirpate the Communists for
good.*

*There was another example of "Perfidious Albion" in the British
policy on Palestine. The British had made pledges to the Arabs and the
Jews which made this the twice-promised land. With the war approaching, Mike Pearson's friend, Malcolm MacDonald, had to resolve this
double-dealing.*

MALCOLM MACDONALD

The Arabs wanted the Jewish national home abolished, and the
Jews, on the other hand, being terribly persecuted in Germany,
wanted more and more immigrants and more and more land
sales, and an enormous growth of the Jewish national home. Well,
I had the awful job of trying to reconcile these points of view.
One shouldn't go into detail, but I tried to get the Jews and the
Arabs together with ourselves at a Palestine conference in St.
James's Palace in early 1939 so that we could get an agreed settlement; but needless to say, the Jews and the Arabs didn't agree;
they didn't even meet sometimes. We had to meet the Jews in the
morning and the Arabs in the afternoon and so on. In the end the
conference broke up without any agreement at all.

So we in the British government had to announce our policy: it
was a policy which was rejected by the Jews on one side and the
Arabs on the other side, but it went much further to meet the
Arab point of view than the Jewish point of view because war was
looming and we in the British government felt that there was
going to be a war and that we would have Jewish support in any

case—there was an element of cynicism in this—but it also refused the Arab view that there should be a complete stoppage of immigration, but we reduced immigration very considerably because it was essential, in our view, that the Arabs should be on our side in the war; otherwise we might lose the war.

We thought, of course, that this was in Britain's self-interest, which was our prime motive: but we also thought this was in the longer-term interests of the Jewish national home in Palestine because if we lost the war and the Nazi Germans won, there would be no Jewish national home in Palestine. They would be just dispersed again as they were two thousand years ago. Therefore, in the interests of the Jewish national home, as well as in the interests of Great Britain and the democratic powers, we wanted Arab support in the war.

Ever since Dr. Riddell's initiative in proposing oil sanctions was repudiated, Lester Pearson found himself in opposition to the foreign policy of the government as expressed by the minister, Prime Minister Mackenzie King. That did not hinder his work, although it could be frustrating. As his country's representative at the League of Nations or any other international meeting, he carried out orders and made the best possible explanation of the government's position even if he thought it was wrong. That was one side of diplomacy; on the other side, in tendering advice, he could and did express his own opinions, which were not always acceptable in Ottawa and may have been the reason why the dispatches from Canada House did not produce the expected results and were so often ignored. Mackenzie King and Dr. Skelton were cautious to the point of doing nothing; while they wanted a Canadian presence on the international stage, they did not want any involvement, which, as Geoffrey Pearson said, was the opposite of his father's passionate belief in collective action.

GEOFFREY PEARSON

They did not think alike on foreign policy although Mr. King saw him as a possible future minister. Mr. King, I think, had some suspicions of his internationalism and his activism, and my father in turn was not sympathetic to Mr. King's view of Canada's role in the world. For Mr. King that role was strictly subordinate to the domestic situation: if we did anything in the world which helped to cause controversy in Canada, then it should be forgotten at once. He [Pearson] felt the opposite way, that to be active in world politics was to help Canada domestically, to bring the two parts of the country together behind causes which were, if you like, patriotic ones. There was a difference of generations also, perhaps, and a difference of personalities.

On May 1, 1937, George VI was crowned king of Great Britain, Northern Ireland, and the British Dominions beyond the seas, as well as emperor of India. Besides being an usher or "gold stick in waiting" for the coronation service in Westminster Abbey, Lester Pearson was also acting as secretary to Prime Minister Mackenzie King and the Canadian delegation attending the Imperial Conference, which was being held at the same time as the coronation. The request for the latter appointment had come from the prime minister, and while Pearson found this flattering, he did not look forward to the assignment, not because of any antipathy toward the Liberal government's policies, but because the job of secretary meant that he would have to help in speech-writing and Mr. King was a notoriously hard taskmaster in that regard. Actually, Pearson spent most of his time in housekeeping, securing adequate accommodation for the members of the delegation in a grossly overcrowded London, and seeing that they were comfortable and reasonably contented.

It was in the days after this conference that Mackenzie King went on a secret mission to Berlin and had an audience with Adolf Hitler, which was said to have been arranged by the British. Certainly, the Canadians in London had nothing to do with setting it up. The Nazi leader made such an impression on the Canadian prime minister that he returned to Canada believing that he was a man of peace and that there would be no war. In his diary Mackenzie King said that Hitler would be seen as "a very great man" and compared him with Joan of Arc. The prime minister wrote that he was sure that the German Führer was a fellow spiritualist and felt that he was not only the deliverer of his people but could be "the deliverer of Europe." Some time later, if the Kirkwood study of External Affairs is right, Mr. King sent for Mike Pearson, who happened to be in Ottawa then, and asked him his view on the Nazis and the situation in Europe. Pearson replied that he was convinced that war was inevitable—a reply that did not please the prime minister, who felt that there was a lot lacking in Pearson's judgment. After that, according to Kirkwood, "External

Affairs jobs assigned to Pearson were not of top importance."

However, there is no record of Mackenzie King's having talked to Pearson at that time, although he did see him just before the outbreak of war. The Pearsons had returned to Canada on home leave and were enjoying a family holiday at Lac du Bonnet near Winnipeg when the news that the Nazis were threatening Danzig and the Polish Corridor made Mike Pearson feel that he should be back at his post in London. He caught the next train to Ottawa and persuaded Dr. Skelton that he should leave immediately. When the prime minister heard that he was in the capital, he invited him to dinner that evening at his country estate, Kingsmere. Mr. King told Pearson that he was being foolish, that he had seen Hitler, and that Hitler would not risk a war, and advised him to rejoin his family. However, if Pearson was insistent, Mr. King said he would not stand in the way of his departure, although he repeated there was going to be no war.

3 A Diplomat at War

LESTER PEARSON GOT back to his post in London just days before the war began, but he would not have done so if he had not flown. The day after having had dinner with Prime Minister Mackenzie King, he saw the under-secretary of external affairs, Dr. Skelton, and told him that he wanted to go by plane, that he would be too late if he went by ship. Pan American Airways had just started a transatlantic service that summer, but it was so new that no Canadian government official had made use of it up to then. Shaking his head at what seemed an extraordinarily rash request, Dr. Skelton nevertheless agreed and even arranged for Pearson to get a lift on a government plane to Montreal, from where he took a commercial flight to New York. The next morning he boarded a Boeing Clipper seaplane, which took a day and a half to reach Southampton, sometimes flying only a few hundred feet above the waves.

It was remarkably prescient of Mike Pearson to have realized that the war was so close. Almost everyone, with the possible exceptions of Mr. King and Dr. Skelton, knew that there was going to be a war, but to be able to predict, with such confidence, that there were only a few days left was an example of Pearson's superb sense of timing. Or was it just plain luck? Or a bit of both? By now he had become official secretary or second-in-command to High Commissioner Massey; General Vanier had moved to Paris as minister to France. On September 3, 1939, the day that Britain declared war on Germany, Mr. Massey called together the staff in

33

his large second-floor office. Charles Ritchie has a vivid memory of that meeting.

CHARLES RITCHIE

I can see Mr. Massey's rather diminutive form standing under that enormous chandelier in the huge Mussolini-esque office and in quiet tones telling us that war had been declared and indicating that precautions had to be taken and talking to us as a Canadian group.

From the time of that meeting Canada House was a busy place, with officials trying to find passage home for hundreds of Canadians stranded in London and answering a storm of inquiries, although it wasn't until a week later, on September 9, 1939, that Canada declared war on Germany. Unlike 1914, there was no single declaration for the whole British Empire, the independent dominions having the right to make this decision on their own. A Canadian officer, E. L. M. "Tommy" Burns, who was to become the first commander of the United Nations Emergency Force (UNEF) in the Middle East, was attending the Imperial Defence College in 1939. He had come to know Mike Pearson as a man who got things done and when war broke out, he went to see him.

GENERAL E. L. M. BURNS

All the Canadian officers were called back to fill in various slots in the mobilization plan for the Canadian contingent that was to come overseas, and I also had a position—I think I was to be GSO 1 of the First Canadian Division. However, I pointed out to Mr. Pearson and he agreed that it was desirable that there should be a general staff officer at Canada House Headquarters because a number of questions were coming up which required staff dealing with. The only officer there was Colonel Logie of the Ordnance Corps who was there mainly on the question of procurement and also the sale, so to speak, of munitions and other equipment. He was a very good officer, but he wasn't on the general staff side. Mr. Pearson agreed with me, especially as swarms of people who had served in Canadian forces in World War One and who had settled in England were coming in and wanting to get taken on the Canadian forces for World War Two, the commissions, pay, and pension being somewhat better, or so they perceived. So he sent telegrams to Ottawa and eventually it was agreed that I should stay there waiting to serve under General Crerar, who was coming up to set up Canadian military headquarters. He arrived, as I recall, in October sometime [1939].

Although the air raid sirens wailed a few minutes after the eleven o'clock deadline for the declaration of war on that Sunday morning, September 3, 1939, it turned out to be a false alarm. Aside from the sinking by a German U-boat of the Cunard liner, Athenia, *which was full of returning Canadians, nothing happened in the West; the British and French sat in the Maginot Line or remained immobile on the frontier while the Nazis completed the destruction of Poland and its division with the Soviets. London was in for the long siege of the* Sitzkrieg *or Phony War. It was a trying time for Pearson.*

CHARLES RITCHIE

During those months there were all sorts of questions about Canadian policy and whether the British were seriously going to go ahead. It was very hard on the nerves—it was easy, once the war really began, to feel that you were, diplomatically anyway, on the front line, if not militarily.

I think that the muddle and the slowness of the British in adapting to war methods and standards made for a lot of pessimism abroad. I was rather pessimistic always—not that it mattered because I was obscure. I don't think I was a defeatist but I was pessimistic. Mike was not ever pessimistic. He didn't go about doing a Pollyanna or being a ray of sunshine, but he never believed the British would give in. He was pretty stouthearted, and never expressed his private doubts. But then, of course, it was very deceptive about Mike because in spite of his accessibility and his easiness and our long friendship, he was one of the most reserved men about his own feelings and sometimes about his real objectives.

In the early months of the war Pearson spent much of his time looking after a succession of Canadian Cabinet ministers and listening to their complaints about the muddle-headed British and the way that they were being treated as colonials. The arrival of the First Canadian Division help to break the monotony of the Phony War. Then came the spring of 1940 and burgeoning military activity. There was the ill-conceived British plan to stop the ships carrying Swedish iron ore to Germany—it would mean a violation of Norwegian territorial waters but the excuse given was that Nazi submarines were using these waters. However, grave doubts were expressed and Pearson records in his diary: "The dominion high commissioners have been telling Eden the proposal is a most unwise one, that whatever advantage accrued from stopping the iron ore would be more than neutralised by the Nazi invasion of Sweden and Norway." The British went ahead, with dire consequences: the Germans overran Denmark in a few hours and swooped down on Norway. A Canadian contingent was to be used in an operation against the northern Norwegian port of Trondheim, the news of which alarmed Pearson, who confided in his diary: "If the whole thing turns out badly and they cannot drive the Germans out of Norway, then I would not wish to be in McNaughton's shoes if he agrees to the use of Canadians in this way without prior authorization from Ottawa." General A. G. L. McNaughton, the Canadian commander, had agreed, but the whole explosive issue fizzled out because of the military debacle in Norway, and the Canadians were returned from the embarkation ports to their Aldershot base.

On May 10, 1940, the all-out German assault on the West began, and Mike Pearson watched with growing amazement and anguish the Nazi Blitzkrieg as it smashed Holland and Belgium on its way to victory over France. At the beginning of June he wrote in his diary: "The whole thing still seems unbelievable; that the much-vaunted French army would fold up; that the lauded Gamelin was no good and some of his army commanders worse; that the Germans could wander at will in parts of France which they couldn't reach in four years in the first war; they could take towns without difficulty on which British communications depended; that they can now look across the Channel from Boulogne; well, it just doesn't seem possible."

The miracle of Dunkirk. And the former history professor could not miss the opportunity of being an eyewitness to history in the making. He and Charles Ritchie used all the pull they had to get the necessary passes and permits, and, on a Sunday morning, in glorious summer weather, drove to Dover. There were reports that volunteers were needed to man the little boats, and this was the explanation of their presence in a

restricted area that they gave to an officer. He was not impressed by their
offer, but he let them stay to watch the evacuation.

CHARLES RITCHIE

It was a most beautiful day. I remember the boats coming in
with the returning troops and the prisoners. One forgets that
there were a few German prisoners taken at that time, and the
peaceful life going on in Dover—the old ladies trundling up to
church because it was Sunday with their prayer books in their
hands and the children with their little gas masks playing and
somersaulting in the fields just outside the town. And then this
scene of these returning troops and the German prisoners sham-
bling out and small French naval craft and the inescapable feeling
that we were really where history was actually taking place.

The war had really begun, as Lester Pearson said in his diary. And
life at Canada House became so hectic that he wrote to George Ignatieff,
whom he had known as a Rhodes scholar in the immediate prewar days,
telling him that he had passed his foreign service exams and begging him
to come and work for the Canadian high commissioner because they had
the authorization of Prime Minister Mackenzie King and Dr. Skelton to
recruit him. At the time the war began, George Ignatieff had finished at
Oxford University and was doing a Ph.D. (which he never completed) at
London University. He had taken the exam for the Department of
External Affairs while in London. Since he could not join the Canadian
Armed Forces, while living in England, he volunteered for the British
Army and, because of his languages, was seconded to an intelligence unit
that had its quarters in the stables of Woburn Abbey, the Duke of
Bedford's estate. George accepted the Canadian offer and got his brother,
Nick, to take over his intelligence job.

GEORGE IGNATIEFF

I was given the job of taking care of the needs of all displaced
Canadians and getting them home. Also, all the people who
wanted to get their children to Canada, I had to arrange transport
for them. Since this was all based on the arrival of transports
carrying the Canadian First Division, reinforcements, supplies,

and that sort of thing, I had to work closely with Canadian military quarters, which was next door. As the ships came into the Clyde or Liverpool or wherever, we had these people to put on board all ticketed. It all had to be done under most difficult conditions because of the bombing of London which had started. We used to assemble people, boatloads of them, in a small theater on Charlotte Street in Bloomsbury. Then I would escort them to the boat and see them aboard. Mike was in charge of the operation and I was working under him.

There was a certain amount of anti-foreign feeling which led to a panic decision to intern everybody who was of German or Austrian or Italian origin. The internment was a general order, it was carried out very unfairly, and it led to a very messy situation because it turned out, of course, that people who were sent, for instance, to Canada, were intense anti-Nazis and anti-Fascists. It then fell to Canadian internment operations to sort this whole thing out. You'd get great savants like Gregory Baum, for instance, who is one of the great professors of theology at the University of Toronto, who arrived here originally as one of the interned people with a German name. He was intensely anti-Nazi, but everybody was interned, and then we were left to straighten this out.

I was very unhappy about it at the time. However, the War Office and the Home Office just said that they were facing an imminent danger of invasion, they just couldn't sit around trying to sort people out. The only thing to do was to ship them all out and that's how it happened.

Then, from that experience, I was turned on to handling all the prisoners-of-war work. That is, all prisoners of war—real prisoners of war who began to be captured from sunken U-boats, operations mainly at sea, or downed airplanes brought down during the Battle of Britain—they were shipped out to Canada. Now, that was a different operation, these were *bona-fide* prisoners that I had to handle.

During the Blitz, when air raids were incessant, there would have been no work done at all in Canada House if the officials there had obeyed the sirens and had gone down into the shelters. So Mike Pearson organized a watch on the roof of the building: when the officer on duty saw a certain flag raised on the Air Ministry which could be seen from Trafalgar Square, he knew it was the signal that the Luftwaffe was over London and pushed the panic button, as George Ignatieff called it, and everybody went down into the CMHQ (Canadian Military Headquarters) shelter. However, the flag could not be seen at night, and those working then had to judge the closeness of the attack by sound; they would go on coding and decoding until Canada House shook from the explosions; then they would pick up their helmets and gas masks and go below. There were bunks in the shelter and they could sleep there, and often did.

Besides his regular diplomatic work, Pearson did a weekly broadcast for the BBC that was beamed to Canada; he used a pseudonym, Michael Macdonald, and these broadcasts were the forerunners of the sort of commentaries that Leonard Brockington did later. George Ignatieff felt that Pearson could have been an extremely effective press correspondent, as he put it. He said that he was a very good teacher and an inspiring person to work with.

This was a time when the British stood alone, and the Western Allies consisted of Canada and the remnants of the national forces that had been defeated in Europe, the Free French, the Free Poles, the Free Norwegians, and so on. That was the situation in Britain (no one was counting the Australian, New Zealand, and Indian forces in the Middle East as far as this was concerned) and the question arose as to how the war should be conducted.

GEORGE IGNATIEFF

Should there be the re-creation of the War Cabinet structure of 1914–18 under Lloyd George or some version of it, or should there be certain statesmen including Canadians, brought into the British Cabinet or an Imperial War Cabinet, or should there be a War Conference, an Allied War Conference? I remember Mike Pearson calling me in and saying, "George, I know you're busy but I just haven't got time to do a first draft; you just go though the press and prepare an analysis of all the various types of suggestions that were made. Let me have it."

He worked this out into a fairly comprehensive report. I mean, one of the options that was mentioned was that General McNaughton, as the commander of the one organized command which was capable of taking the field, should be invited to join the

British War Cabinet. It was as specific as that. Some newspaper ran that idea. Anyway, Mike made this collection and put it in the form of a dispatch and Mr. Massey signed it. Some months followed and Mr. Massey showed me a letter, handwritten, signed by Mr. William Lyon Mackenzie King, reacting to this dispatch.

It dismissed all the options except the one option that he was prepared to come to a conference with Churchill, that he was not prepared to have any representation of Canada on the War Cabinet, that was a situation that might have worked back in the days of 1914–18, but now the situation was that the Canadian government was solely responsible to the House of Commons in Ottawa, that the proper decisions to be taken about the war or any aspect of the war had to be taken collectively by the Canadian Cabinet and that, while he was willing to come and take counsel and arrive at consultive decisions, the actual Canadian decision had to be taken with his colleagues in the Cabinet.

According to George Ignatieff, Mike Pearson had extraordinary political judgment and a spontaneous sense of public relations. He knew how to deal with prime ministers and with common soldiers by instinct. There were many complaints about the behavior of Canadian troops in Britain and Pearson was able to resolve these problems graciously and without creating the least kind of incident.

GEORGE IGNATIEFF

For instance, to give you an example, I definitely remember getting a letter saying that Private So-and-So of Such-and-Such Canadian regiment had been in the habit of spending his weekends at our home, as a result both I and my daughter are pregnant. Not that we hold that against this man, but when he last left, he took my daughter's bicycle, she needs same for going to work, signed Mrs. So-and-So. Now, Mike would know how to handle that kind of thing without creating any ill feeling.

On January 28, 1941, Dr. O. D. Skelton died suddenly while returning to his office from lunch; within an hour or so, according to Max Wershof, Prime Minister Mackenzie King, who was also secretary of state for external affairs, appointed Norman Robertson as acting under-

secretary. Lester Pearson made no secret of the fact that he thought that he should have been Dr. Skelton's successor. Although Hume Wrong had joined the year before he did, Wrong had spent all his time in missions abroad and had had no service in the department. Pearson, as he himself put it, was the only officer of senior rank who had served both in the department and abroad; he was certainly much senior to Norman Robertson, having been taken on as a first secretary in 1928, the year before the latter joined as a third secretary. He admitted that he was disappointed not to become deputy minister but said that his disappointment was lessened by the fact that Robertson was such a close personal friend.

Shortly after the appointment of the new under-secretary was confirmed, Pearson left London the day after the heaviest air raid of the war, to return to Ottawa for a new posting.

MAX WERSHOF

It was perfectly natural for Mike to have thought that either he or Hume Wrong should have been appointed under-secretary to succeed Dr. Skelton. As a matter of fact, during the period between the death of Dr. Skelton and the confirmation of Norman as under-secretary, Mike and I believe Hume Wrong himself both made it known to Mackenzie King that they ought to be considered for appointment.

When Mike came back he served under Norman Robertson as under-secretary with complete loyalty and devotion, so that their friendship was certainly never disturbed for one minute. The working relationship between Mike, who was considerably older than Norman, and Norman Robertson—well, one could see that it was just a wonderful working relationship. It was clear, even to junior officers like myself, that among Mike's many fine qualities was his complete lack of anything that could be called jealousy. There was no resentment on his part at the fact that Mr. King in his wisdom had passed over him in favor of Norman Robertson.

Lester Pearson became Robertson's assistant or, as he said, second-in-command; his main responsibility was administration, to make the department an effective working organization, but there were other concerns, such as relations with London and Washington. It was a happy if busy time for him to be back with family and friends in Ottawa, but it did not last for long. Early in 1942 he was informed that he would be going to

Washington as minister counselor in the Canadian Legation; the minister was Leighton McCarthy, a prominent Toronto lawyer and businessman who was an old friend of President Roosevelt. During the short time that he was at home there had been a drastic change in the nature of the war: Hitler's invasion of the Soviet Union and the Japanese attack on Pearl Harbor[1] had turned it from being largely a European conflict into a world- wide struggle. Overnight the USSR became "our gallant ally" and greatest hope for victory, but, as Pearson found, it took the Royal Canadian Mounted Police some time to adapt to the new circumstances and to stop treating the local Communists as dangerous subversives who ought to be locked up. The entry of Japan into the war meant that arrangements had to be made through neutral countries to bring the Canadian diplomats in Tokyo back to Canada.

Although it was a wrench to be on the move again, Pearson was delighted with the appointment since Washington had become the nerve center of the whole Allied war effort. He could look back on the fact that he was the assistant and chief diplomatic officer in London—the "univer- sal joint," as the West Coast journalist, Bruce Hutchison, described him— at a time when London was the most important place in the War. Now he was to be assistant and chief diplomatic officer in Washington when the United States capital was the most important place in the war. It was a sign that his skills and talents were fully appreciated and recognized, and this helped to assuage any hurt he might have felt at being passed over as deputy minister.

The first thing the Pearsons had to do was to find accommodation in overcrowded wartime Washington. Fortunately, the Canadian military attaché, Major C. M. Bud Drury, was being transferred overseas, and

---

[1]At the time of the attack H. F. Temp Feaver was on a Japanese ship just off Pearl Harbor. There were few ships plying the Pacific at the end of 1941 because everyone knew that war was imminent, and when Feaver heard that the *Tatsuta Maru* was sailing to Los Angeles to pick up Japanese nationals who had been evicted from the Panama Canal Zone, he booked a passage on the liner—he was due for home leave from his post with the Canadian Legation in Tokyo. On December 8 there was a great deal of excitement aboard, with the radios blaring, and Feaver heard about the attack, but although it had occurred at dawn, the *Tatsuta Maru* kept steaming eastward until one o'clock, when the Japanese authorities ordered the ship about. "It was beautiful, the wake was like a huge white feather boa on the blue Pacific," Feaver said. He was arrested on the arrival of the *Tatsuta Maru* in Yokohama. However, a kindly Japanese policeman consoled him by saying, "We've sunk the American Navy at Pearl Harbor. We've sunk the British Navy off Singapore. So the United States and Britain will be asking for peace in two or three days. You'll be free in a week." Feaver remained interned in the Canadian residence in Tokyo for seven months and was repatriated in the middle of 1942.

they were able to take over his place in Chevy Chase—a large house that had been a summer residence in the old days but had been winterized, and there were some fruit trees in the garden. William P. Bundy, who became an important official in the Johnson administration during the Vietnam War, remembered a story that his father-in-law, Dean Acheson, told about a dinner party at the Pearsons'.

WILLIAM P. BUNDY

There were a lot of people there, including the Achesons, and they were having a jolly good time on a summer's evening when the area was hit by one of those summer thunderstorms that can be really quite severe. The rain was beating down outside this screened porch and somebody, who was obviously feeling no pain at all, said, "Let's take to the boats, take to the boats." So they all got up on top of one of the tables on this verandah, and they played that they were on a lifeboat and they would accept certain people and they wouldn't accept others. It was a rather colorful episode which two or three other participants seem to recall. Both men [Pearson and Acheson] had gaiety and *joie de vivre*, and they enjoyed sharing it when they were both relatively carefree. They found each other's company quite delightful.

In Washington, Lester Pearson's main concerns were the same as they had been in London; they were the military and political problems that arose from the need for Allied cooperation in the war effort, only there was a difference. In London, while he might have been annoyed by the patronizing and colonialist attitude of some of the British officials, the Canadians were consulted and kept fully informed, whereas in Washington they were as likely to be ignored. Of course, the situation had changed: in the early years of the war, and especially after the fall of France, Canada was Britain's most important ally and the acknowledged arsenal of democracy, but, with the entry of the Soviet Union and the United States into the conflict, the Canadian role diminished, as it was bound to do. The United States became the dominant factor in the Alliance and the workshop of victory. The British and Americans dealt directly with each other in joint civilian boards and combined chiefs-of-staff committees; they were the Big Powers and there was no room in their counsels for lesser powers, Churchill and Roosevelt worked closely to-

gether and hardly ever took Mackenzie King into their confidence.

As Pearson wrote in his memoirs, "We were not consulted about plans and decisions at high levels unless our agreement was essential, and this was seldom. Often we were not even informed in advance about those plans nor our interest in them recognized except as part of a 'British Empire.' Indeed, the Big Two saw nothing incongruous in deciding to meet, or to have their representatives meet in Canada without telling the Canadian government about it beforehand." Whenever the British and Americans felt they had gone too far in slighting Canada, as in the case of the Quebec Conference, they would go out of their way to placate Mr. King: as Pearson said, Churchill and Roosevelt would pose with him for pictures or write him fulsome letters.

Then there was the vexing question of Canadian sovereignty, particularly in the Northwest where thousands of United States troops drove the Alcan (Alaska-Canada) Highway through a forbidding wilderness at Blitzkrieg speed and built a chain of airfields that were to be the staging posts of a supply route to the Soviet Union. There were few Canadians in the area, and the Americans behaved as if they were in their own country. The issue came to a head when the British Columbia authorities insisted on trying a black American soldier for attacking a white woman; the U. S. military immediately ordered court-martial proceedings. As a result of Lester Pearson's negotiations, a reciprocal agreement was reached whereby the Canadian government granted the American authorities the rights of jurisdiction over their forces in Canada. At the time the Alcan was built, it was understood that it would be an international road, but the Canadian government paid for the construction of the airfields along the highway that the Americans had built. Max Wershof, who was posted to Washington in 1942, recalled delivering the check.

MAX WERSHOF

Actually, earlier, when I'd been in Ottawa, I was involved in my legal capacity with some of the aspects of the negotiations for the exchange of notes that set up the Alaska Highway proposition so that some of the problems that arose afterward about payment would come over to my desk in Washington. I recall that one of the amusing and pleasant things I did was to go down to the State Department one day carrying a check for, I forget whether it was eighty million dollars or hundred million dollars, some stupendous amount—in those days eighty million dollars sounded like eight billion dollars today—to present this to Jack Hickerson, who was the expert on Canada, among other things and in charge of all Canadian affairs.

I gave this check with an accompanying diplomatic note to Hickerson and he was so astonished to be handling a check of this size that he engaged in a form of high school humor, going down the corridor in the old State Department Building and dropping into different offices and saying, "Oh, I have a little check here; do you think you could cash it for me, I'm short of money." He then presented this check for eighty million dollars.

As the war progressed, and the United States became totally involved, more and more Canadian officials were sent to Washington; almost every department in Ottawa found it had to have one or more representatives with the various agencies that ran the great American war machine. These officials were mainly concerned with such matters as priorities and procurement, as well as production sharing; they were outside the greatly expanded Canadian mission although they came under the supervision of the head of the mission. At times there seemed to be utter confusion in Washington, as Lester Pearson noted, but there was also abounding energy and, despite often contradictory policies, the Americans got things done and the war won.

One of the men from the Canadian Ministry of Munitions and Supply in Washington was Sidney Pierce, who was to join External Affairs after the war and become a distinguished Canadian envoy and ambassador. He met Mike Pearson as a result of the baseball games that Mike organized between members of the U. S. State Department and some of the Canadians stationed in Washington.

SIDNEY PIERCE

The first couple of games were walk-overs for the Canadians. We clobbered the Americans, we really did. Mike, of course, was quick to realize that a crisis was developing. Canadian-American relations, which we hoped to strengthen by these baseball games, were becoming severely strained. The question was, what to do? The idea of, you know, of throwing the game and deliberately playing to lose was repugnant, of course, to people like us, but Mike found a way out. He arranged to have a large supply of martinis placed in a bucket of ice just by first base. Every player who reached first was given a martini. So the oftener you got on first base, the more martinis you had, and the more martinis you had, the less likely you were to get on base.

Well, from then on, this is what would happen on a Sunday morning. We Canadians would pile up a large lead in the first few innings and from then on, as our euphoria increased, we would happily watch the Americans catch up. By the time they caught us, neither they nor we gave a hoot who won.

In the summer of 1944 Lester B. Pearson became Canadian ambassador to the United States, succeeding Leighton McCarthy, who had decided to retire and return to private life. The mission had been elevated from legation to embassy a few months before, a move that Prime Minister Mackenzie King resisted and only agreed to when he was assured that it would cost no more money. It was pointed out to him that it would be ludicrous if Canada maintained a legation while every Latin American banana republic had an embassy in Washington. Pearson was frankly surprised that Mr. King should have appointed him because he knew that the prime minister was suspicious of his activist approach to diplomacy and was afraid that it would get Canada involved in too many foreign entanglements. It was also unusual for a promotion such as his, from a subordinate position to becoming head man, to be made within a mission.

At the time the Canadian ambassador's residence was a suite on the second and third floors of the embassy, one of the great mansions on Massachusetts Avenue; the chancery and other offices were on the lower floors. When Geoffrey Pearson visited Washington on holidays—he was a boarder at Trinity College School near Port Hope, Ontario, while his father was ambassador—he was tremendously impressed by the magnificent surroundings. He remembered the butler and other servants and the state dinners, and among the guests he recalled were Mr. King and the governor-general, the Earl of Athlone, and Princess Alice, and the Achesons, and a journalist friend, James "Scotty" Reston, who was a reporter on the New York Times *then.*

Geoffrey was not in Washington when the atom bombs were dropped on Hiroshima and Nagasaki but learned about his father's reaction from talking to him later.

GEOFFREY PEARSON

It was one of disbelief at first. He was aware of the development of the atomic bomb because Canada was part of the picture, but I don't think he ever realized just what it entailed. I think he had a very hazy scientific understanding, and I don't think he ever grasped the concept of nuclear energy except in a political sense. He understood what it meant. The explosion shocked him deeply and then the dropping of the bomb in Japan—he could accept that rationally, as a way of ending the war, but I am sure he couldn't accept it emotionally.

He also felt slightly guilty about Canada's own part in all of this. I never really talked to him about that, and he doesn't say much about it in his memoirs. It may be that he felt that Canada should have thought more about the effects of this new source of energy. Of course, it was a very tightly held secret and, as I say, I think the nonscientific civilians were not too much aware of what it meant. But his views on nuclear weapons were put in a dispatch to Ottawa fairly soon after the explosions in Japan, and that dispatch has been quoted by a number of writers on Canadian foreign policy. One can see from it that he did feel strongly, but also constructively. He wanted to use this new threat to do something about international organization. His favorite Shakespeare quotation was "From this nettle danger we pluck this flower safety." He often saw crisis as a way of getting things done constructively.

4 Postwar Hopes and Fears

Even when the war was at its worst, preparations were made for peace, and Lester Pearson was involved in them from the beginning. As early as June 1942 the Canadian government agreed to an American proposal that an international relief agency should be set up, and Pearson worked long and hard on the organization of the United Nations Relief and Rehabilitation Administration (UNRRA). In fact, Max Wershof says that he spent at least a third of his time, and maybe half, away from the legation and at the building in Washington where the international committee met. There was the old problem: while Canada was expected to be one of the main suppliers, only the Big Four—the United States, the United Kingdom, the Soviet Union, and China—were to be on the Central Policy Committee, the controlling body of UNRRA. The Americans were quite adamant about this; they said that if Canada were allowed on the committee, then they would have to let Brazil or some other Latin American country have a place, and the Soviet Union would be upset. The Canadian government was indignant, and there was talk of "no contribution without representation."

Finally Pearson came up with the compromise proposal that Canada should be chairman of the Suppliers or Supply Committee and, as such, participate in the deliberations of the Policy Committee; but it required a good deal of hard selling on his part to get the Canadian government to agree to this solution. Pearson was made chairman of the Supply Committee and attended the first UNRRA Council meeting, which was held at Atlantic City in November of 1943 and laid down the principles and procedures to govern the agency's work. It was there that Mitchell Sharp,[1] *who had been in the grain trade in Winnipeg and had recently joined the Finance Department in Ottawa, got to know Mike Pearson. Sharp recalled helping to write a speech for Pearson, in which he paraphrased Lincoln's famous line "No nation can survive half free and half slave" by saying that the world could not survive half fed and half clothed.*

On May 17, 1943, the first formal conference of the United Nations was held in a luxury hotel at Hot Springs, West Virginia; Pearson was one of the five Canadian delegates to attend this meeting, which was concerned mainly with the basic questions of food and agriculture. An interim commission was set up to continue the work of the Hot Springs Conference in Washington, and Pearson was elected its chairman, which he described as his most important responsibility up to then. Out of the commission grew the Food and Agriculture Organization (FAO), and Pearson also chaired the founding conference of that UN agency which was held in Quebec City during the latter half of October 1945.

All this must have been a matter of deep satisfaction to Lester Pearson because he believed passionately in a world order. In fact, his son Geoffrey said that he was an internationalist, if not a world federalist.

GEOFFREY PEARSON

If he was not a dreamer I think at least he hoped that the UN would grow into a body which would be able to prevent war through collective machinery and collective security. The phrase that he used most, I suppose, was collective security. That was the ideal which statesmen of the time wanted to bring into effect.

Among the younger members of the department who echoed his words on collective security was Ernest Côté. To Jean Fournier and others, nationalism and sovereignty had become dirty words. There was talk of One World and a One World Movement sprang up. Escott Reid, another Rhodes scholar who joined the department at the end of 1938, could be counted among the idealists. John Holmes, a wartime recruit to the foreign service, was secretary of the Post Hostilities Planning Committee.

[1]Almost a quarter of a century later Mitchell Sharp was to become Prime Minister Pearson's second finance minister. (See *Lester Pearson and the Dream of Unity,* Toronto: Doubleday Canada Limited, 1978.)

JOHN HOLMES

I think what you had in the department were, as someone said, two wings of opinion, although that's a bit too categorical. There was, in a sense, the Washington wing, which was Mike and Escott Reid, who tended on the whole to be somewhat more utopian. In Ottawa, you had Norman Robertson and Hume Wrong who were certainly idealists but who were much closer to the political process. I think they knew much more of what Mackenzie King and the government would take. They were aware that everybody was using fine words which sounded like world federalism, but I don't think they really meant it. I don't mean that there was deliberate hypocrisy. These are the words you use, "one world" and there was a great deal of talking and Mike himself constantly spoke about the need to surrender sovereignty to a super-sovereign body. I think Wrong and Robertson thought more in terms of the functionalist approach to these things. There's less emphasis on surrender of sovereignty, which is a kind of a meaningless and beautiful phrase, much more on the concept of constructing international institutions on the basis of what you can do.

Perhaps on the one hand, Escott Reid tended to like constructing institutions, he was a beautiful draftsman, and did a marvelous job of setting up NATO—the rules of procedure of the General Assembly owe a great deal to him. That sort of thing. Mike was philosophically attracted by that. I think what was very useful in the department at that time was that you had Escott Reid on one side and Hume Wrong on the other, and they countered each other a good deal. Escott was constantly pressing out farther and Hume was the person who could adjust the moves. I think Mike was sort of torn between them, which was very good. It was a very constructive dialogue within the department.

GEORGE IGNATIEFF

There was an organization called the One World Movement and I remember that we used to get constant communications from this organization centered in Washington. Now Mr. Pearson, I don't think, was ever idealistic to the extent of saying that we could, by some miracle, become one world. What I think he was saying was that there had to be effective collective security, that an effort, a conscious effort, an untiring effort, had to be made to prevent a third world war. He went about it somewhat pragmatically, he didn't say that we must imagine ourselves as one happy family. He was aware of the realities, of the difficulties, for instance, of the relations with Russia. He was aware of the difficulties of relations between the United States and Britain and how Canada could be made a victim of this kind of great power play.

What he was trying to do was not to build pie in the sky but to catch this moving momentum toward a world organization and make it into something which Canada and Canadians could relate to—in which we'd have a role in proportion to our contribution. If we didn't want to contribute, we wouldn't have a voice; if we did want to contribute, we would have a voice, and there would be no compromise on that.

CHARLES RITCHIE

I think it's a great mistake to imagine that anyone in the Department of External Affairs had any dewy-eyed illusion about a new heaven and a new earth following the war, or the United Nations being the organization to bring them about. Mike had had a long experience at the League and had been a strong supporter of it, of course. His wish and his policy was to make the United Nations something more realistic and more effective than the old League. We knew that it was going to be heavy going. Then on top of that in those very peculiar years after the war by an accident of history most of the industrialized nations of the West and East had been laid low, Canada played a part way out of proportion to any part that we played before or since. When we went to San Francisco as the middle power or the upper-middle power, our influence was deemed by ourselves and others to be very important and Mike was one of the architects of policy.

I might just say a word about his methods as I experienced them over many years. He approached his objectives indirectly, not by method of head-on confrontations. He was incredibly persistent. He would back away from something and then come back to it, come around to it again. It was fascinating to watch. It was a form of gamesmanship of a most accomplished kind and his footwork—not a bad analogy for him with his interest in football—was expert. Very seldom was there a fumble.

The first conference on the establishment of an international organization for the maintenance of peace and security was held behind closed doors at Dumbarton Oaks in August 1944; the discussions were confined to the representatives of the Big Three, the United States, United Kingdom, and the Soviet Union—later, expanded to the Big Four with the inclusion of China. It took all of Lester Pearson's diplomatic skills to find out what was being done and to keep the participants, particularly the British and the Americans, informed as to Ottawa's views on various points. The Dumbarton Oaks draft of a charter for a world body was made public on October 10, 1944, and was the subject of a thorough study and review by all concerned, including the Big Three at the Yalta Conference in 1945. A few changes were made.

As the date for the founding conference of the United Nations at San Francisco approached, Pearson was satisfied that Canadian preparatory work had been thoroughly done. Yet he knew that it would be a struggle, that the United States government, in order to gain the support of Congress, had insisted on what amounted to an American or Big Power stranglehold, and that some of the most important people had little or no regard for a world organization. Prime Minister Mackenzie King had given lip service to the covenant of the old League of Nations and did not believe in the concept of collective security. Dean Rusk, who was an up-and-coming young official in Washington then, said that there were high officials in the State Department who were opposed to the United Nations, while Averell Harriman was sent to see Stalin to persuade him to treat the San Francisco Conference seriously.

AVERELL HARRIMAN

As far as Roosevelt was concerned, his principal objective was to get an agreement about the United Nations; he didn't want to make the mistake that Woodrow Wilson had made over the League of Nations after the war. He wanted the American people committed and he wanted Stalin committed. And, of course, in that connection he wasn't too successful because he did get agreement from Stalin on a number of points that were open—it was not easy, there were a great many differences. You know the veto really was Roosevelt's, not Stalin's, and President Roosevelt didn't think he'd get the United Nations agreed to by the Congress without a veto because they [Congress] didn't want to give up sovereignty, but, unfortunately, Stalin was not overly keen on the United Nations.

Before Roosevelt's death Stalin said he was going to send [Andrei] Vyshinsky [to the San Francisco Conference], and I remember going to see Stalin after Roosevelt's death—it was only a day or two after his death. Stalin was very much moved and very much concerned about the future of the world and recognized the role Roosevelt had played in the world. I said, "Well, you can do a great deal to show the world that we are working together," and he said, "What can I do?" And I said, "Well, you can send Molotov instead of Vyshinsky." Molotov turned around and said—my interpreter told me he said, "No, I can't go, I've got engagements." Stalin said, "No, you will go." And it was done under the moment of concern at the loss of President Roosevelt.

As I said, Stalin was none too keen; he thought that the Americans would dominate the United Nations. He kept talking about our—that we would control the twenty-one Latin American countries and he thought we dominated them. You know, he thought anybody that was friendly to you, you dominated. He didn't accept our idea of friendly nations being one of equality and he knew that he'd be outvoted and he was rather concerned about it.

There were several questions still open which I settled. They were related to the right of an individual country to bring a complaint to the Security Council. Stalin wanted to make that a substantive question which would let the veto apply and we wanted it to be a procedural question which would make the voting on a majority basis. We won and he finally agreed to that.

The other question was the right of the [UN General] Assembly to debate matters. He wanted to restrict the Assembly's discussion only to those subjects that the Security Council assigned to it as an agenda. Stalin was concerned because he thought that the United States and the West would have control of the United Nations and of course, in those days, that was true. It's quite changed now.

DEAN RUSK

Dean Acheson had very little, if any, respect for the United Nations. He thought that was a waste of time. He had almost contempt for the United Nations. Mike Pearson had a much clearer view of what the United Nations ought to do and try to accomplish than Dean Acheson did, and I think that led to some margins of impatience on Dean Acheson's part with Mike Pearson occasionally.

It was in a mood of fin de guerre *euphoria that the San Francisco Conference met on April 25, 1945, a mood that was heightened by the fact that VE Day occurred in the midst of its deliberations. Despite the chaos and confusion at the opening, Lester Pearson remembered it as a busy and exciting time: the Canadian delegation, he said, worked hard and effectively and was responsible for some of the compromises that were necessary if the United Nations Charter were to be accepted by all of the fifty founding nations. However, the euphoria did not last long. It soon became evident that there was nothing united about the United Nations and that the world was split into two suspicious and antagonistic power blocks.*

A first symptom of this mutual distrust and hostility, which came to be known as the Cold War, was the Gouzenko Affair. In September 1945 a cypher clerk at the Soviet Embassy in Ottawa defected and turned over to the Royal Canadian Mounted Police documents that purported to show that an "atom spy ring" was operating in Canada, but it was not until February 1946 that news of this was made public and the first sensational reports appeared. The revelation of Russian espionage came as a rude shock to the young idealists in the Department of External Affairs who were advocates of international cooperation and interdependence. It wasn't cricket, as Louis Audette said. The royal commission's report on the Gouzenko Affair came out at the beginning of March 1946, just a couple of days before Churchill made the speech at Fulton, Missouri, in which he accused the Soviets of lowering an "iron curtain" across Europe, and asserted that under no circumstances should the United States share the secret of the atom bomb with anyone, including the United Nations. This speech came to be regarded as a Western declaration of the Cold War. As the Canadian ambassador in Washington, Pearson was asked by Churchill to read the speech before it was delivered; aside from suggesting a couple of small changes, he seemed to approve of its contents.

So the Cold War could be said to have begun shortly after World War Two ended, and Arnold Smith was able to confirm this timing. He remained in Moscow when the Canadian ambassador, Dana Wilgress, left to attend the San Francisco Conference, and at that time the Russians seemed ready to be cooperative, and Wilgress reported such to Ottawa. However, in the late summer of 1945, there was a sharp policy change, and the Soviets decided, as Smith said, to grab Eastern Europe and impose totalitarian control, and to hell with the West. Averell Harriman quotes the Bulgarian American revolutionary, George Andrechin, as attributing this Soviet policy change primarily to the atom bomb; Andrechin said that the Kremlin, which was proud of the Red Army's achievements during the war, was shocked to learn that American possession of the bomb once again exposed Russia's comparative weakness. John Holmes, who was sent to Moscow as chargé d'affaires—for a time after the Gouzenko Affair, neither Canada nor the Soviet Union had ambassadors in their respective countries—spoke of Russian fears and suspicions.

There were other causes of the Cold War: the confrontation in Berlin and along the demarcation lines, and American threats of Soviet destruction at a time when the United States war machine was being dismantled.

JOHN HOLMES

The Americans had the atom bomb; they had developed it in cooperation with the British and ourselves; they had developed it for a specific wartime purpose—and everybody agreed the Allies had to get it before the Nazis did. They had it. I don't think they brandished it. Obviously it frightened the Russians that somebody who could be hostile to them had this thing. Anybody sitting in Moscow would have got a little nervous physically about it. Sure, some senators and generals made crazy speeches, things like that, but the fact is they didn't use it. But there it was. It was a form of blackmail in a sense even if you weren't using it and if you didn't want to use it.

DEAN RUSK

After VJ Day the United States demobilized almost completely almost overnight. By 1946 we did not have a division in our army or air force that could be considered ready for combat. Such ships of our navy as remained afloat were being manned by skeleton crews. Our defense budget for three fiscal years, 1947–48–49, came down to about eleven billion dollars. So perhaps—and the same thing was true throughout much of the West—so perhaps we exposed Joseph Stalin to temptations during that period. He saw all our divisions melting away. I suspect that had a lot to do with his attempt to keep his troops in Iran; his demand for the two eastern provinces of Turkey; the coup in Czechoslovakia; the guerrillas in Greece; the blockade in Berlin; the green flag he gave to the North Koreans to go after South Korea.

We were trying to find answers to problems without the use of forces which we did not have at that time. Those who afterward said that we should have used armed forces to break the blockade of Berlin would have to answer, "Which armed forces?" The Soviets were sitting there with massed forces and we didn't have them. So we used an airlift to try to find a diplomatic solution, which we succeeded in doing after a few months. But these were all difficult and complex and challenging issues, and Mike Pearson was always pretty cool and level-headed, but nevertheless completely loyal to the notion of a Western alliance, the accumulated interests of the West, and loyal to the idea of the United Nations himself.

I might add that he was a somewhat unusual person in that he strongly supported both NATO and the United Nations. A good many members of the NATO alliance, when they saw NATO coming into being, tended to neglect the United Nations or treat it with contempt, as though it didn't really matter very much. Other countries never caucused on United Nations matters like other groups caucused. Mike Pearson understood that alongside of NATO we must consider the United Nations a very important organization. As a matter of fact, in our own country, Senator Arthur Vandenberg, in supporting NATO, wanted to make it very clear that under no circumstance was NATO to be considered a substitute for the United Nations. Sometimes some of our friends in NATO lost sight of the importance of the UN. Mike

Pearson always recognized that this was a very important forum and we ought to pay attention to it, support it.

GEOFFREY PEARSON

My father thought of NATO as not a second UN but a kind of halfway house: if you couldn't make the UN work, then you got off the train for a time and took a smaller train on more narrow tracks, but you went in the same direction. Presumably at some point you got back onto the main train. That's what he expected, that NATO would be a short-term solution to the Cold War and as soon as the Russians saw that they couldn't get away with anything, then you got rid of NATO and went back to the UN, where all the main passengers were anyway, to use the train analogy. By that time the Russians would cooperate in the UN and you'd have the UN working the way it should work.

This was one theme of his thinking, but with that was what was most certainly a contradiction, and that was that NATO would become the main train. It would develop in such a way that it became an Atlantic community; all countries around the Atlantic would belong to it and you'd have a kind of federation of some sort which would—its sovereignties would eventually merge and it would be the Western group acting as one. Presumably that group would join the UN—he didn't give up the UN but perhaps he thought of that group as in a sense having a single membership.

Both these ideas were not very carefully worked out. Again, he wasn't a philosopher, he didn't have long-term blueprints, but he wanted in either case to reduce the importance of national sovereignty and increase the importance of international institutions and decision-making. So both these vehicles served his purpose to some extent. But NATO was definitely in his view, I think, a secondary organization; the primary one was still the UN and if one had to wait until the Russians changed their behavior, well then one just had to wait.

There was no doubt that the North Atlantic Treaty Organization was a direct response to the Cold War; the military alliance was also a reaction to the devastation and chaos in so much of Europe which provided conditions that the Communists could exploit (subversion was also a facet of the Cold War). Revolutionary strikes had brought France to a standstill and had turned off the lights in Paris; the British were shivering in the dark, but this was due to a lack of coal being mined; Greece was divided by civil war with the Communist guerrillas holding the countryside and the government forces bottled up in the cities; the Western Zones of Germany had not even begun to pick themselves up from the rubble and the ruins.

At the end of 1947 the statesmen of the victorious powers of Western Europe made an effort to bring about stability and order; they negotiated, with American encouragement, an alliance known as Western Union — the Americans must have wished that they had chosen some other name than one that was to be confused with a telegraph company. The Brussels Treaty bound the participants to joint action against an aggressor. But it was not enough. In February 1948 Ernest Bevin, the British foreign secretary, proposed a military alliance between the United Kingdom and the United States. But this was going too far too fast for American opinion.

ESCOTT REID

The Americans were holding back. They were saying, "Let's see what you people can do in the Brussels Treaty before we discuss what role the United States might play." Then two things happened. One was the Soviet *coup d'état* in Czechoslovakia. The other, and as frightening, was a message from Norway that they feared they would soon face Soviet demands for a pact which would reduce Norway to the level of a Soviet satellite. Norway, at that time and I think ever since, has been regarded as a pretty stable, sensible country, not given to panic, and when the Norwegians had this fear and you had the coup in Czechoslovakia and Jan Masaryk's death, which came as a great emotional shock to people who had known him, this made possible the opening of the discussions on the North Atlantic Treaty.

In 1948 the Cold War reached a climax with what became known as the Berlin Blockade. This was the attempt by the Soviets to force the British and the Americans out of the former German capital by closing the Autobahns and other overland routes connecting the city with the Western Zones. The excuse given was that the roads and the railways needed repairing, but the real reason was that the Western occupying powers had approved the issue of a new currency for the Western Zones which the Communists realized posed a threat to their East Zone. The world teetered on the brink of nuclear warfare. Winston Churchill, who was out of office at the time, urged that the atom bomb be used to break the blockade, but British Cabinet papers reveal that his proposal was rejected by Prime Minister Attlee and President Truman. An airlift kept the beleaguered city going while negotiations (in which Lester Pearson participated) went on at the United Nations and elsewhere. Finally, in May 1949, the blockade was lifted.

However, it was not the fear of Soviet military aggression, of the Red Army driving westward, that prompted the formation of the North Atlantic Treaty Organization, which was essentially an anti-Communist alliance. It was rather the fear of revolution, of coup d'états, of subversion, which was a side of the Cold War. John Holmes made this clear in his dispatches from Moscow, and so did Escott Reid, who was Pearson's second-in-command and one of the principal Canadian negotiators on NATO.

JOHN HOLMES

For the most part, I was repeating what the British and Americans were thinking, on the grounds that it was very important for us to know what their estimates were, whether we agreed with them or not. They were both fairly sober, their views were that the Russians were nervous; they also had a feeling of weakness, *vis-à-vis* the United States in particular, and they would probably be pretty cautious about striking. I know that my view was that it was unlikely that you would have a military push to the Atlantic; that the great danger was not a Soviet march to the North Sea; that it was the kind of things that could happen in France and Italy that happened in Czechoslovakia, where the Soviet troops simply sat on the border. You'd get that kind of a push if you had Communist take-overs in Paris and Rome. The whole situation then would be pretty dangerous. That was the real worry.

There was an interesting dispatch from Dana Wilgress [former Canadian ambassador in Moscow] commenting on one of mine. I think his view, which I certainly shared, was that it was desirable for the Western powers to look firm, not to look as if they would scatter, but at the same time not to go too far, because you could frighten the Russians and they would take some rash actions. This was the balance [that we had to maintain].

ESCOTT REID

It was not so much a fear that the Russians would invade Western Europe. The dominant fear was that by a process of gradual penetration, they would take over one Western European government after another, beginning with Italy. We believed then that there might well have been no First or Second World Wars if it had been made clear to Germany on both occasions that, if war occurred, they would eventually face an unbeatable coalition.

The moral to be drawn was that it was prudent to make clear to Stalin that if a Third World War broke out, he would face an unbeatable coalition, and we'd form the coalition in advance so that the war would not occur. St. Laurent put this very clearly on the day that the treaty was made public in a document which he wrote in his own hand. I had drafted a statement for him, but he wrote a much improved statement in his own hand.

Pearson was a good deal more optimistic about the results of the San Francisco Conference than Norman Robertson was or St. Laurent, certainly more than I was, and he was very depressed, worried, and apprehensive by the failure of the United Nations to fulfill his expectations. As a result, he felt we had to move to a military alliance and [he wanted it to be] more than a military alliance.

At the end of 1946 Lester Pearson was recalled to Ottawa after having been ambassador in Washington for a little more than two years. He was appointed under-secretary of state for external affairs, succeeding Norman Robertson, who went to London as high commissioner. It was a triple shuffle, with Vincent Massey retiring and Hume Wrong becoming ambassador to the United States. When the first informal discussions began on a North Atlantic Treaty, Pearson was under-secretary, but on September 10, 1948, he was sworn in as secretary of state—by which time the NATO negotiations had reached the halfway mark—so that he spent half of the time at the conference table as an official and half of the time as a responsible minister, although none of the other participants noticed any difference. That was the trouble, as far as Mackenzie King was concerned, and the diaries show the prime minister hovering around like a querulous old maid, grumbling about Pearson as an official taking a too prominent role and getting the government into an obligation "from which we will find a great difficulty in being free." However, Mr. King retired at the end of 1948, and, as minister, Pearson served under Prime Minister St. Laurent, with whom he saw eye to eye on almost every international issue.

The first preliminary meeting on NATO was held in Washington and was confined to the United States, United Kingdom, and Canada; the meeting was at the official level, and Lester Pearson, who was undersecretary then—it was in March of 1948—represented Canada. The security was such that the site of the talks was the Pentagon's war room. As Escott Reid said, we kept the meeting secret from everybody but the Russians. Donald Maclean, who was later to be exposed as a Soviet agent, was a senior officer with the British Embassy in Washington at the time and attended these discussions.

At first the United States proposed a unilateral guarantee for Western Europe rather than a military alliance, but Canada was opposed to this.

ESCOTT REID

The main reason was that if it were a unilateral U.S. guarantee, called an extension of the Monroe Doctrine to Western Europe, there would be no particular reason why Canada should join in. There was no place for us. There would be no reason why Canada should follow the United States in making a unilateral guarantee of Western Europe. The problem would still remain of defence cooperation between Canada and the U.S., and we would then have a defense alliance with the United States rather than an alliance in which Canada and the United States were both members. It is a constant objective of Canadian foreign policy that we shouldn't be left alone with the United States. There was safety, as Mike Pearson said, in numbers: to call in Western Europe to redress the balance in North America.

A unilateral guarantee, in our opinion, was also a weak instrument. It could have been accompanied by a Congressional resolution, a resolution of both Houses of Congress, but it wouldn't provide the same certainty of American assistance in resisting aggression in Western Europe as would an alliance. Also, it could be regarded as an act of charity on the part of the United States. One thing St. Laurent insisted on from the beginning was that what was needed was not an act of charity from the United States, or from North America. What Western Europeans needed was our assistance.

GEORGE IGNATIEFF

I do remember that there was a strong difference of views in Washington between those who really wanted nothing more than just an outright American guarantee of Western security in view of the Soviet threat and not get involved—it may have been due to this colonial business, not only Palestine but the problems of Algeria and all the rest of it—and those like [Jack] Hickerson and Escott [Reid] and Mike who wanted [an Atlantic] community. There were various stages in between but the pace was really set by George Marshall and [President] Truman, namely, that there would be a guarantee of European security in answer to the Brussels pact. That's where the starting point was.

Once the participants had rejected the idea of a guarantee and decided on an alliance, the question of a name came up. Hume Wrong suggested "Western Alliance." However, there was general agreement that membership should be limited to the North Atlantic countries; it was not contemplated in the early stages of the negotiations that Italy, let alone Greece and Turkey, would be members. Lester Pearson was even opposed to the inclusion of Portugal. Thus, the alliance became known as the North Atlantic Treaty Organization, or NATO for short, and, as a result of American pressure, not only Italy but Greece and Turkey became members.

It was obvious that the supreme commander of the NATO forces in Western Europe was, in fact, appointed by the United States, but Escott Reid did not know how it was formally done, whether or not the North Atlantic Council, which was supposed to be the ruling body of the alliance, ratified the nomination.

ESCOTT REID

Mr. Pearson put in the first speech he gave as foreign minister in Kingston that we wanted the organs of the alliance to be constitutionally responsible to the alliance. We didn't want, in the event of another war, the arrogation of power by two or three countries, which had happened in the Second World War.

One of the reasons why Pearson was opposed to including Italy, Greece, and Turkey in the alliance was that it would make it just that much more difficult to achieve his concept of a North Atlantic community. There were few ties, if any, that bound those three countries to the others—not even geographical ties. From the very first meeting on NATO, he had made it clear that Canada wanted something more than a military alliance. When St. Laurent was external affairs minister, he told the Canadian House of Commons that "nothing in the Charter precludes regional political arrangements or agencies provided that they are consistent with the purposes and principles of the United Nations and these regional agencies are entitled to take measures of collective self-defence against armed attacks until the Security Council has acted." Later, in April 1948, St. Laurent, in a speech undoubtedly written by Pearson, said that if the North Atlantic alliance were to endure, it would have to have political, social, and economic foundations and that the Canadians were being realists rather than idealists in pressing for this.

However, Pearson soon found that most of the delegates, and certainly those of the major powers, were less than enthusiastic about making NATO more than a military alliance. Some of them said that it was mixing apples and oranges. However, they did agree to Article 2 of the treaty, the social and economic provision that was meant to bring about the greater integration of the members of the North Atlantic pact, although they only gave it lip service in the end.

JOHN HOLMES

I think NATO was as much a Canadian idea as anybody's. A lot of the thinking came from us—at least Article 2 and our emphasis that it should not simply be a military alliance, that it should be based on a sense of community and economic and other questions. However, there's a fundamental misunderstanding of what we intended by Article 2. It's implied simply that Canada wanted to turn NATO into an economic organization. But that wasn't really the point. I think maybe Escott [Reid] would have liked to do that—he at heart was a world federalist. But that wasn't the view of Norman Robertson. I know his feelings because I was working with him in London at the time, and the thinking was this: if we're going to militarize, we have to have some kind of political solidarity; it's not that we're going to have a common foreign policy or anything so naïve as that, but that we have to consult each other and consider each other's interests, because if we're going to get involved in a war, this has to be. Everybody in NATO accepted that.

Really in a sense what we were saying was that this has to extend to economics, that, in our dealings with each other economically, you must not start a cut-throat war, because that would break down the alliance faster than any political difference about something or other. That's what we meant.

ESCOTT REID

From the beginning MacKenzie King believed that the North Atlantic alliance should be more than a military alliance. I don't know how far this was spontaneous or how far Pearson had put this into King's mind, but he didn't like military alliances. My guess is—and I remain of this opinion after refreshing my memory by studying the documents in the External Affairs files—the idea that a treaty that was more than a military alliance would be more popular in Canada than a military alliance did not enter into the minds of St. Laurent and Pearson at the beginning. It was simply what they wanted, what they felt was desirable, and their own feelings, as would any good politician's, were the views of the Canadian people. Constantly in their public speeches they kept emphasizing that their idea of a North Atlantic Treaty was a treaty which created an institution which was more than an alliance. Then they found that this was one reason why they were gaining such general support in Canada.

A little later they discovered, and I remember some shock when they discovered—it must have been the end of '48—from a study of the French language press in Quebec, that there was a great deal of opposition in Quebec to the treaty. It was then that we used the argument strongly in Washington that for domestic political reasons in Canada we required a treaty that was more than a military alliance. It was to diminish opposition in Quebec and to get the support of the CCF [Socialist] Party. But I don't think this was the original reason why St. Laurent and Pearson argued for Article 2.

GEOFFREY PEARSON

He was always unhappy with NATO's purely military aspects because he was afraid that it might lead to what he was always hoping to avoid which was war. His own experience suggested that military alliances wouldn't work in the long run, and therefore they had to be more than military and have a more permanent life and function. I think in some ways this is a Canadian illusion that military alliances are bad because they lead to war, but my father certainly shared it and was always therefore trying to transform NATO into something else.

This led to a lot of skepticism and a lot of veiled criticism by the Americans and this is one of the things that Dean Acheson claimed he could never understand Canadians were trying to do, because in the American view, and especially Acheson's view, the purpose of NATO was a short-term military alliance. Any idea of an Atlantic community to them was mere sentiment, and that was one of the sources of tension between my father and the Americans.

I think the Europeans also felt we were being romantic about this, although the British shared some of our thinking. The French didn't and the continental Europeans generally didn't. All of that business about building up a community went into the European Economic Community anyway and the idea of an Atlantic Alliance community was dropped from about 1955–56 on.

DEAN RUSK

There was considerable skepticism in this country about Article 2, partly because it looked a little bit as though Article 2 might be some kind of substitute for the United Nations, but also because Article 2 might, from the United States point of view, be looked upon as a continuing commitment for such things as the Marshall Plan, that we were not willing to undertake. So there was skepticism about Article 2 in the United States.

CHARLES RITCHIE

I recall his crusade for Article 2 in the North Atlantic Treaty and his hope that this would be what he used to call a signpost to the future of economic cooperation and closer ties and the development of the alliance from its military framework into something more permanently political. He adhered to this. I remember when Wyn Plumptre was sent over to Paris—I suppose this must have been considerably later on—to see what foundation there was for this hope in economic terms, and he came back with a very, very pessimistic report, saying more or less there's nothing in it in practical terms when it comes down to nuts and bolts. I recall being there when he was putting this report to Mike and Mike listened to it the way he would listen to unpleasant news, but he wasn't really convinced. He still believed that it was essential to hang on to this because he was a great man for the general concept. It was the direction that counted with him.

It took more than a year from the first informal meeting of officials in the depths of the Pentagon's war room for the final draft of the North Atlantic Treaty to be approved and signed. The 1948 American presidential election campaign intervened— it would not be the only time that the United States democratic process would get in the way of orderly international negotiations, as the diplomats were to find out. The considered opinion in Washington was that the Republicans would win, and, as a result, the American representatives were not willing to move on a text for the treaty until they knew the results of the election and could size up what kind of support there would be in the U.S. Senate. It so happened that the presidential election campaign almost coincided with the by-election in the northern Ontario riding of Algoma East, where the newly appointed minister of external affairs, Lester B. Pearson, was making a successful bid for a seat in the Canadian Parliament.

Besides the American presidential election, there was another matter which interfered with the smooth course of the NATO negotiations, and that was the Palestine Question. This led to serious differences between the British and the Americans. Just after the war ended, President Truman, who did not hide his Zionist sympathies, had pressed London to allow more Jewish refugees to enter the promised land, but the British felt that they could not do this. The U.K. Foreign Office became convinced that the United States government was conniving at the shipment of arms and munitions to the Jews in Palestine, and there was evidence, according to British state papers, that U.S. officials in the Allied Control Commissions in Germany and Italy were actively involved in the illegal traffic of Jewish immigrants, and that American crews were manning the refugee ships. Finally the British threw up their hands and turned over their mandate for Palestine to the United Nations.

However, this did not stop the bickering, and there was a message from Dean Rusk that seemed to indicate he sought Pearson's good offices in this dispute, but it was resolved before there was any need for him to act. George Ignatieff saw the issue as part of the problems arising from the break-up of the British Empire.

ESCOTT REID

My recollection of Rusk's message to Pearson was that he had warned the British that if their policy and American policy remained so much opposed on Israel, it would be difficult for the United States to secure the necessary public support for the North Atlantic Treaty. It was roughly that. I assume that Rusk told us in the expectation we might pass the message on to the British, which as far as I know we didn't, and it had, as I recall, no effect on British policy on Israel. But what I say in my book [*Time of Fear and Hope: the Making of the North Atlantic Treaty, 1947-49*] is that if Rusk attached so much importance to the Israel issue, what would have happened if the British Labour government had not in 1946–47 agreed to the independence of India. If the Indian issue had continued to fester—and the Americans were always in favor of Indian independence—if the British had not given up India, I doubt very much if there could ever have been a North Atlantic Treaty. There couldn't have been that cooperation between Britain and the United States in the postwar period if the British had not granted independence to India.

DEAN RUSK

We were concerned at that time, during the formation of NATO, that the Western alliance would get off to a very bad start indeed if the issue of Palestine was a bitterly divisive issue among the members of the alliance. As a matter of fact, it didn't turn out that way, but we were concerned about it and had some discussions about it at the time.

I don't remember the date of the message, because, after the British put the question of Palestine before the United Nations— the NATO Treaty was not signed until some time later—the Palestinian problem had ceased to be a divisive issue. After all, we'd had the partition resolution in the United Nations. We had the fighting in Palestine that led to the *de facto* situation. The state of Israel had been declared; it had been recognized by the United States immediately. And so it more or less disappeared as a major element that could have intruded itself upon NATO by the time the NATO Treaty was ready for signature.

George Ignatieff saw the issue as part of the problems arising from the break-up of the British Empire.

GEORGE IGNATIEFF

I remember this much— that Dean Rusk, who wasn't a very influential figure at that time, worked with me on the Palestine Question. One thing which he said to me many times was, "Why should we be picking up the pieces and trying to put the Humpty Dumpty of the collapsing British Empire back together again?" That was a view which many of us felt: this business of having to patch up the Empire. One must remember that it wasn't just Israel and Palestine. We'd gone through the same thing over Kashmir with India and Pakistan, and the blood shed on that was just dumb. And then, to have the Middle East dumped on us— and all about the same time!

In 1947 Canada succeeded Australia in what was then regarded as the British Commonwealth seat on the U.N. Security Council. General A. G. L. McNaughton, the distinguished soldier-scientist who had been the

*first commander of the Canadian Army during World War Two and
briefly defense minister at its end, was chosen Canadian representative at
the United Nations; George Ignatieff was sent to New York as General
McNaughton's assistant.*

GEORGE IGNATIEFF

I think it is true that we were totally unprepared, with no real
preconception, when the British brought this Palestine issue to the
Security Council and said, "What would you do with it?" Now,
we had had rather similar situations, when two peoples were
claiming the same territory as in the case of India and Pakistan
[over Kashmir], a partition had been applied—and the partition
had been tried in Ireland—the natural thought was, therefore, let's
have a partition plan. Anyway, Canada was brought into this
business, not because of Mr. Pearson, but because of our membership in the Security Council. There's no doubt that General
McNaughton was not really very sympathetic to the Jewish
cause, but he was an extremely honest man, such an honorable
man. I was there on the spot, working with him, and General
McNaughton asked me to represent him when the problem of
Israel was being discussed. I think it was such a great stand [to
take].

It was thus that I went to meetings with the Jewish Agency, and
my relations with the agency were partly facilitated by the fact
that most of the representatives from Palestine were Russian-
speaking Jews, and I used to chatter away in Russian to them.[2] In
fact, I think they were all from Russia in one way or another, and,
despite the sad history of relations between the Russians and the
Jews, it is a strange paradox that whenever Jews and Russians get
together, they usually seem to be able to face [each other] and feel
a kinship of some sort because of certain historic, though very

[2]When George Ignatieff was introduced to Chaim Weizmann by members of the Jewish
Agency in New York, the Zionist leader, who was the first president of the state of
Israel, said that he did not think that he would want to shake hands with anybody by
the name of Ignatieff. "Oh," said the Jewish Agency official, "you're thinking of his
grandfather. His father, as governor of Kiev in 1905, stopped the pogroms." "Don't
let's live in the past," George said. "I accept you as the president of Israel," and told
Weizmann that his mother-in-law, Maude Parkin, had been a colleague of his at the
University of Manchester in England. They had a friendly meeting.

unsatisfactory, relations. It may be partially the reason why the
Soviet Union supported the creation of the state of Israel. There
is, of course, the policy of trying to get a sphere of influence in the
Mediterranean, which has been a consistent Russian imperialist
policy. But at the time of the Palestine debate, they must have
thought that the chances were much better with a people who, as
I say, in spite of the histories of persecution and pogroms and
heaven knows what, had all had Russian associations and spoke
Russian. This isn't true, of course, in the present generation, but it
was true at the time of the founding [of the state of Israel].

*The first step that the United Nations took to deal with the Palestine
problem was to set up a committee, the United Nations Special Committee on Palestine (UNSCOP). Canada was one of the eleven nations that
made up this committee and the Canadian representative was the respected
jurist, Mr. Justice Ivan Rand. Since the United Kingdom wished to avoid
any further responsibility, it was excluded from membership, as were the
Arab states and the Jewish Agency, which had been established under the
British mandate to look after the Jewish interests in Palestine. Mr. Justice
Rand was one of the main contributors to the work of the committee and
was a strong supporter of the UNSCOP majority report, which recommended the partition of the territory into a Jewish and an Arab state, with
a demilitarized Jerusalem under United Nations trusteeship. There was
also an UNSCOP minority report that proposed a federal state for
Palestine.*

*As might be expected, the prominent part that Lester Pearson played in
the Palestine negotiations did not please his political master, W. L.
Mackenzie King: the latter's diaries indicate that he refused to allow
Pearson to become chairman of The Palestine Commission ". . . as prime
minister, I had said that he, as under secretary of state, could not take on
that obligation." Mr. King was against any effort of the United Nations
to impose a settlement, and the Liberal government only agreed to
partition when it was convinced that there was no other solution. It was
James Ilsley, the minister of justice and senior minister, and not Lester
Pearson, who made the main Canadian statement at the United Nations
during the Palestine debate. Ilsley was worried about the conflicting
promises made to the Jews and Arabs, according to George Ignatieff, and
insisted on getting both sides of the story before accepting the partition
proposal.*

While Lester Pearson tried to be impartial, most of his friends and colleagues agreed that he was sympathetically disposed toward the creation of the state of Israel. Certainly, the Arabs felt that he was on the Jewish side and, years later, they were to tell Tommy Burns how Pearson put his arms around Ben Gurion when he greeted him at the United Nations, although the general, who was to be the first commander of the United Nations peace-keeping force in the Middle East, supposed that he could not have done anything else if Ben Gurion had clasped him to his bosom. Elizabeth McCallum, an Arabist on the Canadian delegation, said that the Jewish Agency went out of its way to win Mr. Pearson to their cause, and that Moshe Sharett waited on him almost every day. While no one denied that the Jews were persistent—and why shouldn't they be?— Ignatieff asserted that the real trouble was that the Arabs were unable to present their case in the same concentrated manner that the Jews did; that there was a "mélange," as he put it, of Arab interests but no equivalent Arab organization to the Jewish Agency. Mike Pearson seemed to be aware of his own predilections because he was quoted by Arnold Smith as saying that the Canadians had a balanced representation at the United Nations: "we have Sheikh McNaughton and Rabbi Pearson."

GEOFFREY PEARSON

I do know that the Americans were unhappy and the British were unhappy, and that Canada naturally found itself in a position of trying to help this misunderstanding [over Palestine] or to change it, partly because my father was the chairman of the ad hoc committee of the Assembly which set up the new state of Israel. He was the chairman, I think, for reasons that have nothing to do with the British and the Americans but simply because he was active at the UN, well known at the UN, and they needed a chairman and he was available. This was before he became minister. He was a civil servant, and he was therefore a neutral chairman. He was, I think, fairly neutral about that issue. He wasn't committed to a state of Palestine, although he felt he knew a lot of the background. All the biblical knowledge which he got from his parents helped him, I think. He knew all those places; he hadn't been there but he knew the Bible from one end to the other, so a lot of the geography was familiar to him.

I think he was genuinely impartial and unlike the British, who were committed to the Balfour Declaration, and the Americans, who were acting the part of a great power, but I don't think he had strong views on that subject. He was associated with it almost by accident. In that context I think he gave less importance to the Palestine issue, but he was important in the solution that was reached, and he supported very strongly the new state of Israel once it was on the map and never wavered in that support. I don't think he thought it would be the kind of issue that it became. I think he hoped that it would be accepted as a *fait-accompli* by the Arabs.

GEORGE IGNATIEFF

It's assumed a little too easily that Pearson started with a prejudice toward Zionism. I don't think so. One of the truest things that one of his closest friends who knew him much better than I did, Hume Wrong, ever said about him was that Pearson never seemed to act on grounds of rationally arrived principles which could be stated and clearly expressed as motivation. He said that, to understand Pearson, you have to think of him as a sort of a Houdini: you tie him up, stick him in a mess, and without telling you how, why, or when, he'll get himself out and in the process help all the others who are involved.

And it's so true because, you know, people have said, "How could you have been associated with Pearson in such a strictly pro-Zionist, anti-Arab situation?" I don't remember that—that wasn't the impression at all. I remember he'd worked tremendously hard and that he was under very strong Jewish pressure— yes, I admit it—and moreover he was a pragmatist. He and the Canadian government, to whom he was responsible at that time, in common with the United States government, were clearly more responsive, shall we say, to Jewish pressure and influence than they were to Arabs because they'd say that there were far more Canadians who were of that persuasion. I remember Brooke Claxton saying to me once when we were in doubt how to vote. "Don't forget George, I don't mind how you vote but," he said, "Don't forget that I have no Arabs in my constituency and I have I've forgotten how many hundred Jews."

For the first time Canada was on the Security Council and

Brooke Claxton said, "We're in this mess, which has been deposited on our doorstep by Britain, and both for the reason that she is a close ally and a mother country for a great many Canadians, we can't turn our backs on this issue." Yes, it's true, that there were more pressures on us from one side than from the other but I think it would be wrong to say that Pearson started from a preconception. I can't say that he did.

In the end the state of Israel was created by force of arms. Shortly after the adoption of the partition plan by the UN General Assembly, fighting broke out between the Arabs and the Jews, and the Palestine Commission, which had been set up to supervise the division of the territory into a Jewish and an Arab state, never left New York. On May 14, 1948, a provisional government formally proclaimed Israel, and Lester Pearson noted with some disgust that within sixteen minutes of this declaration, the United States recognized the new country. The fighting went on in the Holy Land, and after repeated attempts the United Nations mediator, Ralph Bunche, was able to bring about a cease-fire; but there was no armistice agreement.

Although Pearson had become external affairs minister when Israel was admitted to the United Nations (May 11, 1949), he had been undersecretary during the difficult negotiations on the partition plan. It was an awkward situation because he knew that Prime Minister Mackenzie King was worried about the prominent part he was playing on the international stage. Mr. King confided to his diary: "He [Pearson] likes keeping Canada at the head of everything, in the forefront in connection with U.N. affairs. He does not see that the Big Powers are using us, that we will count for little or nothing once the struggle comes and we have served their purpose."

The Palestine problem led to bitter disagreements between the British and the Americans which threatened the harmonious relationship needed for the North Atlantic alliance. Lester Pearson was external affairs minister when he signed the treaty at a ceremony in Washington on April 4, 1949, but once again most of the work was done when he was undersecretary. Mackenzie King noted sourly in his diary that Pearson "does not hesitate to advise both the United Kingdom and the United States as to what it is wisest for them to do," and this was one occasion when Pearson did help to bring together the two great English-speaking powers.

GEOFFREY PEARSON

He did see Canada, I think, partly as a go-between. This is not new for Canada, but he himself, having served in London and Washington, was very aware of the understanding between those two capitals, and he was himself part American and part British in the sense that he understood both, liked both, had lived in both countries, had loved his student days in England and had many friends in both places. So he was a go-between in a very personal way. He found it natural that he should act this way officially and politically. I don't think he had a theory about Canada being a go-between, but as long as the British remained influential in world politics, then British-American relations were important. For Canada they were more important than for any other country, so that it wasn't until Britain lost this role, which was well into the Fifties, that the Canadian role became less important. So, without working it out—and you won't find a theory about it, I don't think, in his speeches—he certainly believed in it.

The missing factor, it seems to me, is France, and again it's this matter of understanding French and he didn't know many French politicians or diplomats. France tended to be left out although in Canadian terms France is important. I think he was conscious of this. This was so to some extent when the European Economic Community was created, and he could look at Europe in terms of both Britain and France. But the overwhelming preoccupation in those early years was Washington and London. I suppose if you looked at the telegrams going into Ottawa, my guess is that more than half came from those two capitals, and that probably measured the importance for Canada of those relationships, both economic as well as political, trade as well as culture.

So he just symbolized something which was true anyway, and he happened to be very good at it, but it was an Anglo-Saxon kind of diplomacy. It wasn't world-wide or it wasn't European. Norman Robertson, Hume Wrong, his two most prominent fellow diplomats and closest friends, had also served in London and Washington and nowhere much else, although Wrong spoke some French. But it was curious that they should be a trio who—of course, Mr. St. Laurent balanced this a bit, and that was a happy circumstance—but I don't think they ever spoke French with him.

So that the go-between was London–Washington, and later, perhaps even then, it also became New Delhi–Washington, and later still New Delhi was the go-between between Peking and Washington; with Ottawa acting as a kind of helper. I think one can exaggerate this role a bit, but there was something to it. After twenty years I think it was over, twenty years from 1948–49, and that's why Mr. Trudeau in effect said that's enough of this.

When Lester Pearson returned to Ottawa at the end of 1946 to become under-secretary of state for external affairs, he was a world figure and sufficiently famous as a diplomat to have been proposed as secretary-general of the United Nations. He had had ten years experience abroad, in London and Washington, and was regarded as a founder of the Canadian foreign service and a father figure by many of the bright young people joining the department. Sidney Pierce was one of them, and he recalled asking Mike Pearson what advice he gave officers who were going off on their first posting abroad, as he was. Pearson's reply was: "When you get there, take your time, have a good look around, and try to select one member of the government or of the civil service who you think is both able and likely to succeed—concentrate on him and try to gain his confidence." Sidney Pierce knew that he had given the same advice to others, but what about Pearson himself? According to Pierce, Mike, when he first went to Washington, picked Dean Acheson as the man most likely to succeed.

As under-secretary, Lester Pearson was responsible for putting the department on a peacetime footing. There had been a tremendous expansion, from seven missions abroad when World War Two began to twenty-two by the time it ended, and much more was to come. In the immediate postwar world, Canada loomed large as a sovereign state just below the rank of the great powers with a strong economy, and almost every nation in the world wanted to have diplomatic relations with Ottawa. It was an exciting and challenging job for the new deputy minister. Once again, his timing could not have been better—or was it just luck? If he had been appointed under-secretary on Dr. Skelton's death, as he thought he should have been, he would have missed Washington and all the preparations for peace and the exposure on the international stage; if he had become deputy minister in 1941, he would probably have sought a prestigious posting abroad after the war, as Norman Robertson had done, and might not have been taken into the Cabinet. Instead, he returned at the right time, just before Prime Minister Mackenzie King handed over the portfolio of external affairs to Louis St. Laurent as a first step toward retiring. Bruce Hutchison and others have said that Mike Pearson would never have joined the Mackenzie King government because he profoundly distrusted King's views on foreign policy. However, he was in complete agreement with St. Laurent's internationalist outlook, and when St. Laurent succeeded King, Pearson was ready and available.

He was sworn in as minister of external affairs on September 10, 1948, and elected the Member of Parliament for Algoma East on October 25 of that year. In outlining his views on foreign policy, Lester Pearson said that Canada must not be timid or fearful of commitments but activist in accepting international responsibilities. "To me," he wrote, "nationalism and internationalism were two sides of the same coin. International cooperation for peace is the most important aspect of national policy." That was his credo, collective security. There was no doubt that Pearson's leadership of the Department of External Affairs, first as deputy minister working with a sympathetic minister, and then as the responsible minister, marked a great change in Canadian foreign policy, an about-turn from the cautious isolationism of Mackenzie King and his principal adviser, Dr. O. D. Skelton, to the ardent internationalism of a United Nations peacekeeper. As Paul Martin said, "We wanted law and order to be the instrument by which the disputes between nations would be resolved—Mr. King, who represented an older generation and Dr. Skelton, they thought that this was idealism gone mad."

In his memoirs Lester Pearson noted that "the countries whose political policies now concern us most would be not Great Britain but the United States. That country was now the super-power. Washington, not London, would determine, with Moscow, whether peace, progress and even survival were possible." He came to that conclusion in 1946. After the war British influence declined rapidly, but it could not be said that any one particular event marked its nadir, although after 1949 Canada and Mr. Pearson were to concentrate their attention mainly on Washington.

5 Nonrecognition: the American Heresy

WHILE THE ATTENTION of Canada and the Western world was fixed on the Berlin airlift, the greatest revolution was raging across the ancient landscape of China. If a plane carrying coals or other supplies to the beleaguered German city were to crash, there would be a collective shiver of fright, and the delegates and diplomats, including Lester Pearson, would meet in the corridors of the United Nations and agonize over the situation. Europe seemed to be teetering on the brink of a nuclear war, and the Berlin blockade tended to obscure the awesome developments elsewhere. In January 1949 the great bastion of Peking fell to the Chinese Communists when the Nationalist general, Fu Tso-yi, capitulated; at the end of April of that year three great masses of troops known as the Eighth, the Fourth, and the Second Route Armies, swept across the Yangtze River in an armada of junks and open boats and engulfed the nationalist capital of Nanking. It was now just a question of time before Chiang Kai-shek, with American assistance, would flee to the island sanctuary of Formosa (Taiwan), with short-lived stop-overs in Canton and the old wartime capital of Chungking. On October 1, 1949, Mao Tse-tung proclaimed the establishment of the People's Republic of China in the old imperial capital of Peking.

Although the Russians entered the war against Japan after the first atom bomb had been dropped on Hiroshima and only days before the surrender, they took most of Manchuria, or Manchukuo as it was called; they turned over Harbin and the main cities to Chiang Kai-shek, whose

77

troops had to be flown in by the Americans; but they left the countryside firmly in the hands of the Chinese Communists. At the same time the Red Army and Soviet-trained Korean troops crossed the Yalu River and moved down the Korean peninsula, only to meet United States forces and their Korean allies moving up from Pusan and other ports in the south. Thus, the country was divided along the thirty-eighth parallel, and the two great powers confronted each other in Korea as they did ten thousand miles away in Germany. If anything, the Far Eastern confrontation seemed the more dangerous, and Averell Harriman, when he left Moscow on the completion of his mission, decided to take a look for himself and returned to Washington via Korea and Japan.

AVERELL HARRIMAN

I took considerable interest in [Korea]. I came back from Russia in January 1946 and went to see [General] MacArthur before going on to Washington. I recommended that we get more Russian experts [for our occupation zone in Korea], a recommendation which was not followed. However, there was nothing we could do because the Russians closed that border [thirty-eighth parallel] just as they did the border in Europe, and there was no way you could penetrate. I think that Stalin was very anxious to get control of Korea, which would give him a base right close to [Japan]—after all, Korea's a dagger pointed at the heart of Japan. I know that Stalin wanted Hokkaido [North Japan]—I know that because he asked in my presence for the island of Hokkaido as a zone of occupation, and some Americans were not opposed to this. I was very much opposed to it and had a hand in preventing it happening. I wouldn't say I did it myself but I did have a hand in it.

Not only was Averell Harriman afraid of what was happening in Korea, but so was Prime Minister Mackenzie King. It may have been due to his political intuition or "psychic communication," as George Ignatieff suggested, but Mr. King had a premonition about the danger of a Soviet-American confrontation there—which proved to be so right. At any rate, he said that, as long as he was prime minister, Canada would not become involved in the affairs of that benighted country, and Canada had just been made a member of the United Nations Temporary Commission on Korea (UNTCOK), which had been set up at the United

States' insistence to supervise the elections in both halves of Korea. The Soviet Union was adamantly opposed. Lester Pearson was given the unenviable task of getting Canada released from this obligation; he was dispatched to Washington to tell President Truman that Mackenzie King would resign rather than have any Canadian on the commission. Although he was somewhat bemused by the assignment, Pearson realized that the situation was serious and there was a Cabinet crisis.

According to Jack Pickersgill, the prime minister's secretary, this "very curious incident" had its beginning in November 1947 when Mackenzie King stopped over in New York on his way to London and the wedding of Princess Elizabeth and Prince Philip; Pickersgill was accompanying Mackenzie King on this trip.

J. W. PICKERSGILL

We arrived in New York in the morning. A private member of Parliament who was on the [Canadian] delegation named Joe Bradette had made a speech in the General Assembly of the United Nations the day before about Korea. Mackenzie King read an account of this in the New York *Times*, and he was incensed. He said, "Joe Bradette! What does he know about Korea? He doesn't even know where it is!" which was perhaps a little unfair to Joe Bradette because all he did was to read a speech which had been written by External Affairs—he was the one who was called on to deliver it. But this little incident, I think, put Mackenzie King on edge about Korea.

Then, he also claimed that Truman had told him that it was a very dangerous place, Korea, and that even Roosevelt before that had told him... I've always had some doubts about this. There are those who say that Roosevelt spoke to him in one of the séances about Korea. I suspend belief about things like that. However, what happened was that Mackenzie King was away for a critical period, and he didn't know what was going on at the United Nations. And during this period J. L. Ilsley, who was the minister of justice in those days, was head of the delegation in New York and Pearson, I think, was there a good deal of the time. The Americans put great pressure on the Canadian delegation to support the establishment of a committee of the United Nations to supervise free elections in Korea, both North and South, with a view to uniting them and getting rid of the occupations of both the Soviets in the North and the Americans in the South.

Neither Ilsley nor Pearson was enamored of this commission or wanted to be on it, but they didn't see any very strong reason for objecting. They didn't think any great national interest was involved as far as Canada was concerned, or that it was of any great importance at all, because I think they were both very skeptical— I know Pearson was—about whether there would ever be any elections in Korea anyway, and quite rightly so. Mr. St. Laurent was acting prime minister as well as the secretary of state for external affairs. It was considered of so little importance that he wasn't even consulted about it. But when he was told about it he didn't dissent in any way because he didn't think it was of any importance.

Well then, after Mackenzie King came back to Ottawa, oh, a month or so later, the question of appointing a Canadian member to this Korean commission came up in the Cabinet. Nobody had spoken to Mackenzie King about it beforehand; it was just brought up cold in the Cabinet by Mr. St. Laurent. Korea, apparently... he [Mr. King] had an almost Pavlovian reaction to Korea. Never, as long as he was prime minister, would we take any part in this. A real Cabinet crisis developed. So Pearson was sent on a mission to ask Truman[1] either to agree to Canada withdrawing from the commission or, better still, to say that the commission couldn't operate at all.

Truman wouldn't agree to this. It would have been a sensible thing if he had, because the commission was an utterly useless thing anyway. But he wouldn't agree. Instead of that, he sent a very strong appeal to Mackenzie King to change his mind and appoint someone to the commission. And this appeal, Mackenzie

---

[1]In his account of his mission to Washington, Pearson says that he saw Robert Lovett first and found that the acting U.S. secretary of state could not understand what all the fuss was about. Then, accompanied by Lovett, he went to see President Truman; both were anxious that the press should not find out about the visit and the split between the two countries. So they entered the White House by the back door. Pearson had made up his mind that if discovered, he would throw the press off the track by telling them that he had come to see the President about Korea—and, as he commented, "that would have sounded so fantastic they would have assumed I was joking and that I really was there to talk about dollars or fuel oil."

King drafted the answer personally; then he showed it to Pearson. Pearson said, "Well, shouldn't this go to the Cabinet?" Mackenzie King was affronted at the suggestion and said there was no need. So then Pearson said, "At least it should be shown to the secretary of state for external affairs," and Mr. King agreed that it should be shown to Mr. St. Laurent.

And that provoked the real confrontation, which was not between Pearson and Mackenzie King directly, but I think there's no doubt that if St. Laurent had resigned, Pearson would have resigned too. I've always felt that he felt so committed both to St. Laurent and to the policy that he couldn't have carried on. It was the biggest crisis I have seen in all my experience of government over the smallest and least important question.

It ended with Mr. St. Laurent telephoning me one evening and saying that he must talk to the prime minister, and he said, "It's quite possible that I won't be a minister tomorrow." Well, I had been kept well informed about what was going on by Pearson and also by Brooke Claxton, who was very worried about the whole thing, about the danger of breaking up the government. But at any rate, when I put Mr. St. Laurent's request to Mackenzie King, he said, "Tell him to come to dinner at Laurier House tonight." And Mr. St. Laurent went to dinner, and we all sat around in our various homes.

In fact, I went to bed. I wasn't feeling very well. Anyway, I had a telephone by my bed, and Brooke Claxton telephoned me and said, "Have you heard any news?" And I said, "No, I haven't heard anything yet, but I'll tell you what happened." And I gave him an account that turned out to be very similar—not quite the same, but very similar—to what occurred. He had just hung up when Pearson telephoned me, and he repeated to me Mr. St. Laurent's account of the conversation and the skillful way in which Mr. St. Laurent, after making it perfectly clear that he was not going to back down, found a face-saving device by which Mackenzie King appeared to win the substance of his point.

He pointed out that the terms of the resolution of the United Nations provided for an election in the whole of Korea; that there couldn't be an election in North Korea without the assent of the Soviets; and therefore the commission could never have anything to do because they'd [the Soviets] already said they wouldn't assent. So that it was a nullity anyway; and that in accepting a position we would take the view that the commission had no function unless there were elections held in both Koreas. I may not have the precise definition of it, but that's the substance of it.

Now subsequently, the commission did agree, when the Canadian representative was out of the room, to supervise the elections in South Korea. But we dissented from that, though we didn't withdraw from the commission. It didn't amount to very much, and it certainly wasn't really responsible for the Korean War in 1950, although Mackenzie King always thought so.

The last time but one that I saw Mackenzie King was... or was it the last time? I'm not quite sure, but it doesn't matter. It was in July of 1950 anyway, and he died in July of 1950. I saw him out at Kingsmere and he told me that he had been all through his diaries for the end of 1947 and the beginning of 1948, and that the position he had taken at that time was completely justified by the outbreak of the Korean War at the end of June 1950. I smiled and he asked me to convey this information to Mr. St. Laurent, which I did. And Mr. St. Laurent smiled, and said no more about it.

In 1949, even before the proclamation of the People's Republic of China, Mike Pearson, who was external affairs minister now, was under pressure to recognize the victorious Communist forces. Chester Ronning, the Canadian envoy in Nanking, kept cabling the department and recommending that Canada establish diplomatic relations with the Mao Tse-tung government as soon as it was officially organized, which was to be on October 1, 1949. Although Ronning was only chargé d'affaires — the ambassador, General Victor Odlum, had left the previous year and not been replaced — he assumed the leadership of the diplomatic corps or what remained of it after April 23 when the Communist armies took Nanking. Not only could Ronning speak Chinese — he had been born in China of missionary parents and had himself been a missionary and was so fluent in the northern Mandarin language that he had a local Hupeh accent — but he knew Chou En-lai and many of the Communist leaders. He acted as an interpreter and spokesman for the Western diplomats, most of whom could not speak Chinese, at the meetings the Communist authorities called and where they were invited to begin negotiations for diplomatic relations.

There were no principles or precepts that stood in the way of immediate recognition of Communist China. The Canadian government tended to follow the British practice of extending diplomatic relations to a government when it was obvious that it was in control of a country. Certainly, Ottawa, as John Holmes said, did not relish the American position that recognition was some sort of award for good conduct. Thus, the intention was there, and Pearson himself was, from the beginning, fully in favor of establishing relations with the Peking government as soon as possible.

ARNOLD SMITH

I urged Mike in 1949, when I was deputy representative to the UN Security Council and at the time acting representative, that we ought to recognize China by the end of December 1949. We knew Chiang Kai-shek was planning to withdraw his last division to Formosa by the end of the year. I didn't know anything about China, but I knew a lot about Russia, and the West had done itself grave damage by taking fifteen years on the average to recognize that the Soviet regime was here to stay. We just helped Stalin create xenophobia among his people and build an iron curtain around Russia. I didn't want to see this mistake repeated with China. I wanted to get recognition of China, and I thought it should be done right away, and I urged this on Ottawa.

While Arnold Smith felt that Mike Pearson was on the side of the angels on the issue of Communist China, the new minister had to contend with human prejudices and emotions. The Americans were opposed, and, while they were not as much against the Peking government as they became as a result of the Korean War, they would argue that recognition was not a good idea now and that the Canadians should not be in a hurry to talk to the Communists. Smith had said to Ernie Gross, the American official who was his opposite number at the United Nations, "we must not repeat the mistake we made with the Russians," and Gross assured him that Washington was taking the matter very seriously and would not make the same mistake, but said the U.S. recognition was a "very valuable counter in negotiating" and there were problems to be resolved such as consulates and trade agreements, and they wanted some six to eight months or more of time to work these out.

Then there was the state of public opinion: the Americans had been led to believe that, compared with the British and French and other impe-

rialists, they had been the only true friends of China, with their open-door policy, and here were the perfidious Chinese repaying all their kindness and good intentions by embracing their rivals and enemies, the godless Communists. So many Americans, in Sunday schools and churches across the nation, had given nickels and dimes to "Save China" appeals; they had been assured by the missionaries that China was being rescued, that it was becoming part of the Kingdom of God, that Generalissimo Chiang Kai-shek had been converted to Christianity and certainly Madame Chiang was a Christian. A similar attitude prevailed in Canada, although the Canadian missionaries tended to be more realistic, and this was partly the reason for Pearson's hesitations and caution in approaching the question of relations with the Peking government.

Henry Cabot Lodge, the grandson of the senator who was the nemesis of President Wilson and the League of Nations, was appointed by President Eisenhower U. S. ambassador and permanent representative to the United Nations; he took up his post at the height of the anti-China feeling. Lodge acknowledged that the United States was "very anti-Peking government for years and years and years" and put down this country-wide paranoia to two factors: first, the Americans had backed Chiang Kai-shek, although they knew that his regime was hopelessly inefficient and corrupt[2]; and, second, "we thought that Peking was the aggressor in Korea," and, while Lodge did not say so, the worst thing of all was that the Chinese Communists had entered the fray and driven the United States forces back from the Yalu River—it was a blow to national pride.

It was taken for granted that Canada would recognize the new government of China in due course. There was no rush, and, as John Holmes said, the question being debated in Ottawa was whether the Communists really wanted anything so old-fashioned as diplomatic relations. There was American opposition hanging like a dark cloud on the horizon, and divided Canadian opinion, and when faced with a problem like this, Lester Pearson was inclined to find out what others thought. There were consultations with members of the Commonwealth but nothing came of them, and there was certainly no unanimity, no chance of

---

[2]An American general told Henry Cabot Lodge about the way Chiang Kai-shek was selling U. S. arms to the Communists. He said that he marked rifles that were being issued to the Nationalists with a red stripe. His office was in downtown Chungking, and, a couple of hours later, the general would see Communist soldiers marching by his window with these same marked rifles.

the Commonwealth's acting as a body. The subject was going to come up at the Commonwealth Foreign Ministers' meeting, which was scheduled to be held in Colombo, Ceylon, January 9-14, 1950, and Pearson put off making any decision until he had a chance to discuss it further there.

CHESTER RONNING

It was Pearson's intention first to consult all the members of the Commonwealth and then reach a decision—his idea was that they should all recognize the new government at the same time. But the members of the Commonwealth delayed so long that India did not wait and established relations on December 26, 1949, approximately three months after the new regime was established in Peking. Mike Pearson was to get in touch with me in January. But already, on January 6, 1950, I received a wire from the department instructing me to rent a house in Peking, and I did so through the British Embassy—it was not accepted by the Chinese as the British Embassy then, only as the British negotiators residence.

Mike Pearson had planned to recognize China toward the end of January 1950. You will remember that on January 6 the United Kingdom and Pakistan recognized the People's Republic of China. Mike Pearson tried to get in touch with me on his way home from the Columbo Plan organizational conference in Sri Lanka [Ceylon] but he was unable to get through on the telephone from Hong Kong. So the matter of our recognition was delayed until toward the end of January 1950. Then there was so much pressure from the United States on Canada and within Canada itself, there was a difference of opinion as to whether or not we should recognize the People's Republic of China and the matter was postponed.

Later I was instructed to negotiate with the Chinese in regard to the terms of recognition. I did so with the intention of simultaneous announcements in Ottawa and Peking that recognition had been given and that recognition had been received by the Chinese. However this was postponed and postponed and postponed until the day that the Korean War broke out. That same day, I received instructions from Ottawa to negotiate, and on that day the North Koreans came storming over the division between North and

South Korea—whether or not they were the ones that initiated that, I don't know—but, at any rate, they came across and further consideration of recognition was stopped.

JOHN HOLMES

There were a lot of things to be done and Ronning was pressing from Nanking for action and the government was considering what to do. We really wanted to wait and see, but there were practical matters; we needed to have a place in Peking. It kept being put off but the government finally took a decision on Friday, June 23, 1950, to instruct Ronning to go to Peking and begin negotiations. Now that wasn't a deliberate decision to recognize, it was a decision to open negotiations for exchange of diplomatic relations, but the decision was taken. That was done on a Friday and the Korean War started on Sunday, June 25, 1950.

Obviously, the Korean War was not the time to initiate any talks with the Chinese Communists, but it remained a fixed Canadian policy to recognize the Peking government when the air cleared and the passions aroused by the war had died down. The decision was simply postponed until the appropriate moment. However, when the appropriate moment seemed to have arrived and Lester Pearson was on the point of offering to begin negotiations, something always happened. According to John Holmes, the Chinese started shelling the offshore islands of Quemoy and Matsu, or there was about to be an American election, or some trade arrangement got in the way. It was aptly described as a period of Hamletian indecision, a period that went on into the Fifties and Sixties and redounded to no one's credit.

The result of the nonrecognition of a fully accredited major power, one of the five permanent members of the UN Security Council, was very damaging, if not disastrous, for the United Nations, which could not deal with any issue in which China was involved or had an interest, and was by-passed by international conferences on Asian affairs such as the 1954 and 1962 Geneva Conferences. There were Western diplomats who claimed that if the Communist regime had taken over China's seat in the United Nations at the beginning of 1950, the Korean War would not have occurred.

Arnold Smith called nonrecognition "the American heresy"; he said that the idea that a regime would go away if it were not recognized was deeply embedded in American mythology. It used to work with Latin American coups in the old days; then, American recognition or not of a new regime did tend to make the difference between the regime lasting or not. But, as Smith pointed out, Fidel Castro and his Cuban government did not disappear and certainly not Mao Tse-tung and Chou En-lai and the People's Republic of China. Only in the United States was there this delusion that they had vanished, and in the UN's glass tower on Manhattan, the only China that existed was the semicolonial China of the prewar days when the Chiang Kai-shek government was able to collect and publish some statistics: it was a much smaller China, a quaint country of four hundred and fifty million, including many women with bound feet. The American press and news media played along with nonrecognition and insisted on calling Peking (Northern capital) Peiping (Northern gate), which was the name given it by Chiang Kai-shek, who had his capital in Nanking (Southern capital), right into the Seventies.

CHESTER RONNING

I recommended that Canada should recognize the People's Republic of China when it came into power on October 1, 1949, because whatever advantages were to be derived from it would disappear inversely as the square of the length of time it took Canada to decide after the People's Republic of China had been formed. Well, it actually took twenty-one years and about thirteen days before Canada finally recognized. But I left China in 1951.

It was the absence of the Russian representative at the Security Council's horseshoe table that allowed the UN to become involved in the Korean War and take the first collective security action against an aggressor. If Yakov Malik had not been boycotting the meetings of the world organization as a means of protest against the way the Peking government was being denied China's seat, there would have been no doubt that the Soviet Union would have vetoed the first resolution calling on the North Koreans to cease fire and all the subsequent resolutions that cast the mantle of the United Nations over what was essentially an American military expedition.

Lester Pearson realized that it was only "in theory" a United Nations operation—and international lawyers were to argue whether the Security Council had the legal right to act in the absence of one of its permanent members—nevertheless, the external affairs minister felt "very excited about this historical precedent," as he described it in his memoirs, "a most valuable precedent for the future of the United Nations." However, it was not to happen again. The Russians would not repeat the mistake of boycotting the Security Council—but what was surprising was the time they took to realize that it had been a grave error to leave the United Nations open to the schemes of the Western powers.

The first Security Council meeting was hurriedly called for the afternoon of Sunday, June 25, 1950, at the UN's temporary quarters in a former bombsite factory (Sperry Gyro works) at Lake Success on the outskirts of New York City. Two days later there was another meeting during which a resolution was adopted calling on member states to assist the Republic of Korea (South Korea) in repelling the armed attack. President Truman did not wait for the passage of this resolution before ordering United States forces to go to the support of the South Korean government and the Seventh Fleet to protect the island of Formosa. It was not till August 1 that Yakov Malik returned to the Security Council: August happened to be the month when it was the turn of the Soviet delegate to be chairman. By that time there had been many meetings of the Security Council and a United Nations Unified Command was set up which was really a United States command (from then on there was confusion of the United Nations with the United States). As chairman, Malik rode roughshod over the Security Council and declared that the North Koreans were not aggressors but were merely responding to attacks by the South Koreans. However, Averell Harriman was to say that Stalin had given the green light to Kim (Kim Il Sung), the North Korean leader.

After the Security Council resolution of June 27 condemning the North Koreans as aggressors, Canada was under pressure from the United States, which was organizing the collective security operation as the UN's agent, to announce the form of Canadian participation. At first the Canadian government hoped to get away with a couple of destroyers and a few planes, and it came as shock to the Cabinet to find that much more was expected. Mike Pearson was in favor of sending ground forces; otherwise Canadian support would have been no more than a token gesture, and Geoffrey Pearson quoted his father as saying, "we mustn't let the Americans take this over to the point where the United Nations was simply a screen." On July 22, 1950, Mackenzie King died, and on the special train bringing the government back to Ottawa from the state funeral in Toronto, there was a heated debate about the Korean War. Some of the ministers wondered what Mr. King would have done, and Pearson replied that he would not have got involved. Prime Minister St. Laurent supported his external affairs minister, and, after a series of Cabinet meetings, it was decided to send a volunteer brigade.

Perhaps the greatest irony was the fact that the United Nations forces, in the first test of collective security, should be put under the command of General Douglas MacArthur, a military leader with a Napoleonic complex. The general, who had been the American ruler of Japan since the war, was not used to taking any advice from anyone, including his own president and commander-in-chief. When asked about the danger of the Chinese entering the Korean War, MacArthur told a New York Times reporter that, given a handful of American pilots, flying the best equipment, he could wipe out the whole Chinese Communist army.

Lester Pearson and most of his aides were horrified by the UN commander and his excesses, and worried that the Korean War might expand into a world war, especially after MacArthur insisted on advancing above the thirty-eighth parallel, the dividing line between North and South Korea. Pearson resisted giving him this authority (which he had already taken), arguing that the United Nations had accomplished its task by driving the aggressors above the parallel. However, he found that Canadian participation in UNTCOK, which the late Prime Minister Mackenzie King had been so much against, came back to haunt him as the Americans argued that this meant Canada had agreed to the unification of Korea.

ESCOTT REID

I must have been acting under-secretary when the resolution came up which in effect authorized MacArthur to cross the border. The language, as I recall, was obscure, but this was the effect. I sent message after message to Pearson in New York putting forth the arguments for our opposing this resolution. I felt I was getting nowhere and I went around to see Norman Robertson, who was then secretary of Cabinet, and I said to Norman, who agreed with me, "Could you talk to Pearson?" Norman phoned him to urge him to oppose the resolution, and Mike said, "Norman, you have no idea what the pressure is like down here. I can't."

DEAN RUSK

When the North Korean forces were driven north of the thirty-eighth parallel, they didn't say anything about peace on the basis of the status quo. They didn't lay down their arms. They began the process of regrouping and reorganizing and getting ready to renew the fighting. So the army in the field, though it had been badly injured, was going to start shooting again. Then the United Nations had strongly supported the idea of the unification of Korea. There had been a commission [UNTCOK] sent out to Korea and so forth. They would have no luck in getting any moves toward unification through the commission. There was no attempting, therefore, with the North Korean forces in disarray, to look and see whether we could bring about the United Nations policy in Korea by unifying the whole country. That was one of the motivations of the move north beyond the thirty-eight parallel.

Mr. Pearson was, I think, skeptical about the decision of President Truman in 1949 to withdraw our combat team from Korea. He said, "Look, this can invite trouble," and he was right. He was nervous and skeptical about General MacArthur when General MacArthur was commanding out there. Even the United States government was also nervous about him. So there were some differences of view. I think, as I recall, that Mr. Pearson went along with the United Nations declaration of policy with respect to unifying the whole country. That was passed by the UN General Assembly.

Although Dean Rusk would admit that there were only "margins of discontent" between Mike Pearson and some of the American representatives, George Ignatieff spoke of the Korean War as being a period of the greatest possible strain in Canada-United States relations. The Canadian government had been advised by Prime Minister Nehru that the Chinese would not stand idly by if the drive above the thirty-eighth parallel continued and approached the Yalu River, and Pearson had passed on this information to the Americans; it must have been galling for him to have this warning disregarded and even pooh-poohed. The so-called United Nations Command under General MacArthur paid no attention to it, with disastrous consequences. Not only did New Delhi have a man in Peking (Ambassador K. M. Panikkar), but Chester Ronning visited the

Communist capital at the time of MacArthur's drive north, and, while he had no diplomatic status, he did have excellent contacts, and he also told Ottawa about the Chinese concerns.

DEAN RUSK

A good many people did warn us at the time that the Chinese might come in; I don't remember in particular about Mike Pearson, but I suppose he did. Even the Indians said that they weren't sure they believed what the Chinese had said. But I think Mike Pearson was very cautious about this notion of going beyond the thirty-eighth parallel.

CHESTER RONNING

I was convinced, as a result of previous conversations with Chou En-lai, that the Chinese were sending their forces up to the Yalu River to defend the power stations there. That was the only power available to North China for industrial purposes. I had warned Ottawa that there was no doubt about the intention of the Chinese, that they were determined to prevent the United Nations forces under General MacArthur from advancing on the Yalu River and capturing the power stations.

Well, the Chinese stormed across, in such overwhelming numbers that they immediately defeated the South Korean Army, which was most anxious to take over the Yalu River. Then the Chinese paused in order to settle the question peacefully. But General MacArthur had no intention of settling it peacefully as he was absolutely confident that he could wipe them out. So the Chinese attacked and drove the United Nations forces under MacArthur out of North Korea and they didn't stop until they came to the boundary between North and South Korea.

The winter of 1950-51 was an agonizing time for the United Nations and Lester Pearson. The Chinese had entered the Korean War, as Pearson had warned that they would, and their presence on the battlefield was made known in a communiqué from General MacArthur's headquarters on November 5; actually, the so-called Chinese Communist "volunteers" had begun moving across the Yalu River in mid-October, but after a few bloody battles with mainly South Korean forces at the beginning of

November, they broke off all contact. This may have been a demonstration on their part that they were offering a truce, as Chester Ronning suggested, but it could be interpreted as endorsing General MacArthur's contention that the Chinese had no capacity and could be wiped out by the latest American warplanes. At any rate, on November 24, the United Nations commander launched his campaign to end the war and "bring the boys home by Christmas"; at about the same time the Chinese forces began a massive counter-offensive. On November 28 General MacArthur notified the United Nations in New York that "we face an entirely new war," which made Pearson comment that, for once, the general was not making an overstatement.

As the United States Eighth Army and its South Korean allies rolled back in defeat, Pearson became more and more worried about the Korean War becoming a nuclear conflict. General MacArthur talked about using atomic weapons to stop the enemy, and during a press conference at the end of November, President Truman seemed to say that MacArthur had the authority to use these weapons if he so decided. This really made us shudder, Pearson wrote. Prime Minister Attlee rushed over to Washington to add Britain's voice to those crying that to drop the atom bomb on Asians again would be madness. In letters to his son, who was at Oxford at the time, the external affairs minister made several references to his disagreement with American policy. There was growing hysteria in the United States over the retreat in Korea, and Geoffrey Pearson said that his father was very uneasy about American public opinion and the editorials being written about the Communist or Chinese menace.

In December 1950, during the darkest days of the United Nations action in Korea, Lester Pearson joined a "cease-fire" committee that included Nasrollah Entezam of Iran, the president of the General Assembly, and Sir Benegal Rau of India. This proved to be one of his most frustrating assignments because the members of the committee spent so much of the time sitting around their hotel suites waiting for a telephone call that never came.

It so happened that on November 24, the day that MacArthur had picked to launch his "home by Christmas" offensive, a Chinese Communist delegation had arrived in New York. As might be expected, the cease-fire committee seized on this opportunity to negotiate with representatives of the enemy. However, General Wu Hsui-chuan, who headed the delegation, had refused to have any dealings with the committee. The Chinese had come, at the invitation of the Security Council, to present

Peking's views on the question of Formosa (Taiwan), and that was all they were going to do. Obviously, General Wu was not a high enough official to discuss a cease-fire and said as much; he was a tough soldier who sounded like a drill sergeant as he delivered a ferocious attack on the United States at the Security Council meeting. Despite the pleas of Secretary General Trygve Lie, General Wu and his delegation left on December 19; the United Nations was to have no further contact with the Chinese Communists for more than twenty years.

Now there was no way of delaying the Americans from bringing in a resolution condemning China for aggression, which they did in January of 1951. Lester Pearson resisted as long as he could, describing it as "premature and unwise," but had to vote for it in the end. Just as he had to support, reluctantly and against his better judgment, a further resolution imposing an embargo on China.

JOHN HOLMES

I was unhappy with the decision [to vote for condemnation]. I would have liked to oppose it. I think, though, that this is a rather important thing in understanding part of this philosophy. This isn't necessarily intended as a justification; it's more of an explanation. I think people have assumed and, understandably, tend to see this as a lack of gumption or submission to pressure. But it stemmed from Pearson's whole attitude toward the alliance, particularly with the United States. It comes out in various places. First of all, this does not mean that you submit to the will of the powerful leader. You argue against, you argue your case, you tell him when you think he's wrong—people talk about his quiet diplomacy, but they forget about his loud diplomacy. He said pretty bold things to the Americans, made fun of John Foster Dulles's massive retaliation.

On the other hand, he had this feeling that ultimately, because of the importance of maintaining the solidarity of the Western countries, you recognize that you do owe something to your leader, that he should not be weakened or humiliated, so he actually believed in the necessity of solidarity. So what, in a way, he was doing was making a clear statement, which is: "We don't agree with this tactic of the Americans, and I'll go on record as saying I don't agree with the tactics. But, in case you chaps on the other side misunderstand, this is our leader and we stick with them and we'll be solid and don't get any ideas you're splitting us." I think this is the message.

ESCOTT REID

The resolution naming Communist China as an aggressor was stupid because from then on the Americans used it as an argument for keeping Peking out of the United Nations. In all these issues—recognition of China, seating representatives of Peking in the United Nations—you get what is a constant in Canadian foreign policy: if you consider that the United States is proposing to do something unwise and dangerous, and not in the interest of world peace and world prosperity, how far do you go in standing up to them and opposing them in public? You have to make this assessment, day after day, as you have to ask yourself: "Is the cost of opposition truly in the national interest of Canada?"

Pearson, as you know, was often accused of sacrificing Canadian national interests through his desire to play a big role on the international stage, of sacrificing Canadian national interests in the international interest. Eisenhower said to St. Laurent and he said to Diefenbaker: "If Communist China is admitted to the United Nations, the United Nations will leave the United States and the United States will leave the United Nations." The first would have been a damn good thing—for the United Nations to leave the United States. To put the headquarters in New York was wrong from the beginning, and if the seating of Peking's representatives in the UN had led to that, it would have been excellent. I believe that the American bluff—and I think it was a bluff—of leaving the UN could have been called. I cannot believe that the United States would have left the United Nations in the mid-Fifties, leaving it in the hands of the Third World and the Soviet Bloc, its assets, its good will, its everything. But perhaps they would have, and the effect would have been disastrous. Perhaps the risk wasn't worth taking.

In the constricted sixty-member United Nations of the early Fifties, there was what was described as an automatic Western majority of forty-five votes, consisting of the United States, the Latin American client states, the NATO nations, and others bound to Washington by alliances. In the same sense, there was an automatic Soviet minority of five, the USSR and its satellites. The rest were non-aligned Asian and Arab countries. However, India and Burma joined the Soviet Bloc in opposing the resolution condemning China for aggression—the crucial vote that was to stultify the United Nations for more than a generation: forty-four in favor, seven opposed, and nine abstentions. It was not a very satisfactory outcome for the United States, but the American press made the best of it, claiming an overwhelming majority for censuring the Communists. Sir Benegal Rau was to remark that the seven who voted against represented more people than the forty-four who voted for.

After the condemnatory resolution, Lester Pearson realized that any hope for an early cease-fire in the Korean War had vanished. It was therefore important to find out what the United States wanted and what its long-term plans were; there had been a good deal of confusion about this with contradictory statements being made by American officials. The external affairs minister sent a long dispatch to the Canadian ambassador in Washington, Hume Wrong, in which he said that it was "essential for us to know as precisely as we can what present United States objectives are as regards the Far East in general and China in particular." Pearson did not feel that the ambassador should make any suggestions as to what the policy should be—"we may have been giving them too much gratuitous advice lately"—but he did express the view that there should be "agreement that our objective in the Far East is the defeat of aggression and not the use of the United Nations to overthrow Communist governments." Hume Wrong met with Dean Rusk, and, since the information he received was so sensitive, he wrote a personal letter to Pearson in which he said: "Mr. Rusk states the belief or the hope that the attitude of the Peking government may be changed by some kind of upheaval within the regime," and added that this analysis was based on very secret intelligence that the American official would not reveal.

When he was interviewed about this some seventeen years later, Dean Rusk said that he doubted very much that he had made such a statement. He described as "total garbage" the suggestion that the American objective was the overthrow of the Mao Tse-tung regime, and asserted that there was no prospect of this happening, and that he did not know of anyone in the American government who seriously felt that the Mao regime was going to fall.

In the spring of 1951 Pearson had been warned by the British that

General MacArthur was contemplating launching an invasion of mainland China from Formosa, but within a few days the United Nations commander was to be fired by President Truman. There was some question as to the value of American intelligence on China because of the damage done to it by the anti-Communist witch hunts, but Mr. Rusk felt that this had been greatly exaggerated and that, in any case, there was an exchange of information with Great Britain and Canada during the period.

In his dispatch to Ambassador Wrong, Pearson had expressed "the desirability of doing everything possible to drive a wedge between Communist China and the USSR." Dean Rusk was asked whether he felt that any concessions to Peking at the time of the Korean War would have strengthened the pro-Moscow group in the Chinese government.

DEAN RUSK

I don't recall thinking about it particularly in those terms, in terms of relations between Peking and Moscow. I thought then and I still think that there's not much point in our trying to play cute games between Moscow and Peking, trying to work one against the other, because they are much too intelligent in both capitals to let us do that. We deal with our relations with each one separately and do what we can to improve them, but not try any kind of game or maneuver between them or try to make judgments as to whether a group here or a group there within their system are going to move this way rather than the other.

At the opening of the Seventh General Assembly in October of 1952 — the first to be held in the great new Assembly Hall of the United Nations, which was as brightly lit as a Hollywood set for the television cameras — Lester B. Pearson was nominated for president. In the consultations that had gone on among the permanent delegations in New York, the names of a few other possible candidates had been mentioned, including that of Madame Pandit, Prime Minister Nehru's sister, but it was obviously the Canadian diplomat's turn. Furthermore, Pearson had become very well known at the United Nations and almost identified with the world body, largely because of the Korean War and his untiring efforts to stop the fighting there. (Since General MacArthur had been relieved of his command, and General Matthew Ridgway had taken over, the front

Canadian diplomat George Ignatieff and Under-Secretary L. B. Pearson at the UN Security Council meeting, Lake Success, New York, on January 6, 1948. (*Public Archives Canada PA 122003*)

Escott Reid and Pearson before going to Colombo, Ceylon, in January 1950 to attend the Commonwealth Conference. (*Public Archives Canada PA 121700*)

Lester Pearson, president of the seventh session of the UN General Assembly, held in the new building in New York City in December 1952. (*Public Archives Canada C 18725*)

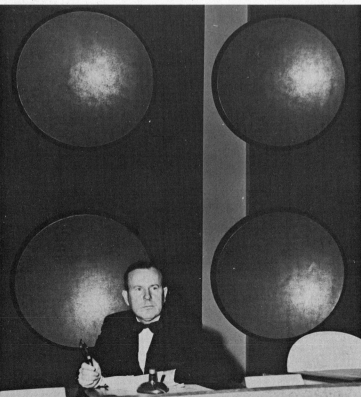

President Eisenhower meets with Prime Minister Louis St. Laurent at the White House in May 1953. With them are Canadian Ambassador Hume Wrong, Foreign Minister Pearson, and U.S. Secretary of State John Foster Dulles. (*Wide World Photo*)

Henry Cabot Lodge, Jr. (left), permanent representative to the UN, Lester Pearson, secretary of state for External Affairs, and Dag Hammarskjöld, president of the UN General Assembly, at the signing of the Korean armistice agreement in July 1953. (*Public Archives Canada C 76068*)

Lester Pearson and actress Helen Hayes share a joke before receiving
honorary degrees at Princeton's commencement ceremonies in June 1956.
Pearson was cited for his contribution to the development of the UN and
NATO. (*Wide World Photo*)

Lester Pearson addressing a UN Correspondents' Association luncheon
meeting in 1955. At left is author Peter Stursberg. (*Courtesy Peter Stursberg*)

Major General E. L. M.
Burns, commander of
the UN Emergency
Force in Egypt,
January 1957.
(*United Nations Photo*)

Canadian delegation to the UN during the Suez Crisis in 1957 (from left to
right): John Holmes, Geoff Murray, Dr. Robert Mackay, Allan McGill, and
Lester Pearson. (*Public Archives Canada PA 117597*)

External Affairs Minister Paul Martin greets U.S.
Secretary of State Dean Rusk as he arrives in Ottawa to
attend a NATO ministers' meeting in May 1963.
(*Canadian Press photo*)

Lester Pearson welcomes Averell Harriman to Ottawa in August 1965.
(*Public Archives Canada PA 113496*)

Prime Minister Pearson chats with President John Kennedy at Hyannis Port on Cape Cod in May 1963. The weather was chilly but the greetings were warm as the chief executives met for two days of talks. *(Wide World Photo)*

had become stabilized near the thirty-eighth parallel, and negotiations had begun in the summer of 1951 first at Kaesong and then at Panmunjon between the representatives of the North Koreans and the Chinese on one side and the South Koreans and the Americans on the other; they went on in acrimony and recrimination, and the fighting went on and there was always the danger of its spreading and becoming a nuclear war.) Pearson was elected president by a large majority—only the Soviet Bloc voted against him and the Arab states abstained because of his support of Israel.

GEOFFREY PEARSON

I remember we visited him, my sister and I and my mother, and he obviously enjoyed being president and having a car and having a special office and being a big man at the UN. He took us to the private dining room and showed us all around. He obviously enjoyed that. He was always a bit of a schoolboy; perhaps he couldn't imagine that he was really where he was, and he got a kick out of it. I think he probably liked pomp and circumstance, sometimes anyway—not as a general thing, but for a man who had come from a very modest background, he rather enjoyed being surrounded by people who did what he wanted them to do, but he never ordered people to do anything.

It was a parlous time to be president because many felt that the United Nations could not last. Chester Ronning, who was back in Ottawa now, recalled that the British delegate, Sir Gladwyn Jebb, when on a Canadian visit, told division heads of the Department of External Affairs that there was not the slightest possibility of the United Nations' continuing after the next meeting. Ronning felt that this was a predominant thought, as he put it, in Mike Pearson's mind, that he was not going to preside over the disintegration of the United Nations.

While he was president, Pearson became a leading candidate for the office of secretary-general, succeeding Trygve Lie who had resigned. This was not the first time that he had been nominated to run the world organization; back in 1946, at the First Assembly of the United Nations in London he was very seriously considered for the job. The Labour Party, which had recently come to power in Britain, was anxious to have him. The Americans, according to Geoffrey Pearson, while favoring him, were only lukewarm because they did not want anyone as active as his father who might cause them trouble. Stanley Knowles, who was on the Canadian delegation and had close ties with Prime Minister Attlee for party reasons—the Socialist CCF Party was the counterpart of the Labour Party in Canada—remembered Hector McNeil, one of the Attlee's junior ministers, coming to see him privately to find out why the British could not have Lester Pearson as secretary-general. Knowles's reply was that Prime Minister Mackenzie King was opposed, that he had other plans for him.

On March 11, 1953, the Security Council met to choose a new secretary-general. The Americans put forward Brigadier General Carlos Romulo of the Philippines, and, when he was rejected, supported the nomination of Lester Pearson, which was vetoed by the Soviet Union. There was no doubt that Pearson wanted the job and hoped that the Russians would accept him, and, according to his good friend Walter Gordon, nobody knew what the Soviets were going to do until the last minute. There is some evidence that the Russians might have agreed, as Trygve Lie said that they wanted a delay, but the Americans moved quickly to get an agreement on Dag Hammarskjöld of Sweden. Pearson had spoken to Prime Minister St. Laurent about the possibility of his becoming secretary-general and, according to Arnold Smith, St. Laurent did say to him that he might become his successor as Liberal Party leader and prime minister.

GEOFFREY PEARSON

I know he talked it over with Mr. St. Laurent, who had not said no because the prime minister was not the kind of man to stop people from doing something that they wanted to do. I think also the prime minister indicated that he'd also be glad to have him stay. I don't think the prime minister encouraged him. I think my father would have enjoyed doing it because his stay as president had intrigued him to go on as secretary-general and [it] would have interested him very much. But whether he actually thought he had a chance I don't know. I think he did because he was not anathema to the Russians. He may have thought they would come around, but I don't think he lobbied for the job. In fact, I am almost sure he didn't. He didn't lobby for things much. He had the kind of self-confidence that implies you don't blow your own horn. If you don't get something, there are always other things to do. So he wasn't all that disappointed. That's also an advantage of not taking goals too seriously: you're not too disappointed, and I don't think he was. I think he would have been glad to have it, but not having got it, he was just as pleased to go on because it could hardly be said his job was uninteresting in those days. Canada was still an important country and he was an important foreign minister.

PAUL MARTIN

I was very close in his zeal and his desire, in his plans to become president of the United Nations. I was also very close with him, but we had differences of view as to the possibility of achievement when he wanted to become secretary-general. My view was that he couldn't become secretary-general. The Soviet Union would not agree to an appointee from the West, and especially from NATO. But if he had become secretary-general, he would have been a very great one. That was an area where he was especially adept, and he brought not only zeal and dedication but a sense of how to operate. He would have been like Dag Hammarskjöld, in my judgment. And it was a very bitter disappointment to him that he didn't [become secretary-general].

It was hardly surprising that the so-called "armistice negotiations," which were being conducted in the midst of the Korean War, should not rise above the level of a Cold War slanging match. Averell Harriman, who was special assistant to President Truman at the time, complained that the Chinese were very obstinate, very difficult to deal with then; the only thing they were doing was shouting. It soon became evident that the main obstacle to any kind of a truce was the question of the prisoners of war: the Communists insisted on the letter of the Geneva Convention of 1949, that all POWs should be repatriated, while the Americans would not agree to what they called "the compulsory repatriation of prisoners of war"—to have done otherwise, as Harriman said, would have been unconscionable.

As these negotiations were going on, although achieving nothing, it was decided at the Sixth General Assembly, which was held in Paris during the winter of 1951-52, that there would be no discussion of the Korean War. As a reward for serving as Indian delegate to the UN, Sir

Benegal Rau had gone to The Hague as a judge of the International Court, and Krishna Menon showed up for the Seventh General Assembly. He had been an agitator for Indian independence, and was a good friend and confidante of Prime Minister Nehru and he had come to New York especially for the Korean debate. Since he conceived that the main task of the president of the Assembly was to resolve this conflict, Lester Pearson found himself involved in countless consultations with Menon while drinking numberless cups of tea.

GEOFFREY PEARSON

I remember my father talking about Krishna Menon and about [Sir Benegal] Rau, who was a judge and a very moderate man and easy to get along with. Krishna Menon was a politician and much more difficult. My father did his best to understand Menon and I think gained Menon's rather grudging respect but never his trust. I don't think Krishna Menon trusted anybody really. He was a tremendous egotist: the world turned around Krishna Menon, and the Americans couldn't stand him literally. They could hardly stay in the same room. My father stayed in the same room for hours and hours, but they were never friends really.

I can imagine how that negotiation went. My father always saw what other people were after even if he didn't agree. He was never really nonplussed by anyone, even Vyshinsky, the notorious Russian at the UN. He understood Vyshinsky's motives. He didn't like him, of course. He had a sort of respect for him.

He would know what Menon wanted even when he was very devious, and he would pass this on to the Americans, who would simply not or pretend not to understand because they assumed that Menon was an ally of Peking. I think the Americans assumed Menon was taking orders from Peking, which I don't think my father believed. I think he felt that Menon was very pro–China but was loyal on the whole to Nehru, and Nehru was not a Chinese servant of any kind. He had a great respect for Nehru. Mr. St. Laurent also had respect for Nehru so that they took Krishna Menon's word and the Americans didn't. I think on the issue of the prisoners my father probably didn't feel very strongly one way or the other. His main concern was to get the thing settled without widening or re-igniting the war. On the whole he managed to do that.

By the time the Seventh General Assembly met, the Panmunjon talks had broken down over the repatriation of the prisoners and had recessed indefinitely. Thus, the Korean War, which the United Nations had deliberately eschewed for a couple of years, was now taken up as a matter of urgency. Shortly after the Assembly opened, the countries with troops serving under the unified command, which included Canada, put in a resolution backing up the stand taken by the Americans at the armistice negotiations, while the Soviets put in one supporting the Chinese and North Korean position. For a month a desultory argument went on in the UN's First Political Committee, but the debate was getting nowhere. Meanwhile the United States delegation, and Dean Acheson in particular, perhaps out of a sense of frustration at being "lame ducks"—the Democratic administration of President Truman had just been voted out of office and General Eisenhower elected as a Republican president—began to be suspicious and critical of Mike Pearson because of his dealings with Krishna Menon.

WILLIAM P. BUNDY

The issue that did divide them [Acheson and Pearson] rather sharply was the question of Canada's attitude toward the repatriation of prisoners, Chinese and Korean, in the negotiations on Korea. Acheson has told in his memoirs of visiting Canada in November of 1952, after it was clear that he was a lame duck but while the issue was still a burning issue, and of his telling the Canadian Cabinet as a whole why he thought the position that Pearson had certainly been urging was just plain wrong from the standpoint of the United States and, as he felt, of a responsible outcome of the War. There's no question that he thought that Pearson was being carried away by rather abstract idealism and was prepared to abandon a very important principle for the sake of a compromise agreement. I think that particular incident had a rather searing affect on his judgment of Pearson.

I'm only saying that the account that Acheson gives in his memoirs is, if anything, milder than his oral account to his family and close friends in that period. He was very critical of the position that Mr. Pearson took on that issue, and tended to feel that a good deal too much free advice had been offered by Canada on an issue that was absolutely central to the United States and not nearly so central to Canada. I'd single that out as a very important episode in the relationship.

GEOFFREY PEARSON

Over Korea there was real tension. It didn't disturb their personal relations. They saw each other a good deal. He went to visit Acheson on his farm near Washington several times with my mother, and likewise the Achesons came to Canada two or three times and stayed with—I don't think it was with my parents but with mutual friends anyway, and they saw each other a good deal socially and enjoyed each other's company. But they were very different people and there was substance to the arguments they used to have.

Of course, my father never knew whether Acheson was a front for the military or was protecting his rear against Congress. I think he felt sometimes that Acheson had to take positions which he might not have wanted to personally, although Acheson himself never said that. I think Acheson believed what he said; certainly he spoke with great conviction, and my father may have rationalized their disagreement in this way.

[In their arguments] voices weren't raised, as far as I know, not like the time when Lyndon Johnson came to Canada and voices were raised over Vietnam—at least Johnson's voice was raised anyway. I don't think Acheson ever spoke like that. He didn't bully in that way. He was a gentleman; he was courteous, but he was ironic and tough-minded.

Lester Pearson, in his memoirs, dealt with Dean Acheson's claim that there was a Canadian conspiracy with the Indians, and that he (Pearson) had joined Krishna Menon's cabal and become enmeshed in an illusory proposal that amounted to a Canadian about-face, presumably on the resolution in the First Committee, which Canada had cosponsored, supporting the American stand at Panmunjon. Acheson had also implied, in his book Present at the Creation, *that the whole matter was cleared up at once when he saw Prime Minister St. Laurent, which Pearson described as "a travesty of the facts." In the light of the grave concern that Dean Acheson felt about Pearson's activities, the most surprising statement was to be made by Dean Rusk, who asserted that he was familiar with the kind of moves that went into bringing about a Korean armistice, and did not recall any major Canadian role.*

Even before it was voted out of office, the Truman administration had reached the end of its tether: it had been paralyzed by the McCarthy witch hunt and had lost all ability to maneuver. The investigation of alleged Communist activity in the State Department had had a devastating effect. The United States delegation to the United Nations was locked in a Cold War stance that equated neutralists with Communists: anyone who was not for was against, which accounted for the distrust of Pearson. It was not a happy time for American liberals, who felt that somehow they had been betrayed by the Indians and non-aligned Asians, the very people they had befriended and helped.

On November 17, 1952, there was a briefing in the White House for the Republican president-designate and some of his closest aides, and, according to Henry Cabot Lodge, Dean Acheson minced no words about the seriousness of the situation at the United Nations over Korea. The retiring secretary of state said that there was a resolution pending that, while it paid lip service to the principle of nonforcible repatriation of prisoners of war, created a commission the actual purpose of which would be to send the prisoners back. This was the resolution that Krishna Menon had discussed at so many meetings with Lester Pearson, who, as he said, had taken upon himself to mediate between the Americans and Indians on the means of bringing about an armistice.

When the plan was presented to the General Assembly, the Soviets turned it down and Andrei Vyshinsky attacked it as if it were a Western proposal; the Americans then supported it and Dean Acheson praised Krishna Menon. But here he was saying that the resolution completely circumvented the idea of nonforcible return of the prisoners. While Acheson may have impressed General Eisenhower, Henry Cabot Lodge insisted that there be no mention of the question of the POWs in the communiqué to be issued after the White House meeting because he did not want the incoming Republican administration to be compromised in any way.

The next day General Eisenhower and his party visited the Pentagon.

HENRY CABOT LODGE

Upon arrival at the Pentagon, we were met by General [Omar] Bradley and taken down to the briefing room. There we were given a thorough briefing on Korea. The map to which General Bradley pointed showed the bloody front, which was not far from the thirty-eighth parallel. Fighting had been going on for almost two and a half years and had been costly and indecisive. Twenty-one thousand Americans had been killed, ninety-one thousand wounded, and thirteen thousand were missing.[3] The enemy had dug a network of interlaced, underground entrenchments with positions organized in depth. The possibilities submitted to General Eisenhower were (one) to let the war drag on without a change in policy, or (two) to attack to the north so as to win a military victory by conventional means. Eisenhower thought both proposals were "intolerable." After much thought and study he finally decided to make a major effort and negotiate a truce, and on July 27, 1953, six months after his inauguration, the truce was signed. It was accepted by public opinion. Obviously Eisenhower was not worried about political adversaries at home saying he had lost Korea.

Although the change in administration in Washington and President Eisenhower's determination to end the war did a lot to bring about a Korean armistice, the United Nations also played a role. It was Krishna Menon, with the assistance of Lester Pearson, who developed the formula that resolved the problem of the prisoners of war. The course of events was as follows:

On November 19, 1952, Krishna Menon made a speech in the General Assembly introducing the Indian resolution, which was one of the longest on record with seventeen operative paragraphs, the most important of which was a proposal to establish a neutral nations' repatriation commission to which all the prisoners would be turned over. At first the Americans were opposed, but after many amendments and the Soviet rejection, they turned around and supported the resolution, which was adopted by fifty-four votes in favor, five against, and one abstention, on

---

[3]Total United States casualties in the Korean War were 140,806: 33,729 killed, 103,284 wounded, 10,218 captured (those who died as prisoners are listed twice under killed and captured). South Korean casualties were 300,000: 70,000 killed, 150,000 wounded, 80,000 captured. Canadian casualties were 1,641: 406 killed or died, 1,202 wounded, 33 captured. Enemy POWs in South Korean camps numbered 171,000: 151,000 North Korean, 20,000 Chinese.

December 3. As president of the Assembly, Pearson received telegrams from the Chinese and North Koreans, saying that the Russians were speaking for them. There were reports heard in the new UN Building that the American military did not want to resume negotiations following on the Indian resolution because they were preparing a big offensive that would win the war. If nothing else, General Eisenhower's visit to Korea at the end of December 1952 put a stop to those plans.

Then the United Nations Command, which was now under General Mark Clark, proposed an exchange of sick and seriously wounded prisoners, which seemed to break the deadlock. The Panmunjon talks were revived. At the end of March, Chou En-lai said that both sides should repatriate "all those prisoners of war who insist on repatriation and hand over the remaining prisoners of war to a neutral state." This was interpreted as a qualified acceptance of Krishna Menon's resolution and led eventually to the war ending on July 27, 1953.

It was the most difficult negotiation that Lester Pearson had ever had—the diplomatic equivalent of squaring the circle to get a resolution that would satisfy both the Indians and the Americans and would, at the same time, have a chance of being accepted by the Chinese and North Koreans, as it was. He was to say in his memoirs that he had never worked harder in his life.

6 India: the Asian Connection

THE WAY THAT Lester Pearson worked with Krishna Menon at the United Nations to produce an acceptable resolution that would end the Korean War, the long hours that he spent discussing the wording and the probable American reaction, was a vivid demonstration of the "special relationship" that Canada had with India during the Fifties. As Escott Reid said, that special relationship, which, simply put, was a recognition of the predominant position of Pandit Nehru in Asian affairs, had a healthy effect on Canadian foreign policy, making it "less Eurocentric." It began with Indian independence, reached its full flowering with the Korean armistice, and ended in ugly recriminations and disagreements on the Indochina commissions.

Because the critical Commonwealth Conference of April 1949 happened to coincide with a Canadian election campaign, Prime Minister St. Laurent could not attend and asked Pearson to take his place. Thus, the most junior minister who had only recently joined the government as secretary of state for external affairs became the senior spokesman at the conference because Canada was the first overseas dominion and the senior member of the Commonwealth. Actually, this made little difference because Pearson would have accompanied St. Laurent to London if he had been able to go, and would have done most of the negotiating to keep India in the Commonwealth. The prime minister was aware of the crisis that had developed as a result of India's becoming a republic; he was most anxious that the country should continue as a member of the association

106

and had instructed the external affairs minister to find a solution to the problem.

When Pearson arrived in London, he found that the British had devised a formula whereby the Crown would be regarded as "Head of the Commonwealth," which, they believed, Nehru would accept. The difficulty was to get the right wording and not make the declaration appear as if all the members were on the verge of becoming republics, which they certainly were not. In fact, the monarchists, led by Australia and New Zealand, argued that India should be regarded as a single exception to the rule, while Pakistan and Ceylon (Sri Lanka) insisted that any change had to be universal and apply to them, should they wish to become republics. In the end a committee was appointed to work out a compromise, and, at Prime Minister Attlee's request, Lester Pearson joined Sir Stafford Cripps and two senior British officials in drafting a declaration that was accepted by all members of the Commonwealth.

It was during this Commonwealth Conference that Pearson had his first real meeting with Krishna Menon, as Geoffrey Pearson put it; in fact, Geoffrey suggested that his father did most of the negotiating with Krishna Menon, who was Indian high commissioner in London at the time and an adviser to Prime Minister Nehru. Of course, there were many others involved in the historic realignment of the Commonwealth, and Pearson mentioned in his memoirs the wise advice that he received from John Kearney and Bert Mackay, two constitutional experts. Max Wershof, who was with the Canadian High Commission in London then, also contributed a paper.

GEOFFREY PEARSON

My father often said that he'd spent most of his career trying to find formulae which people would accept for this or that occasion. It's true; I think he spent an awful lot of time scribbling out words and formulae for communiqués and so forth. He was very good at it because he was always ready to accept a compromise if it seemed to be the right thing to do, and had the confidence to accept it without worrying about what the prime minister or someone else might think. He had both the ability to find the words and then the confidence to agree to it if the others did.

So it's words; yes, it is diplomacy; that's what they mean by negotiation, and I think that's what he was probably best at, negotiation of that kind, partly because of his personality. He always seemed to take people seriously, whoever they were. They trusted him, but the danger of that is you will be accused of giving away too much. And he was accused of appeasement.

MAX WERSHOF

I did assist Mike Pearson when he was substituting for Mr. St. Laurent at the Commonwealth Conference in 1949—that was the conference that took the fateful decision regarding India. At the time I was actually attending a conference in Geneva, the conference that ended by producing, among other things, the revised Geneva Conventions on Prisoners of War and the Red Cross.[1] I was called back to London for a couple of weeks. I hasten to add that I returned not to sit at the right hand of Mike—in fact, I wasn't at the conference table—but to do a paper from the legal point of view. I remember doing at least one memorandum, which I assume was read by Mike and might have been some help to him.

There was no doubt that that Commonwealth Conference was of crucial importance: it marked the peaceful and harmonious conversion of the old British Empire and the all-white British Commonwealth into the new multiracial and multicolored Commonwealth of Nations. As Mike Pearson said, "Had we been unable to solve the problem of India's admission as a republic, we would not have the Commonwealth we have today with all the new members from Asia and Africa." Thus the London meeting took a landmark decision in the postwar development of the world.

Yet, at the same time, Pearson realized that in making the Crown the "Head of the Commonwealth" and allowing republics to be members, they had broken the institutional bond of the monarchy within the Commonwealth. This meant, as he said, that only self-interest would hold the Commonwealth together—the bond of sentiment between the new members and the old was bound to diminish as new leaders arose who had no feelings for British traditions and values. So that in making this

[1]The 1949 Geneva Convention on Prisoners of War was constantly being upheld by the Communist side during the debates on a Korean armistice agreement at the UN.

change, it could be said that they had sown the seeds of the Commonwealth's eventual disintegration. However, there was no alternative; if the conference had not done what it did in April 1949, the rot would have set in immediately, and disintegration come about much sooner. It did have a beneficial effect because the prominent part that Pearson played in finding a solution to the problem of India's membership as a republic was the beginning of the special relationship between Canada and India.

ESCOTT REID

Before the special relationship weakened, it served a very useful purpose, mainly because it had a healthy effect on Canadian foreign policy. Nehru's thesis from the beginning, from the time he took office, was that it was an oversimplification of a highly complicated situation to see the main problem before the world as communism versus anti-communism; what was as important or more important were the struggle of two-thirds of mankind against poverty and the struggle for racial equality. He was right, and his constant reiteration of this on every occasion, including meetings of Commonwealth foreign ministers and prime ministers, and the fact that we considered Nehru to be the most important statesman in Asia, as he was—this did have an effect on Canadian foreign policy, making it less Eurocentric. This was in our interest and in the general interest. I only wish to God that the Americans had had a special relationship with India during this period which might have made them a little more conscious of the truth of what Nehru was preaching.

I think this [the way the Americans turned against India] puzzled and hurt Nehru. He had been the great idol of American public opinion at the time when he was fighting against the British, and it puzzled him. He felt he remained the same and now he was getting this bitter criticism from the United States government and leaders of American opinion. It's a sad story.

While Churchill swore that he would not preside over the dissolution of the British Empire, his successor, Prime Minister Attlee was under no such imperialist illusion. Yet he and his Labour government did little to prepare for the eventual independence of the colonies, and this despite the fact that it was a tenet of Socialist ideology that the subject territories should be given their freedom. They did not seem to have any plan or give the matter much thought when they came to power at the end of the war in 1945. They would certainly get no help from the colonial officials: the White Man's Burden was administration, not instruction in self-government. The district officers and district commissioners, those heroes of the Victorian and Edwardian periods, had as much political savvy as boy scouts, whom they resembled in other ways. When the inevitable riot occurred in the West African colony of the Gold Coast (Ghana), they became panic-stricken and blamed it all on the Communists, the only evidence they had being an out-of-date British Communist Party card belonging to a little-known nationalist leader named Kwame Nkrumah. However, these bemused and badly frightened officials carried on an anti-Communist propaganda campaign worthy of the Nazis until the Colonial Office in London, which was somewhat more sophisticated, realized that if the people of the Gold Coast had not known about the Communists before, they were learning fast. Heads rolled, and the governor and the colonial secretary were sent packing, the latter to edit a departmental magazine.

In 1946 a negotiating team of three British Cabinet ministers was sent to Delhi with the avowed purpose of leaving an independent India as one country; the mission was a failure[2] and in the end the British had to quit the subcontinent, which was divided hastily between two warring nations, India and Pakistan. Undeterred by this, the Labour government went ahead with a policy, if it could be called a policy, that independence should be granted to large units. Where they did not exist, they should be created. So a conference was held at Montego Bay, Jamaica, in 1947 to set up a federation of the widely scattered British colonies in the West Indies and Central America. There followed the West African economic federation, the East African Federation, the Central African Federation, and the Malaysian Federation. All of these federations failed—some of them never got started and others like the West Indies Federation lasted for a couple of years before breaking up.

[2]The British Cabinet mission negotiators, who were led by Pethick Lawrence and included Sir Stafford Cripps and Lord Alexander, spent three months in India. When it was apparent that they could not get agreement from the Congress and the Moslem League, they left behind a constitution which its author, Sir Stafford Cripps, claimed met the views of both parties: it consisted of federations of the princely states within federations of India and the area that became Pakistan within an over-all federation. It was a brilliant legal exercise but totally unworkable.

*Malcolm MacDonald, who took a particular interest in the Common-
wealth, said that this obsession with creating federations was typical of the
times. People like himself, and he included Lester Pearson, believed in the
one-world concept of the brotherhood of man and did not take into
consideration the impact of nationalism.*

MALCOLM MACDONALD

We recognized that it had to be a step-by-step process. One step
was that colonies which had been dependent should become
independent, and the next step was that those nations should
become interdependent, but again not at first on a world-wide
scale but in federations—this region and that region of the world
which had certain common economic and other interests, common cultures and so on. Mind you, the umbrella or the sun shade
(or whatever it should be called) over it all, pointing to complete
unity in due course, was the United Nations. But we knew that
for a while at any rate that would be a talking shop, a jolly useful
talking shop, but we'd got to build practical cooperation in day-
to-day things on a regional basis, and therefore begin with federations. This was a step-by-step strategy for the gaining eventually
of a happily harmonious peaceful world. But it didn't work out.

It didn't work out in most cases, partly, no doubt, for a reason
which I have, so to speak, hinted at earlier when I suggested that
the first step was that the dependent territories in the British
colonial empire, in the French colonial empire, in the Dutch
colonial empire, in the Portuguese colonial empire, and so on—
their dependent colonies should become independent nations first.
Nationalism was their emotion and understandably so. Therefore,
a new independent nation in East Africa, for example, wasn't
ready to lose part of its independence by joining another East
African nation and having to say, "These chaps next door can help
to settle our international policy." So nationalism was, I suppose,
the chief reason why the federations did not work. We were
trying to go too far too fast for human emotions at the time.

*In Malcolm MacDonald's view, the Commonwealth was a substitute
for all the federations that had failed, and he said that Mike Pearson cared
about the development of the Commonwealth into a world brotherhood*

and used his considerable personal influence and official Canadian influence with the British government in this direction. Escott Reid felt that, for Pearson, the importance of the Commonwealth was that it provided Canada with a counterbalance to the United States. William Clark, the British journalist who was to be Prime Minister Eden's press secretary at the time of the Suez Crisis, said that the Commonwealth was a North-South link, a link between the developed and the developing world.

There were other reasons for Pearson's continuing support of the Commonwealth as external affairs minister and prime minister.

GEOFFREY PEARSON

I think my father's view of the Commonwealth was influenced by his time at Oxford where he met so many people who subsequently played a role in British politics and also Commonwealth politics. He knew a lot of these people who were students at Oxford—Indians, Pakistanis, Australians, South Africans— and he shared this common background of admiration for British law and British sports and British habits. So there was a real sentimental bond and I think he genuinely felt the Commonwealth was an important institution which Canada had in part invented because he was present at the meeting in 1949 when India became a republic, and he worked on the formula and wrote parts of it, which allowed India to stay in the Commonwealth.

LORD HOME

My impression was that he was happy with the old Commonwealth, but happier with the new. The reason was that he thought and felt that if you could get a country like the Republic of India into the organization, although it could cause a good deal of trouble, nevertheless it was very desirable to do so because it would expand the area and scope of consultation between the members and after all, they spanned the globe pretty well.

This was again right up Mike Pearson's street because he was always looking for the widest area of consultation, if not coopera- tion, that you could find. The UN was obviously faltering, and here was something which could, of its own right, be of quite considerable value. I don't think he overestimated what the value could be, but was nevertheless very glad when the problem of India, which was quite a big one, was resolved.

ESCOTT REID

Canadians who attended Commonwealth meetings realized that they were valuable to us because they gave us a chance to correct distortions in our view of the world. Every view of the world suffers from some distortion, and we could correct ours by seeing what the world looked like from Delhi or Karachi or Colombo. People who took part in the Commonwealth discussions had all been brought up in British parliamentary procedures. There were no problems about rules of procedure. They all talked the same language so there was no necessity for interpretation. The Commonwealth, as Alastair Buchan has written—he says from 1952 to 1957 and I would say from 1947 to 1957—had many of the aspects of alliance. Pearson and St. Laurent had this feeling of the Commonwealth: that it was a great multiracial experiment. Commonwealth cooperation is now more difficult because of the great numbers involved. Pearson felt that the Commonwealth also helped to balance the relationship with the United States, just as the North Atlantic alliance did. We're always seeking some balance.

WILLIAM CLARK

I think Mike Pearson saw it as a particularly close link between a group of countries—a half-dozen or a dozen countries at that time—in a world that was becoming more closely linked. I think he saw the advent of India as transforming the white empire into what we'd now call a North-South link and that he regarded Canada as a very important part of that link—the Canadian-Delhi link, which I saw a lot of because Escott Reid was your high commissioner in Delhi when I went there as the *Observer*'s correspondent, which was a very close relationship indeed.

ARNOLD SMITH

I think Pearson had a very realistic attitude toward the Commonwealth and therefore a very favorable one. I think he saw it as an instrument that provided an opportunity for pretty frank discussion and mutual influence among the poorer countries, black and white and brown, and also between Canada and Britain and Australia and New Zealand on attitudes and policies toward the Third World—a real way of harmonizing policies on things that mattered quite a lot. He was always a very constructive supporter of the Commonwealth. And this goes back a long way. I think he valued it very much as an instrument to lessen the dangers of continental alienation and isolationism and so on.

It would have to be a round-the-world trip to go to the January 1950 Commonwealth Foreign Ministers' Conference in Colombo because Ceylon (Sri Lanka) is almost exactly on the other side of the world from Canada, and so Lester Pearson decided to visit various Commonwealth and Asian capitals on his way back from the conference. R. W. Mayhew, a British Columbia businessman who was minister of fisheries in the St. Laurent government, accompanied Pearson on this long-distance mission, and so did Escott Reid, who acted as the external affairs minister's principal adviser at the conference which laid the foundations for the Colombo Plan, the first international aid program for developing countries. The British delegation was led by the foreign secretary, Ernest Bevin, and one of its members was Malcolm MacDonald, who was by then commissioner general of Malaya and entertained the Canadians when they visited Singapore. MacDonald recalled that the two men who played a leading role in initiating the aid program were Mike Pearson and Percy C. Spender, the Australian external affairs minister.

At the opening session of the conference Pearson explained that Canada was conscious of two great dangers: first, the aggressive imperialism, as he put it, of the Soviet Union and, second, the alarming growth of communism through the inability of countries to deal with their own economic and social problems. He went on to say that, to meet the first danger, Canada had joined the North Atlantic Treaty Organization, and, as far as the second danger was concerned, he felt that the best defense against communism was a policy of sound economic development. For that reason Canada would be ready to play a part in any practical scheme that would further such development. There was no idealism in this speech, no fine words about the brotherhood of man; in fact, it was a Cold War statement, and support for the aid program was put on the basis of self-interest. However, Escott Reid pointed out that it was the first time that such a

give-away scheme had ever been considered, and there was opposition in
the Canadian Cabinet, many of whose members, while they may have
admired Pearson as a diplomat, nevertheless felt that he was an impracti-
cal dreamer.

ESCOTT REID

As I remember [that trip], we were in a North Star plane,
which was about the noisiest plane that's ever been created; not
only noisy but a continuous vibration. Looking back, it seems so
strange. We left in a terrible blizzard just after New Year's in 1950.
We stopped in Newfoundland for refueling, we stopped in the
Azores for a meal and refueling, we stopped in Gibraltar overnight. We were supposed to go to the airport near Baghdad.
Something went wrong and we stopped in the Suez Canal Zone
overnight and then went to Karachi. We stayed there overnight
and then flew to Colombo. It must have been something like five
days. I remember, I suppose a day or two before the meeting was
to take place, Pearson asked me after we had arrived in Colombo
to do a draft of the first statement he might make. That kind of
thing at home I could have done in ten minutes; it took me hours.
My mind was full of cotton wool from the noise and vibration.

This was the one and only meeting of Commonwealth foreign
ministers, and a very successful meeting. It was where the Colombo Plan was conceived. Then we went on to India and to
Burma, Singapore, Hong Kong, Japan. After we came back,
Pearson had the job of selling to Cabinet the idea of the contribution by Canada to international development aid under the Colombo Plan, which, at the beginning, was restricted to the
Commonwealth. So it meant aid to India, Pakistan, and Ceylon.
This was one of Pearson's great accomplishments. He had no
support to begin with in the Cabinet except from Mr. Mayhew,
the minister of fisheries from British Columbia.

Mayhew had joined us in India. He had gone out for an ILO
meeting. Mayhew was a man who found it terribly difficult to
give speeches or make arguments but he had the confidence of
Cabinet because he had met a payroll, and of course Pearson had
never met a payroll. Pearson finally won St. Laurent to his side
and then gradually got agreement from the Cabinet, but it was

one of the most difficult problems he ever had because this was something completely new in Canadian history, and in the history of most Western countries, that you should enter an agreement to transfer money from your taxpayers to the government of another country to help it speed up its development. And the first twenty-five million dollars was the hardest.

It seems silly now, looking back at it, but it was extremely difficult to get Cabinet to make that decision; they realized the precedent they were creating. I would put that and the North Atlantic Treaty as two of Pearson's great accomplishments. Another was his contribution to the cease-fire in Korea, and I agree with Chester Ronning that Pearson deserved the Nobel Prize much more for that than for his intervention in 1956 on the Suez affair, or as much anyway.

ARNOLD SMITH

The Australian press certainly gave the main credit [for the Colombo Plan] to the Australian foreign minister, and the Canadian press gave the main credit to Mike. On the whole, the press in other countries put them pretty close together, but Mike was in on it very much at the beginning, and the whole concept of using the tax dollars of Canadians and other Westerners to help improve conditions for foreigners was a pretty radical doctrine at that time. I'd spent two and a half years in the early part of the war in Egypt, where you really saw absolute poverty at first hand when you got out into the villages, and the last two and· a half years of the war in the Soviet Union, and I was worried, of course, about Stalin's ambitions and remembered Lenin's statement that he foresaw an alliance between Soviet power and the colonial peoples of the world. And so both for humanitarian and for basic political strategic reasons I very much favored and encouraged the doctrine of Western help for the development of what are now called Third World countries or developing countries or underdeveloped countries, colonial peoples. I'd urged this, I think, in a dispatch from Moscow in 1944. And I was delighted at the line that Mike took.

I think Mike was a man of enormous breadth of vision. The idea that politics was the art of the possible—I don't remember who first said that—but certainly Mike was a wonderful example. He would always do as much good as he thought he could get away with, and he had his feet very much on the ground and eyes high up and looking a long way ahead and seeing the heavens and the skies.

As Lester Pearson expected, the visit to mostly Commonwealth capitals—Rangoon was on his itinerary and Burma had already opted out—proved to be as valuable in its way as the Colombo Conference: there were insights into Asian problems that he would not have had if it had not been for this opportunity for firsthand examination, and talks to leaders on their home grounds. It was the first time that he had been in the Far East. As a result of this trip he was able to make changes in Canadian foreign policy—they were mainly changes in emphasis and in nuances, although in one case he did make a major adjustment.

When he was in Karachi, he was distressed to find the bitter antagonism there toward India. It centered on the Kashmir dispute, and the Pakistani prime minister, Liaquat Ali Khan, made it clear that the acquisition of Kashmir was a matter of life or death for Pakistan, and that, as he put it, they would go down fighting. However, in New Delhi, he found that the Indians were equally opposed to giving in on Kashmir, and he noted that Prime Minister Nehru seemed to be much more adamant on this issue than he had been at the Colombo Conference, which Nehru had attended because he was also Indian external affairs minister. The British Labour government tended to side with the Pakistanis, and the Commonwealth secretary, Philip Noël-Baker, who happened to be in Karachi at the time of the Canadian visit, begged Pearson to back Pakistan to the limit and argued that if enough pressure were brought to bear on India, she would yield. While Pearson might have felt that the Pakistanis had a better case, he nevertheless considered that Noël-Baker's thesis was, as he said, dangerously incorrect.

He reported the conversations that he had had in Karachi and New Delhi to Ottawa and suggested that "we should extricate ourselves from any special responsibility we might have incurred because of General McNaughton's presidency of the Security Council in December 1949." At that time the members of the Council had asked McNaughton, as president rather than as Canadian delegate, to mediate between India and Pakistan; and the general prepared a plan that had, in effect, been rejected by India. "My visit to India," Pearson said, "confirmed my feeling that there was not much hope now for a solution through the Security Council, and little possibility that any resolution of that Council would be accept-

able to or make any impression on the Indian government."

During the stop-over in Hong Kong, Lester Pearson tried to telephone Chester Ronning, the Canadian official in China, but could not get through, which was hardly surprising since communications with that country proved to be hazardous even some twenty years later. The question of Communist China had come up at the Colombo Conference, and Pandit Nehru had urged on all members of the Commonwealth the earliest possible recognition. Pearson had wanted to speak to Ronning about the steps to be taken in preparation for establishing relations with the new regime, including the acquisition of suitable accommodation in Peking for an embassy.

Some five months after the Colombo Conference, the Korean War began, and, as has been recounted in the preceding chapter, Pearson was to concentrate his attention on that war, which was such a sharp focus of Asian affairs generally.

There were interludes when he went to Europe to attend North Atlantic Council meetings; there, he kept hammering on his theme that NATO should be broader than a military alliance. Geoffrey Pearson said that his father always thought that NATO would not survive if there were not economic and cultural cooperation, as envisaged in Article 2, and particularly political consultation. He wanted NATO cabinet meetings where matters could be discussed informally, and hoped that through this process there would develop a North Atlantic community, if not a federation. In the mid-Fifties, Mike Pearson was appointed to a three-member committee, known as "The Three Wise Men," to examine the nonmilitary side of NATO; but their recommendations for regular consultations and closer cooperation ran into the opposition of John Foster Dulles, the U. S. secretary of state, and others. The Americans and the British as well as some Europeans regarded NATO as a military alliance for the defense of Europe and could not understand what all the fuss was about.

Geoffrey Pearson admitted that his father was "never able to put flesh on the bones of this concept." He said that he tried very hard, as Canadians have tried ever since, but "we were the odd man out." The reason he was so anxious to have this kind of cooperation and consultation was, in Geoffrey Pearson's view, "the fear arising from the Second World War that we would not be consulted about anything, that people would make decisions without consulting us."

One of the many clauses in the Indian resolution that finally stopped the fighting in Korea was that there should be a conference on the unification of the country within a year of the armistice going into effect; since the Chinese Communists and the North Koreans were not members of the United Nations, it was agreed that the conference should be held in Geneva. In the end the 1954 Geneva Conference dealt not only with Korea but with Indochina as well, since Dien Bien Phu, the last great French redoubt in Indochina, fell to Ho Chi Minh and the Vietminh. At first Canada was only a member of the Geneva Conference on Korea but Pierre Mendès-France, who had come to power as a result of the debacle of Dien Bien Phu, begged Canada as a friend and a "French-speaking country" to attend the second Geneva Conference—they were held on alternate days, Korean unification on one day, Indochina on the next.

However, just before Mendès-France took over, there was a nuclear scare—the French government asked the Americans to drop the atom bomb to relieve Dien Bien Phu.

ARNOLD SMITH

It was very secret at the time, but Dulles talked to Eisenhower about this request; he talked to some Congressional leaders, and they said they wouldn't do it unless Canada and Britain agreed. We had an awful lot of heat put on us one weekend to agree to this. Who by? The French.

I always had the impression that Dulles rather favored doing it, but I could be wrong. Eisenhower didn't, and so there was a certain muting of the American position.

The French were all in favor. Anyway, we thought it would be a terrible thing if the West dropped an atom bomb for the second time on Asia. It would really have ended the prospect of understanding between the West and Asia, and we were against it.

The British were against it too. And together, we stopped it. We felt we had really done something quite important—it was a rather critical weekend—in participating in the stopping of what could have been a disastrous decision.

GEORGE IGNATIEFF

What I recall happened was that Douglas MacArthur II—that's

the great general's nephew—and a group of generals came to Ottawa to brief us on behalf of Foster Dulles. As I recollect the proposal, it was that the United States Seventh Fleet, which was patrolling the China Seas to guard the offshore islands of Quemoy and Matsu and which was already armed with nuclear weapons, might in certain circumstances, if an attack seemed imminent, contemplate a nuclear shot across the bow on the mainland of China by dropping an atom bomb.

We weren't asked for our approval or disapproval but we were told that this was a contingency which they were contemplating and that this might require certain contingency planning on our side in the sense of alerting the early-warning system and all the rest of it.

The Americans said that the French were urging that, that there should be some intervention on the part of the United States if they were to stay in Dien Bien Phu. There were arguments about that and I don't think the U.S. government was willing to accept that, but there was serious talk of the possibility of the use of nuclear weapons in a manner which would demonstrate that the United States, if provoked against its known defense position— which included, according to the U.S. definition, not only Taiwan but the offshore islands and Japan—would have to use nuclear weapons to demonstrate its willingness to use the ultimate weapon in defense.

I remember that there was a meeting at which I was present as an adviser; Mr. St. Laurent, Mr. Pearson, the chief of the general staff, Campney, the defense minister, were there. As I recollect, we pointed out that—Sino-Soviet relations didn't reach a breaking point until the Sixties—such a move would certainly risk involving the advocation of the Sino-Soviet pact, that it would risk triggering reaction from another nuclear power in retaliation.

Although Henry Cabot Lodge remembered that President Eisenhower was opposed to the use of the atom bomb and would not agree to it, he did not know about the visit of the American diplomat, Douglas MacArthur II, and his party to Ottawa to brief the Canadian government on the so-called "contingency plan." Lodge thought that the matter came up originally when the vice-president, Richard Nixon, spoke to the annual convention of the American Society of Newspaper Editors in Washington on April 16, 1954. Since the ASE Convention was a "prestigious and responsible forum" (Nixon's own words), the vice-president asked that his remarks be off the record. After delivering a prepared speech, he agreed to take questions from the floor. He was asked whether the United States should intervene in Indochina if the French decided to withdraw and that was the only way to save the country from being taken over by the Communists.

HENRY CABOT LODGE

Nixon is quoted [in his book] as saying: "Given those major reservations, that if sending American forces were the only way to avoid further Communist expansion in Asia, particularly in Indochina, I believe that the executive branch of the government has to take the politically unpopular position of facing up to it and doing it." That means using whatever weapons come in handy, including nuclear weapons. Nixon goes on to say: "It's pretty clear and I personally would support such a decision." However, Eisenhower's position, as I have cited it before, was quite different: it was opposed to any unilateral venture of this kind and favored a joint approach [presumably, the approach of the 1954 Geneva Conference].

Nothing came of the nuclear scare, and few people knew about it, but it was not a happy augury for the Geneva Conferences on Korea and Indochina, which opened at the end of April 1954 and went on well into the summer. John Holmes was Lester Pearson's assistant at these conferences; the external affairs minister was at the first sessions along with the other foreign ministers and attended a few other meetings. Holmes was not sanguine about these conferences; he did not think there was a hope in hell of achieving Korean reunification. Chester Ronning was on the Canadian delegation—to provide a liaison with the Chinese Communists—and recalled a confrontation between John Foster Dulles and Chou En-lai on the opening day of the Geneva Conferences which really set the tone for the rest of the meetings.

CHESTER RONNING

You remember we sat alphabetically at international conferences and China and Canada therefore sat together. I was a personal friend of Chou En-lai and a number of the Chinese delegation. At the first morning coffee break, we left the main chamber and went into the reception room, and there Chou En-lai said to me, "I would like to meet Mike Pearson, if he is willing to meet me."

So I went over to Mike Pearson and I said, "Chou En-lai would like to shake hands with you and meet you and talk with you." He said, "Why, of course, I'd be glad to do that." I went back and told him. Then, I said to Mike Pearson, "I will introduce you and then I will disappear because he understands English and he has a very good interpreter for what he doesn't understand." So they met and they shook hands and they drank coffee together and they talked.

Then, at the end of the period, John Foster Dulles came over toward Mike Pearson, who was walking with Chou En-lai, and Chou En-lai held out his hand because he thought John Foster Dulles was coming to shake hands with him. Dulles turned right around and he looked very angrily at Mike Pearson—I think he, he had words with him afterward, but what he said I don't know. . . . At any rate, John Foster Dulles turned right around and stared daggers at both Chou En-lai and Mike Pearson.

When Henry Cabot Lodge was told about this incident, he was appalled and said that it was ridiculous not to shake hands with Chou En-lai. However, his comment must be judged in light of the fact that it was made almost a quarter of a century later, when the Americans and Chinese were friends; he seemed to have forgotten the depth of feeling there was when they were enemies. Furthermore, at the Geneva Conferences the Americans came face to face with the Chinese Communists for the first time, and the United States attitude was that while they had to deal with the enemy across the table, there should be no shaking hands nor any friendly or informal exchanges. In this instance John Foster Dulles may very well have expressed the righteous indignation of the American people.

The secretary of state was a difficult man to get to know and Geoffrey Pearson felt that his father did not get along well with Dulles; that it was, as he put it, a very uneasy relationship. Yet, at the same time, he did not seem to be as worried by Dulles' moralistic and apocalyptic utterances as he was by Dean Acheson's barbed comments and often sharp criticism of

Canadian policy and of himself. Pearson was opposed to the doctrine of massive retaliation as enunciated by Dulles, and did not hesitate to say so publicly. But this did not disturb Canadian-American relations as much as had his efforts to end the Korean War when Acheson was secretary of state. Such diverse persons as Charles Ritchie and Henry Cabot Lodge both felt that while Pearson and Dulles had their differences, they respected each other.

HENRY CABOT LODGE

I saw them both. I was in New York most of the time whereas Dulles was in Washington most of the time, but Dulles was in New York quite often and I was in Washington quite often. Dulles had an encyclopedic knowledge of history. But I think they got along all right because Mike Pearson was the sort of man who, if he had decided that he ought to get along with somebody, he'd get along with him. He didn't allow little things to interfere with big things.

GEOFFREY PEARSON

These people [foreign ministers] always met each other in two kinds of ways. They met around the table at a formal meeting where they exchanged more or less formal statements and they were surrounded by advisers, and it was the reverse of any sort of normal relationship. There were great tensions sometimes because you got to know people very well just by watching them around the table if you did it year after year. The other way was around a dinner table. After these long meetings they all had dinner and they were formal dinners usually. But if there were women present, they would all leave after dinner and the men would then have a glass of port or whiskey and talk quite frankly sometimes. Mr. Dulles didn't do that; he wasn't a drinker and he wasn't a storyteller and he didn't stay late. Dulles used to come up to Canada—he had a summer cottage in the Thousand Islands—and occasionally they would see each other here [in Ottawa], but they were never friends.

They called each other by their first names and they were cordial enough, but I don't think Dulles had any real friends outside Washington. It was an uneasy relationship because they didn't agree with each other at all. Massive retaliation was the Dulles contribution to the debate over foreign policy and that made my father very uneasy indeed. I think there are many records in the files of conversations in Washington, usually with others present, in which Canadian doubts were expressed about American foreign policy in regard to Formosa and the offshore islands, the Canadians expressing doubts about American threats. The other phrase was "rolling back" Soviet forces in Europe, and that, too, aroused great fears in Ottawa. It all seemed at the time as though we were Mr. Milquetoast and the Americans must have looked upon us that way. We were also clutching at their coattails.

I don't think that Dulles would have said to my father that Canada, that we were a lot of cry-babies, as Acheson did, but he would argue usually in moral terms, that this was the proper and the right thing to do and that we should understand that they were acting out of principle and not out of any other motive. That was rather hard to deal with, that kind of argument.

If nothing else, the 1954 Geneva Conference on Korea proved to be a test of Canadian diplomatic discipline. Whether Mike Pearson was leading the delegation or John Holmes was in charge— which he was when the external affairs minister was not present—there were sharp differences with the Americans and vigorous arguments in the United Nations group (the countries that had forces under the UN command in Korea). "We fought very hard," Holmes recalled. "We thought that the United States attitude was unduly rigid, but in the end we voted as a group." However, the Canadian views were not on the record, so that when the issues came up again, they were able to take the same position as before, but within the group. When it came to the conference, Holmes said, "we were not going to appear disunited," which meant voting with the Americans.

Since Korean reunification was such an impossibility, nobody expected the Geneva Conference to get anywhere and, as a result, nobody paid much attention to it.

JOHN HOLMES

If there were any possibility of reunification, we were bound to explore it, and we did, but there was a fundamental difference with the Americans. I think this was really a Pearsonian difference, although it was in general a Canadian one, but he was at the center of it. The Americans said, "There must be free elections in Korea and they must be run by the United Nations." The Communists said, "The UN has become a partisan in this war on one side. Therefore it can't run the elections." The Americans took the high line: "You can't defy the United Nations, which was set up by God and us," et cetera.

Well, our approach, and the Pearsonian approach, was to say, "Sure, you're right: the UN should be doing it and we fully agree, and we musn't accept anything that doesn't seem to be supporting the UN, or is derogatory to the prestige of the UN. But you're not going to get anywhere that way." Now, Mike... we argued for a formula—the American formula was elections by the UN and I've forgotten exactly our formula, but our formula was one which would involve the UN but didn't necessarily say it would have to run the show. But there again, it's the Canadian idea: you hang on to your principles but you find a way around it.

Also, one of the things I think we were saying to them was: "Look, we can't prescribe to the Communists. This is not a case of unconditional surrender. They didn't surrender. They ended this war as a stalemate. We don't like it. It would have been much nicer if the UN had been triumphant but we weren't. So you've got to bargain." This is again to say, "You have our support in this armistice"—we were not involved in any way in the Indochina discussions, we had no responsibility for the Geneva Conference; but on the whole we agreed that it's far better to get an armistice and stop the fighting. But you have to accept the facts of life, you have to deal with Communists.

As might be expected, the 1954 Geneva Conference on Indochina[3] overshadowed the twin conference on Korea, which was being held on

---

[3]Canadians knew so little about Indochina at the time of the 1954 Geneva Conference that there was no good map of the area to be found in Ottawa. Geoffrey Pearson had just been sent to Paris and recalled that the first instruction he received from External Affairs was to get a map of Indochina from the French. So he went down to the Quai d'Orsay and bought a map and sent it home. At that time most people in Canada did not know the difference between Vietnam, Cambodia, and Laos; Geoffrey said that his father did not know much more, although he got to know a lot about it in succeeding years.

alternate days, if only because it did something. Although its achieve-
ments, in retrospect, proved to be ominous, the conference did bring about
the official end of the French war in Vietnam while preparing the ground
for the much worse American war. The Indochina Conference was
considered to be a negotiating triumph for the British foreign secretary,
Anthony Eden, his last diplomatic success before becoming prime minister.
Eden was able to overcome the opposition of John Foster Dulles, and,
according to Chester Ronning, an agreement was reached on the
unification of Vietnam.

The Geneva Conference set up three truce supervising commissions
(for the three Indochina countries) with Canada as one of the members—
Mendès-France, who had come to power as a result of the debacle of Dien
Bien Phu, had insisted on this, the other members being Poland and
India, as chairman. It was an invidious task but, as Arnold Smith said,
we really did not dare to say no to peace-keeping, especially with the
prospect of Mendès-France resigning. There was a good deal of con-
troversy about holding an election on the unification of Vietnam and
whether the United States did not scuttle this because they were afraid that
Ho Chi Minh would win.

CHESTER RONNING

Canada was not involved as a participant at the Geneva Conference on Indochina, we were there as observers. You remember
an agreement was reached that called for the unification of all of
Vietnam, North and South, after a period of a couple of years. I
don't remember exactly what the agreement was, but the United
States upset that agreement and prevented by military force the
unification of Vietnam. You see, the majority of the Vietnamese
wanted the reunification of the whole country—there's no question about that. But the American puppet regime in South Vietnam kept fighting both the Vietnamese of North Vietnam and the
Vietcong in South Vietnam.

JOHN HOLMES

I don't think there ever could have been elections. The people
who said there should be elections didn't sign the Geneva agreement. Nobody signed it. The only things that were signed were
the armistices, which were between the French and the opposing

Communist forces. Then there was a declaration appended to it, in which it was stated that within two years there will be freely held elections. The Americans were not involved in drafting that agreement; neither were the South Vietnamese. The Americans made a declaration afterward—I think it was to the fact that they would not do anything contrary to the declaration.

It seems to me if you look at that declaration, nobody who made it really had any right to do so, except the French. The French were the only people who had any authority; the North Vietnamese, the Vietminh as we called them then, they said, there will be free elections. The French were off the scene when '56 came along.

My own view was that nobody really had any right to make such a declaration, there wasn't a hope in hell of free elections, you couldn't have free elections in the North; it was a Communist state in the early stages. You'd have had a 98 percent vote, that kind of thing. I don't think you could have had very free elections in the South; it was all very chaotic but the Americans and South Vietnamese, I think, played their hand badly. What they should have said—and I know I argued this in Saigon with South Vietnamese—is: "Sure, we're prepared to go ahead; have free elections; let's look at the arrangements." Sort of put the North Vietnamese on the spot because they had no intention of having free elections.

But instead, the verdict of history was that they were quite willing to have them and that this was stopped by the South, and particularly by the Americans. I think the blame goes all around.

Vietnam was divided at the Geneva Conference between North and South. This was not to be a permanent division; it was an armistice line with a demilitarized zone in between. But it was the old philosophy that you stop the fighting, then you can start talking and you can get a settlement. Above all, stop the killing. I think that's why we felt we had [to go along]. There was never a more unattractive job handed to Canada than that job on the commissions. Nobody liked it, but after all, the armistice was very much in accord with our own kind of philosophy. It's exactly the philosophy we had in Korea: stop the fighting and start talking. That was the way it was put to us. Also, a lot of people who write about this now talk about it as if we were put in as the American agents on those commissions. We went in, in spite of the fact that we knew the Americans didn't agree with them at all and we'd get no support from them.

Despite what John Holmes said, and repeated Canadian claims to an independent role, the fact of the matter was that the Indochina Commissions (ICC) were set up as the sort of troika that Khrushchev advocated for settling international disputes, with one Communist member, one neutral chairman, and one Western representative. While the United States might not have been in favor of the ICC in the beginning, it had to accept them and it considered Canada to be the Western representative. Certainly Dean Rusk thought so. After the recorded interview, Rusk complained to me that the Americans had taken it for granted that the commissions were made up of a Western representative, a neutral chairman, and a Communist—instead of which they found themselves faced, as he put it, with two neutrals and a Communist. Although Rusk was not at the Geneva Conference on Indochina, he was secretary of state during most of the life of the ICC. This official United States view contrasted sharply with the assessment of Canadian officials like Escott Reid, who charged the Canadian representatives with being pro-American and anti-Indian.

There was a great deal of wishful thinking during the Cold War and a notable lack of communication over the Indochina Commissions, with the Canadians assuming that they had an independent role while the Americans felt they had another function. Perhaps part of the problem was that Mike Pearson felt that he had been used as the fall guy with regard to the ICC. John Holmes implied that the Geneva agreement was signed, and Canada made part of it, without much consultation. Pearson knew that this would be a nasty business but he could not very well refuse, and to salve his conscience he made out that Canada would have an entirely independent role on the ICC. In the beginning the commissions did a lot of useful work; only later did they cease to function, and became a sorry spectacle. As John Holmes said, the first two years were the time when they really had some effect—and they were the years of the special relationship when the Canadians and the Indians worked well together.

In 1955 Mike Pearson visited New Delhi and saw Pandit Nehru. Escott Reid, who was Canadian high commissioner there at that time, said that Pearson did not get along as well with the Indian leader as Prime Minister St. Laurent did.

ESCOTT REID

Pearson found Nehru a difficult person to deal with, but he had the capacity to deal with him. He had the capacity to overcome some of the difficulties many foreign ministers and prime ministers had in talking with Nehru. Pearson came to India in the autumn of 1955, and I went with him for his first talk with Nehru. Pearson had visited the Soviet Union and he had gone to the Colombo Plan meeting in Singapore, and on to Indochina. He started off by saying, "You've been to the Soviet Union recently and I've been, and I thought you might be interested in my reflections on my visit"; so he gave him a very interesting statement of his impressions of his visit to the Soviet Union, paused, and Nehru said nothing.

Pearson went on to the Colombo Plan meeting and he talked about the Colombo Plan meeting and paused, and Nehru said nothing. Then he talked about the situation in Indochina and Nehru said nothing. When I say Nehru said nothing, it's probably an exaggeration. He probably said something but it was certainly no great contribution to an exchange of ideas.

I had warned Nehru in advance that Pearson would want to talk about the proposal for an atomic reactor. So Pearson said then, "There are some problems on the proposal for an atomic reactor that I'd like to discuss," and Nehru said, "In that case, I better send for Bhabha," his atomic energy expert. Bhabha came and Nehru talked to me about birds and bees and flowers and trees and Bhabha talked to Pearson about the reactor. The next day we had a discussion with Nehru and it was fine; he was all prepared to talk about Russia and the Colombo Plan and Vietnam. Not many foreign ministers could have managed that.

Contrast it with Dulles. I don't know which year it was that Dulles came to Delhi, it may have been 1956. I was invited to the dinner at the Prime Minister's house given in honor of Dulles. Dulles sat on Indira Gandhi's right and I sat on her left. There had been great discussions in the newspapers for weeks about the conversations that were going to take place between Dulles and Nehru and what they were going to talk about. They met for two and a half hours in the afternoon, and about halfway through dinner Indira Gandhi turned to me and said, "Do you know what those two did this afternoon? I met my father when he came out from the meeting and I said, 'How did the discussions go?' and he said, 'It was only during the last 15 minutes that we talked about anything important.'" They presumably talked about lions and birds and bees and flowers and trees for two hours.

When St. Laurent came to India, we set up a couple of discussions, and there were just the two of them together. We asked St. Laurent afterward what had happened and apparently nothing had happened. The two daughters, Madeleine O'Donnell and Indira Gandhi, talked to each other about this, and they talked to their fathers, and the result was Nehru said to me when we were off to visit the Taj Mahal, "Could you arrange to come back an hour or so before you had intended so that I could have another talk with Mr. St. Laurent?" In that talk they did talk about something.

But Pearson was able, finally, to have a sensible talk with Nehru. I think St. Laurent had more personal rapport with Nehru than Pearson did. St. Laurent was more sympathetic to Asia and underdeveloped countries generally than Pearson, more spontaneously and emotionally [sympathetic]. Pearson wrote to me when St. Laurent was coming to India: "You may find him even too enthusiastic an 'Asian.'" I think he meant more Asian-minded than he was, and St. Laurent was. St. Laurent came to Delhi when the fighting in Indochina between the French and the Vietnamese was still going on, if you remember, and there were one hundred and seventy-five thousand French troops in Indochina. While he was there, we were in the gallery of the Parliament together, and Nehru made an appeal for a cease-fire in Indochina. St. Laurent gave a press conference a day or so later. He was asked what he thought about this and he said he agreed completely, that he would have said it himself but that nobody would listen to him, but that he was very glad that the prime minister of a great country like India had said so. The French ambassador in Delhi saw the telegram from the French Foreign Office to Ottawa about this and he told me that the French were furious. This was just before Dien Bien Phu, just before the collapse.

Pearson would have got out of answering the question in some way and at the same time would have given the Indian newspapermen enough for two columns. Similarly, St. Laurent, in New Delhi and later on his trip around the world, said things about the necessity of eventually recognizing Peking that Pearson would have avoided saying. In the Suez Crisis St. Laurent was the one who was raging mad because of what the French and the British had done—what was it he called them? "The Supermen of Europe."

This is exactly what Nehru would have said. The reaction of St. Laurent to what the British and French did in Suez was exactly the same as Nehru's. Pearson was much cooler about it.

GEOFFREY PEARSON

Nehru was not a man who let his hair down, but I think my father was as close to him as any Western statesman. Of course, they didn't see each other very much—once a year, if that. Probably once every other year at Commonwealth meetings. But I have a book inscribed to him from Nehru sitting on the table here, and the inscription is cordial enough. I suppose that Nehru may have given away these a lot but it reads: "To Lester B. Pearson with warm regards, Jawaharlal Nehru." Well, "warm regards" is unusual for Nehru, I think. He didn't regard very many people that way.

As time went on, Lester Pearson became increasingly uneasy about Canada's membership in the Indochina Commissions. The fact that these commissions had to be set up outside the United Nations was a matter of concern to a good UN man like Pearson: he was worried that they would further weaken the fabric of the world organization, which had been so badly strained by the exclusion of Communist China. Then, there was the way that the ICC, which were supposed to be temporary, were going on and on with no end in sight. Perhaps, his diplomatic sixth sense made Pearson afraid that Canada's membership in these commissions might endanger the special relationship not only with India but with the United States.

While John Holmes tended to play down the election in Vietnam and suggest that it could not be held, Escott Reid felt it was the key to the Geneva agreement and that the United States action in preventing it was the cause of all the trouble in the Indochina Commissions. Arnold Smith did not think that Pearson realized that the Americans would do this when he agreed to Canada's participation in the ICC, but whether this would have made any difference to his decision is debatable. Smith was an early truce commissioner and was in Indochina when the neutralist Laotian government of Prince Souvanna Phouma was overthrown by a rightist coup organized by the United States Central Intelligence Agency.

JOHN HOLMES

As assistant under-secretary of external affairs, I had the Far Eastern Division under my wing and the ICC was largely my baby. Mike was always asking me, "When are you going to get us out of there?" I think he was always bothered by the fact that it wasn't in the United Nations. He accepted the fact that we had to do it and that it was better to have it done by somebody than nobody, but if only it had been part of the UN—we all wished it were because it was an appalling headache. All you did with a UN Force was send the boys off to New York and say, you take over, but in this case [of the ICC] there was nobody to run it.

ESCOTT REID

I considered that the implicit agreement at Geneva was that Ho Chi Minh was to take over the whole of Vietnam as a result of an election, and that we were going to do our best to hold the border between Vietnam on one side and Laos and Cambodia on the other. This is what the Indians believed. They believed the United States frustrated the election because they knew that Ho Chi Minh would win. The Indians believed that Ho Chi Minh was a highly intelligent man, very realistic, that he believed that he had two-thirds of the people in South Vietnam on his side and would agree to any kind of rules for a free election because he knew he'd win it. The Indians believed that we more and more went into the American camp on Vietnam, and the relations between the Canadian and Indian members of the Vietnamese commission got worse and worse.

ARNOLD SMITH

I got to know Ho Chi Minh pretty well. I spent a year as truce commissioner in Cambodia and there were two parties to the treaty that I was supervising. One was Ho Chi Minh and one was

Sihanouk so I spent a lot of time in Hanoi, although I was mainly based in Phnom Penh, and of course I was often in Saigon and Dien Bien Phu. But I got to know Ho pretty well. I liked him. He talked rather like a prophet; he was a tough operator politically, but I think if he'd not been pushed into the arms of the Russians and the Chinese, he would have been a nationalist like Tito.

I remember when I was in Phnom Penh there was a coup in Vientiane in Laos. Souvanna Phouma, the prime minister, was a neutralist and a very fine man. His wife taught me to dance this dance where you don't touch, you just wave your hands at each other. Anyway, Souvanna Phouma left Vientiane on a visit to some of the outlying parts of Laos and was toppled by right-wing pro-Western generals. Of course, the coup was organized by the CIA.[4] To hell with nonalignment; to hell with a third approach; we want pro-Western government and you end up with an anti-Western government. It was a great overreaching.

During the first two years, while there was still hope that an election would be held in Vietnam, the Indochina Commissions worked reasonably well; the senior officers like Arnold Smith who went out to be the Canadian representatives on the commissions for Cambodia, Laos, and Vietnam got along well with the Indian chairmen and felt they had made a useful contribution to the cause of peace and stability in the area. But as time went on and the fighting in Vietnam increased in intensity, more junior officials were sent out from Ottawa, and the commissions' work, particularly the Vietnam commission's work, became an exercise in futility.

However, the extraordinary thing was that most of the Canadian officials who had gone to Indochina with an open mind, if not being against the war, returned convinced that the Americans were right. As one

---

[4]A very important American was in Indochina at the time of the overthrow of Souvanna Phouma, and Arnold Smith told him that he thought this was a very grave mistake, that a nonaligned government was the best the West could hope for, and if we tried to get a pro-Western government, we would end up by getting a pro-Communist government. The American said, "I entirely agree with you. But what can you expect if you take the people who fail the State Department examinations and you give them unlimited resources and no accountability?" Smith felt this was being unfair to all members of the CIA—some of the CIA analysts were much better than the State Department's.

senior official in the Department of External Affairs said, shaking his head as if in disbelief, they returned "raging hawks."

ESCOTT REID

Not only raging hawks, but anti-Indian. I think this had a very bad effect on the External Affairs service. So high a proportion of our officers served in Indochina on one of the commissions, and most of them came back anti-Indian. I was outside External Affairs then. I left External Affairs in 1962, but I think there was less opposition in External Affairs to American policy in Vietnam than there was in the State Department. It was extraordinary what happened, and very sad.

7 Suez and the Nobel Prize

IF THERE WAS ever a watershed in postwar history, it was the Suez Crisis of 1956, the ill-fated attempt of the British and the French to reassert themselves as imperial powers by retaking the Canal. The master plan, which had been worked out at secret meetings of the collaborators, was for the Israelis to attack Egypt; then the British and the French would issue an ultimatum saying that they were going in to separate the combatants. No one believed that the new British prime minister, Anthony Eden, of all people, could have been associated with such a scheme, and many Western leaders, including Lester Pearson, wondered "whether Anthony hadn't gone off his rocker." For Pearson, this was a bitter blow because he had been an admirer and friend of Eden's for many years, and could remember how, as a young Canadian representative, he had looked up to the British foreign secretary in the Thirties and during the League of Nations meetings on Ethiopia. Yet, here he was behaving like Mussolini and engaged in what was the worst form of gunboat diplomacy. Pearson vowed that he would try to find a way of extricating the British and the French from a situation that was becoming increasingly dangerous. "This was 1956 not 1876," he noted in his memoirs, "and their course was doomed to failure and ultimate disaster." However, Eden would do nothing to halt the invasion armada that was chugging through the Mediterranean at the speed of the slowest and oldest minesweeper.

Whatever else the Suez Crisis did—and its consequences are still being argued—it marked the end of Empire for Britain and France. Before Suez, the Commonwealth prime ministers were a relatively small group who could meet comfortably around the Cabinet table at Number 10 Downing Street. In fact, William Clark, who was Prime Minister Eden's press secretary, remembered a Commonwealth Conference being held in 1956—there were the new Asian members, India, Pakistan, and Ceylon, but the Commonwealth consisted mainly of the white dominions, Australia, New Zealand, Canada, and South Africa, which was still a member then. The prime minister of Southern Rhodesia was present and he was, of course, a white man, although Clark recalled that Pandit Nehru dominated the conference. It was the last meeting to be held in Downing Street before the explosion of new members, which occurred after Suez and meant that the largest conference room at Lancaster House was hardly big enough to accommodate this assembly of nations. As for the French, they blamed Colonel Gamal Abdel Nasser, the new Egyptian leader, for most of their troubles in Algeria and went to war to destroy him, but succeeded in destroying themselves. The Fourth Republic was a casualty of Suez. When General de Gaulle took over, one of his first acts was to grant independence to Algeria; then he freed the rest of the French African Empire.

The sequence of events that led to the invasion of Suez in 1956 began with the withdrawal of British troops from the Canal Zone: they could return under the Anglo-Egyptian Treaty of 1954 if any member of the Arab League were attacked (though not if attacked by Israel). Then, there was the Aswan High Dam, which Nasser was determined to build. In mid-July 1956 the British and Americans rejected the project and Nasser turned almost immediately to the Soviet Union. At the same time, on July 26, 1956, he nationalized the Suez Canal in order, as he said, to help finance the dam. It was this action which upset Eden so much; it upset Pearson, too: it was the sort of breach of international law that was against his instincts, according to Lord Home who, as Alex Douglas-Home, was commonwealth secretary and a member of the Cabinet's Suez Committee. Lord Home said that Pearson was "full of sympathy for the predicament that we were in" (over the nationalization of the Canal) although he admitted that he was against the use of force. But even before the nationalization of the Canal, Prime Minister Eden was hinting that Britain might have to go to war.

WILLIAM CLARK

In those days, with Alex Home as commonwealth secretary, there was very close consultation with the Commonwealth, but I must say a word about that word "consultation." I forget who it was who said to me, but I rather suspect it was old Lord Halifax many years earlier, that the British Commonwealth had a very special meaning for the word "consultation." In London it meant telling the Empire leaders what we had decided and thought, and I think there was still a little of that on the Middle East.

In May 1956 we had a visit from Bulganin and Khrushchev, their first visit to the West. There was a rather famous quarrel between Eden and Khrushchev over the threat to our oil supplies which Russian moves in the Middle East presented—Eden did say if we felt our oil supplies were being tampered with, we would fight and Khrushchev got up and left the meeting.

It happened to be just about lunchtime, so people didn't know the meeting had broken up in disorder. I remember we sent really very carefully worded telegrams about that. They went to people who had very different views, like Nehru and his then foreign minister, Mr. Krishna Menon, but they didn't leak. We went on keeping them informed about our concern over the Middle East, and that certainly went on after the nationalization of the Canal on the 26th of July. And through August and September, there was a constant stream of telegrams to the Commonwealth and there was a fair stream back.

It was my particular duty at that time, as press secretary, to warn the public that there was a real danger that Britain, if provoked, would use force. I met once a week with the Commonwealth correspondents and I know that I told them what I could tell them reasonably about our attitudes. I based myself quite largely on the briefing papers which were sent regularly, twice a week, at least, to prime ministers from the Commonwealth Office. It was one of the best ways of finding out what was happening. That may surprise you because you might well suppose that, living in Number 10, one knew everything. It was a frequent delusion. In fact, through the Commonwealth Office, one got all sorts of other feed-ins that made sense of a policy in which one saw a part from Number 10, but a part one didn't see because it was verbally done to the prime minister.

I think that Canada was very well informed of our attitudes through the regular [dispatches] care of Mr. St. Laurent and through good communications with Norman Robertson, the high commissioner, who was a friend of mine. I saw him quite often. They [the Commonwealth prime ministers] replied, they replied politely, sympathetically, but with a growing anxiety about the bellicosity of our statements. I can remember Norman Robertson, in fact, once asking me to lunch and saying that he had been disturbed by the bellicosity of the Foreign Office spokesman. All this went on in a fairly open way and, looking back at it, I think in an honorable way, perhaps mistaken, but totally above board, until about October the 15th.

LORD HOME

During the whole of the Suez negotiations, the Commonwealth were kept fully informed that we might have to employ military action. Oh, no doubt about that! And the United States were too. Dulles knew about the possibility that we would have to use force. Oh yes, the Canadian government knew all about that. Now, I think unless there was some message that I didn't know about between Eden and the Canadian prime minister, I think that you will find that the only time there was a complaint about consultations was in the last few days when the military operation was actually moving, because you couldn't give notice, so to speak, to the enemy.

It was in mid-October that the Suez Canal Users' Association (SCUA) collapsed, and with it the last possible attempt to resolve the problem peacefully—at least, in the British government's view. SCUA was John Foster Dulles's idea; he had dreamed it up during the Labor Day weekend at Duck Island, his summer retreat in Ontario. The association was to provide Britain and other Canal users with some measure of protection against the intervention of the Egyptian government, but its most important function was to give Anthony Eden a way out. Dulles knew that the British and the French were preparing for military action against Egypt, to take place in mid-September. The first plans called for a landing at Alexandria; later, during the many revisions, it changed to Port Said. There was the assurance of the Suez Canal Company that the Canal would come to a halt when the British and French pilots were withdrawn from service, but that did not happen. The Egyptians showed they could run the Canal. It was another triumph for Nasser, and Eden became more and more convinced of the need for military measures.

At about the time of the SCUA proposal, Lester Pearson very firmly told the British foreign secretary, Selwyn Lloyd, that "neither Canada nor the United States would stand for the United Nations being employed as a cover for war," according to Hugh Thomas's authoritative book, The Suez Affair. *Lloyd replied: "If things drag on like this, you know, Israel might take advantage of the situation to move against Egypt. Frankly, I wouldn't blame them if they did. They'd probably win, Nasser would go and most of our troubles would be solved." Hugh Thomas says that Pearson implored Lloyd "not to do any urging in that direction" because he was afraid that such action would unite the Arabs against the West.*

Later Lloyd was to return from the United Nations with six principles that Secretary-General Dag Hammarskjöld had worked out with the Egyptian foreign minister, Mahmoud Fawzi; those principles would have guaranteed free and open passage of the Canal, which meant that Britain need not fear for its oil supply. However, by now the British government and the ruling Conservative Party were committed to the use of force, and Eden was a sick man.

WILLIAM CLARK

The prime minister had a total collapse on or about October 5, when he was in University Hospital seeing his wife, who was in there for some minor operation. He got a temperature of a hundred and five and in the opinion of my medical adviser, who was a regular doctor and postmaster-general at the time, Charles Hill, he had total liver failure and that left him with a real impairment in judgment. But be that as it may, what I'm certain of is that from that date onward he was not his old self, and it's very apparent that after about October 10, roughly speaking—the day on which Selwyn Lloyd got back from the United Nations, where he had agreed to a fairly good arrangement— Eden was pursuing a line which he hadn't pursued before and he pursued it in utter secrecy.

He was a very sick man; he was not reacting normally—for instance, he didn't lose his temper during this time, which he traditionally did. He knew that something terrible had happened and he saw it as a sort of disaster. It's funny, I can remember on that last night, with everything else, he rang me up to say he'd forgotten to thank me for the help I gave him in his broadcast, and that was an extraordinarily thoughtful thing to do and there was no reason for it.

Not only was Eden a sick man, but so was Dulles; the two great protagonists of the Suez drama were both seriously ill. In the midst of the United Nations debate on the crisis, Dulles entered a Washington hospital for treatment of cancer. Did Eden's sickness mean that he pursued a course "in utter secrecy," to quote William Clark? Lord Home denied that members of the Cabinet were kept in the dark, and pointed to the fact that one or two ministers resigned because they did not like what was being done—they could not say that they had not been told. However, British ambassadors and high commissioners and senior civil servants, including the British representative at the United Nations, Sir Pierson Dixon, were not kept informed. What Lord Home was critical of was the fact that Prime Minister Eden had not called for a summit conference of the Big Three on the Suez Crisis.

LORD HOME

I think that the historians will say that the thing broke down because Eden didn't keep in close enough touch with Eisenhower. The contacts were with Dulles. If you're going in for an operation of the magnitude that we contemplated in relation to a problem like the Suez Canal, the prime ministers or heads of state must get together. In fact, this didn't happen and so I think that that was where the criticism would lie.

The question is whether there was collusion between the British and the French and the Israelis in the Suez adventure. Certainly the French and the Israelis had been holding clandestine meetings since the early summer of 1956, and the French premier, Guy Mollet, had been pressing Anthony Eden to join them in military action against Nasser, whom the French were already comparing to Hitler. But when Mollet suggested

*collaboration with Israel, which he is believed to have done during his
first telephone call to Eden at the end of July, the British prime minister
rejected it out of hand.*

*The French knew that the Israeli leader, David Ben Gurion, wanted to
wage a preventive war against Egypt before a United Arab Command
was set up. Later on, the French were to suggest that the dispatch of an
Israeli ship to the Canal might be justification for the Franco-British
invasion, which was then being planned, but the British turned down the
idea because it would align them publicly with Israel against Egypt and so
offend friendly Arabs.*

*Yet the Israeli commander, Moshe Dayan, asserted that the British and
the French encouraged the Israelis to attack Egypt.*

LORD HOME

There were two things about this, really: first of all, the Israelis
were getting increasingly impatient with the Arab encirclement,
and you'll remember that the Arabs set up a high command so
Israel felt directly threatened. Now they were going to break out
somewhere and we didn't know where they were likely to attack.
It was very possible they would attack Jordan. We had a treaty
with Jordan in which we should have been bound to respond and
to support Jordan—it would have been a highly unsatisfactory
situation if that had happened. An alternative was they might
attack Egypt, and really until pretty late on, it wasn't at all sure
which way they'd go. So we had to decide what should be done.

The French had a view, and by and large and after many, many
discussions, we came to the conclusion that the best thing to do
was to stop both sides, if you could, so that the Canal was
isolated. You could then get a settlement for the Canal, both
armies having refrained from advancing. The Israelis did stop but
Nasser wouldn't. This was the plan: to try and isolate the Canal
and stop both sides ten miles each way from the Canal. This is
what has been highly criticized.

Selwyn Lloyd said in his book, if you decided that really Nasser
meant to nationalize the Suez Canal—meant to mobilize the Arab
world, get the British out, and then start a war which could
involve Israel and many other Arab countries—that this was the
best of a very bad lot of choices. I think I agree with that point of
view.

But there was collusion. Selwyn Lloyd was the "responsible British minister" who attended the tripartite meeting at Sèvres, France, with Mollet and Ben Gurion, on October 23, 1956. Lloyd stayed the shortest possible time, and Lord Home says that he signed no commitment, which was true enough. However, he left an official behind to draw up a "declaration of intent" binding the three governments. According to Hugh Thomas's account, Ben Gurion had come to the conference to get a British commitment to destroy the Egyptian Air Force: this would be a precondition to the Israelis advancing across the Sinai. The Israeli leader refused to accept the British official's signature on this document, and insisted on its being sent to London, where a more imposing signature was obtained, although Hugh Thomas does not say whose it was.

LORD HOME

Selwyn Lloyd gives an account of the meeting at which the Israeli representative was present. But there was no commitment. This is the point he makes very strongly: nobody signed and said, "We will do this." But, in the event, the Israelis did, rather to my surprise—because I thought they might go for Jordan—they did go for Egypt and so, the plan to limit the war (that's how I think I would describe it) was put into effect. Now when you say collusion, if you're faced with the particular situation in which you think that one of the parties is going to move, what you do, you try, as intelligently as you can, to assess the situation and say what you would do in the circumstances. So in the circumstances, we decided this was the best plan. [There were] many, many critics, of course, and neither this interview nor the debates in Parliament nor Selwyn Lloyd's book will settle the issue, but I still think that it was a horrible situation in which to be placed.

On October 29 Israeli forces crossed the frontier and captured Egyptian border posts, thus carrying out their side of the Sèvres bargain, the tripartite "declaration of intent." General E. L. M. Burns, the Canadian head of the United Nations Truce Supervision Organization in Palestine, knew about the Israeli mobilization and the French-British build-up on Cyprus which was obviously capable of an invasion of the Suez Canal. He reported on both to the United Nations headquarters in New York, although he did not know that they had been "orchestrated," as he put it.

On October 30 the British government issued an ultimatum to Israel and Egypt to withdraw to ten miles on each side of the Suez Canal, otherwise the British and French would intervene. Since the Israelis were nowhere near the Canal, they accepted the ultimatum in what Eden described as an "absolutely splendid reply"; the Egyptians refused. On hearing of the ultimatum, Mike Pearson rang John Foster Dulles, and, according to William Clark, both thought the other had phoned and both said simultaneously, "Do you suppose that Anthony's gone out of his mind?" and both replied, "Yes." At ten o'clock that night the assault fleet set sail from Malta; the great armada of more than two hundred ships was in no hurry since the plan did not call for it to be off Port Said till November 6.

On October 31 General Sir Charles Keightley, the head of the integrated command, gave the order to occupy Port Said, Ismailia, and Suez in order to "bring about a cessation of hostilities." Meanwhile there were urgent meetings of the UN Security Council, and the British and the French used their veto for the first time to reject a resolution calling for all countries to refrain from the use of force in the Middle East.

On November 1 Pearson flew to New York to see what could be done to resolve the crisis, which was threatening to destroy Anglo-American cooperation, to split the Commonwealth, and, as Pearson wrote, to brand Canada's two mother countries as aggressors. John Holmes accompanied the external affairs minister to the United Nations.

JOHN HOLMES

When we arrived in New York, the UN Assembly was in a state of dismay, and everyone around it. People kept rushing up to me, Secretariat people, all kinds of people, and they would say, "What's he got? We hear Mike's got a proposal. It's high time. Can he do it?" I remember the most enthusiastic were the British, who thought their own policy was just appalling. They had to do something about it.

I don't know what the records will show. The trouble is that everything was done by telephone. I don't quite know how much was done by the British, but they were saying to us that if Mike can make a proposal saying the UN will take over what the British and the French were proposing to do, then we can persuade Eden to get up and say if the UN is taking it over, then we don't need to do it. This is the way you unhook and Mike was trying to help Eden get off the hook. He was trying to find a way for the British to do what he wanted them to do, but we had to be extremely careful because the Arabs and the others were all saying, "You're just playing the British game." This was the beautiful balancing job.

There was nothing new about the idea of a United Nations peace-keeping force. As John Holmes said, everyone had been talking about it without being specific: Anthony Eden and Selwyn Lloyd had spoken of the need for such a force in the Middle East when they visited Ottawa at the beginning of 1956, and John Diefenbaker, who was a Conservative private member then, had mentioned it during a foreign affairs debate in the Canadian Parliament. According to Holmes, none of those involved could say that, at any one moment, somebody proposed the United Nations Emergency Force. And, in any case, it was not the idea that was so important, but the diplomatic performance in getting it accepted.

GEOFFREY PEARSON

I don't think my father would have claimed authorship of the idea of using the UN for peace-keeping purposes because that was an old idea that went back to Korea. After Korea we said in Canada that we would keep our brigade group earmarked for the UN and we urged other countries to do that too, so the next time they would be prepared. And we did; we kept forces earmarked for the UN although we thought we'd be using them for fighting purposes again.

But the idea of the UN force was an old one which we encouraged and my father encouraged. There are a lot of his speeches after Korea about how important it was for the UN not to be caught by surprise and to be ready, and several other countries earmarked forces too. The Scandinavians did after Korea. I don't think the British did and I don't think the Americans did. But both the British and the Americans were quite familiar with this idea. Suez was only four years after the end of Korea—three years. So it was a short time and people could easily say in 1956, "Let's revive the idea of a UN force." So it wasn't anybody's idea. I think it was a matter rather of seizing the opportunity in the Assembly and I think the British did say that they would withdraw if the UN would take their place.

The first proposal that the British put forward was that they should be part of the force. That was their idea, that there be a UN force including British and French troops. My father immediately realized that that would be unacceptable so he, in effect, accepted the proposal on the condition that they would leave, and they must have realized very quickly that they couldn't stay. So if they couldn't stay you had to find others and we offered along with other countries to take their place. I think that was the way it was.

However, both the British and the Americans claimed to be the inspirers, if not the authors, of the resolution establishing the United Nations Emergency Force. Selwyn Lloyd wondered whether telepathy was not involved because Lester Pearson made his proposal for such a force in the UN General Assembly on the same day that Anthony Eden advocated it in the British House of Commons. The explanation was that Pearson had telephoned Norman Robertson, the Canadian high commissioner in London and had learned of Eden's intention to state in Parliament that there must be police action to separate the belligerents, and that if the UN were willing to take over this task, "no one would be better pleased than we." This was Pearson's way of sounding out opinion before making any major diplomatic move. He had his aides, John Holmes, Geoff Murray, and Bert MacKay, who was the Canadian representative at the United Nations, buttonholing people in the delegates' lounge and soon found that the idea of a UN peace-keeping intervention would be well supported.

Meanwhile a United States resolution calling for a cease-fire and withdrawal of forces from the Suez Canal area was adopted by sixty-four in favor to five against (Britain, France, Israel, Australia, and New Zealand), with six abstentions. In explaining Canada's abstention, Pearson said that he would have liked to have seen a provision for a United Nations force in the resolution and promised Canadian participation if such a force was set up. Dulles said afterward that he welcomed this statement and urged Pearson to formulate a proposal for an international force. On November 2 Pearson flew back to Ottawa to get Cabinet approval, returning to New York on November 3.

Immediately after the General Assembly had voted for a cease-fire,

Dulles entered hospital; President Eisenhower communicated directly with the American representative at the UN, Henry Cabot Lodge, and Lodge's claim that the United States was the author of the resolution setting up the UN Emergency Force was borne out by Pearson. In his memoirs Pearson wrote that "the State Department had evidently taken our initiative to heart and had prepared a draft for him [Lodge] which he felt would be acceptable to the Egyptians and consequently to the Afro-Asian group. His text was simpler than ours and with some minor alterations we adopted it as our own."

The draft resolution had been sent to Lodge with instructions that he should not introduce it. This was, as he said, a sagacious move because it would get much broader support by not having the U.S. in the lead. Lodge thought of Lester Pearson first; then, if he could not find Pearson, he would approach Ambassador Joao Carlos Muniz of Brazil, "another first class man."

HENRY CABOT LODGE

I had a little office in the UN Building where I received and answered telegrams. When I got the message from Washington, I stepped out into the corridor. There was Mike Pearson coming through the door toward me and I decided then and there that he was the one: he's going to get it if he wants it. So I said that the U.S. would be very gratified if Mr. Pearson would agree to sponsor the text, which I held in my hand. And I gave him the paper. He looked at it and I don't think there was anybody in the UN that could make up his mind quicker than he could, and could read the thing and see the inwardness of it. If there were any hidden meanings or hooks in it, he could see them too. And he looked at the paper and he said, "Yes," just like that, adding, "Yes, I'll take it."

He went downstairs and went into the General Assembly Hall (the General Assembly was in continuous session at that time). Whoever it was who was speaking, Mr. Pearson—or someone— got him to withdraw or to go away or something because I was still up on the second floor when Mike's voice came over the loud-speaker. He'd been recognized and he was on his feet proposing the creation of the UN Emergency Force.

It was the quickest thing I've ever seen in my life. I have never seen a man in a forum pick up and comprehend a complicated

thing of far-reaching implications and then get out and get recognized and get the floor and propose it immediately. It was remarkable—one of the high points of my political life was the way he
took that thing. Really, my hat was off to him. Because, of
course, everybody had gone over it in Washington, but he had to
run with the ball right away.

*In the early morning of November 4 the Canadian draft resolution was
approved in the UN General Assembly by fifty-seven votes in favor,
none against, and nineteen abstentions: for all intents and purposes, the
United Nations Emergency Force had been created. Lester Pearson was
delighted; he noted exuberantly that even Britain and France did not vote
against the resolution, and said that the reason for this was what Eden had
said in the British House of Commons. How Eden came to make that
statement is told by William Clark.*

WILLIAM CLARK

Mike started, before it became public, making suggestions that
the UN should be moved in and get the British and the French to
withdraw and this was regarded with horror originally in Downing Street. It would spoil the whole thing; I mean, what was the
objective if it wasn't to overthrow Nasser? This would never
overthrow Nasser—and it was regarded with real horror. I remember, though not in detail, the prime minister expressing his
utter horror at this and later the same day, I can remember [Sir
Ivone] Kirkpatrick, the head of the Foreign Office, saying that
this is lunacy, this is just losing the whole thing, and Selwyn
[Lloyd] expressing some reservations, saying it may prove useful
later on. By the end of that day we had written a statement for the
prime minister which said something like: If the United Nations
could take over and prevent the closure of the Canal, no one
would be happier than I—a slight misstatement but ... This was
the solution which Mike invented and was the way in which
Britain and France came out eventually with almost no honor but
without being totally, publicly humiliated.

*The task now was to make the Canadian resolution a reality, and after
a few hours' sleep Lester Pearson met with a small committee consisting of*

Secretary-General Hammarskjöld and the delegates of Colombia, India, and Norway. They had to work quickly because they were faced with the urgency of getting a peace-keeping force into the area: the fighting was still going on and the British armada was still steaming toward Port Said. It was decided that the Great Powers, the permanent members of the Security Council, should not be asked to contribute troops. Hammarskjöld proposed that General Burns should be the first commander of the United Nations Emergency Force. He was the man on the spot, with experience, and his appointment was confirmed by the General Assembly, which met again on the evening of November 4. At first Hammarskjöld had been opposed to the idea of UNEF, but John Holmes did not agree with this version, as he called it.

JOHN HOLMES

I was present at the lunch we had with Hammarskjöld in New York and Hammarskjöld was very depressed. He really thought the British had let him down; he'd been quite hopeful these negotiations he'd been having with Lloyd and others on the Canal [would bear fruit]. What I recall was his saying something would have to be done and he even wondered if maybe the U. S. Sixth Fleet couldn't be used because it was the only force there was to stop the fighting. When I say that, it would be wrong to say that he proposed that the U. S. Sixth Fleet—we were playing with ideas—what could we do, what could you do—and he said maybe that's about the only thing we can do, this kind of thing.

Mike talked about the force. My impression of Hammarskjöld's response was that it was very much like Mike's response. Mike had a habit of treating any idea very negatively to start with. You'd have a meeting, we used to call it prayer meeting, you know, with the secretaries in the morning and, you'd say, "What are you going to do about this?" Somebody would say, "I suggest we do that." "Oh gee, I don't think you can get away with that at all." "How would you read this, how would you read that?" This isn't negativism, this is clearing away the obstacles. If you can convince him that you have foreseen all the obstacles and have an argument, then he'll [go for it]. I think what Hammarskjöld was doing was listening, producing the difficulties, but I remember particularly getting a call from somebody in the secretary-general's office later that afternoon about something or other, and saying that he was already asking them to start some drafts. So that I don't think it was really opposition.

GEOFFREY PEARSON

I think at first, as with all acquaintances of Dag Hammarskjöld, there was a certain distance between them. Hammarskjöld was such an intellectual and a man of great restraint and self-discipline. He was not happy at parties. Small talk was not his strong point whereas my father tended to shine, if not at small talk, at least at small repartée at small gatherings. So they weren't similar. But they became friends and I think on my father's side anyway [there was] a genuine admiration and liking for Hammarskjöld. I have a picture which my father owned inscribed by Hammarskjöld which is a picture of them talking to each other in the General Assembly. Hammarskjöld is leaning over the desk and my father is sitting at the Canadian desk; Hammarskjöld is leaning over and talking about the Emergency Force. It's inscribed by Hammarskjöld "To be or not to be for the UN Emergency Force" or something like that. They were the two architects of the Force, and I think the picture and the inscription do represent a mutual friendship and respect.

In the face of the action that the United Nations was taking, there were efforts made to speed up the slow timetable of Operation Musketeer, as the Franco-British invasion of the Suez Canal Zone was called. The French flew to London to urge vitesse, *but there was nothing that could be done about the great armada, now spread over a wide area of the Mediterranean; the British admirals refused to go ahead without the protection of their minesweepers, and these were the oldest and slowest vessels. However, an adjustment was made to the attack plan: the airborne troops would be dropped twenty-four hours before the arrival of the ships carrying the main assault force.*

At dawn on November 5, some one thousand British and French paratroopers floated down on Port Said: this was just about the time that the General Assembly in New York was voting to establish a United Nations command for the international emergency force. Lester Pearson noted another "ghastly coincidence, to have Anglo-French troops landing in Egypt at the very time the Soviets were crushing the two-week-old Hungarian people's rebellion."

In his memoirs Pearson wrote that he became almost as wrought up about the situation in Hungary as about the Suez business. If he had not been so deeply involved in Suez, he would have been tempted to see if he could get a resolution to have a UN Assembly Committee fly straight to Budapest with the UN flag and some men in UN uniforms. However, John Holmes felt that there was another reason for his inaction over Hungary, and that was that he did not want to hog the international spotlight.

JOHN HOLMES

The Hungarian thing blew up right at the same time, and because of what Pearson was doing over Suez, and also because of his general reputation, someone—I can't think who it was—put some pressure on him to prepare a resolution on Hungary. He said no. I think he had in mind two things. One, he just didn't have time. The other was, this is too much. People like leadership from a modest country, but if it begins to be pretentious, [then there's a reaction]. If he hadn't [said no], he'd have had a resolution on Hungary, a resolution on everything and, in the end, come to be disliked. He never made the kind of mistakes that people like [Herbert] Evatt made at the Paris Peace Conference, proposing about six times as many resolutions as any other delegation, not realizing that coming from Australia, this was just a bit silly.

On November 5 Egypt accepted the General Assembly resolution setting up the United Nations Emergency Force and later that day Israel agreed unconditionally to a cease-fire. But the Anglo-French military action, which was supposed to separate the belligerents and stop them fighting, went on: the bombings continued, the paratroopers were advancing in Port Fuad and Port Said, and the great armada was approaching. Then the Soviets made their move; they had taken some time to do so because of their preoccupation with Hungary, but now they proposed that military assistance be given Egypt unless the British and the French halted their invasion within twelve hours. The Security Council refused to discuss the proposal. After this gesture to the United Nations, the Russians sent threatening notes to Britain, France, and Israel and a simultaneous note to President Eisenhower suggesting that the US and the USSR jointly intervene in the Middle East. Although these notes were rejected, there was alarm in Washington at the reports of Soviet jets flying to Syria.

On November 6 the first ships arrived, on time, and the invasion proper began with all the deliberation of a World War Two D-Day: there was a naval bombardment of the landing beaches, then the troops and tanks went in. But their triumphant advance against little opposition was halted after a few hours. It is not clear why Prime Minister Eden agreed to a cease-fire to take effect at midnight that day. There was the United Nations Emergency Force now being formed and the fact that both Israel and Egypt had stopped fighting. While the Soviet threat tended to be discounted in London, it may have had an important indirect effect. There was a new danger facing Britain in a run on the pound; New York was selling sterling in huge amounts; and, according to Hugh Thomas's account in The Suez Affair, *the chancellor of the exchequer, Harold Macmillan, from being a leading proponent of military action against Nasser, was now insisting on putting an end to the invasion, otherwise the country would be bankrupt. The Americans, who were worried about a possible extension of the war by the Russians, said that the British would not get a penny of a three-hundred-million-pound loan to support sterling if there were not a cease-fire by midnight.*

There was mixed reaction in Britain. Arnold Smith, who was with the Canadian High Commission in London during the Suez Crisis, said that some of his friends in the Commonwealth Relations Office felt they had been stabbed in the back by the United Nations, while others at the Foreign Office said that Lester Pearson's initiative had saved their necks and given them a face-saving way out. Years later, in 1978, only a few months before he died, Selwyn Lloyd said that UNEF was appreciated by the embattled Eden government and that it had got them off the hook. Lord Home said that what Mike Pearson did was a "salvage operation" and that it was "extremely valuable." Arnold Smith spoke of Eden wanting to topple Nasser but the conspiracy failed and the ruse of the British and the French going in to separate the belligerents fooled no one.

ARNOLD SMITH

If they had done nothing, the Israelis, who were stronger than the Egyptians, would have toppled Nasser, but the British by intervening protected Nasser and made him a hero. This is called the Suez Incident in the British folk memory, but it's called a tripartite aggression in the Middle East, and it made Nasser an enormous hero. He had defeated what they think of as the two major powers of the world, or did then—the British, who had ruled a lot of the Middle East at one time, and the French, who had ruled a lot of the Middle East for a long time. It was a completely cockeyed operation.

I think Mike Pearson's initiative was brilliant. It wasn't a one-man show; it was using his machinery in London and in the UN; I mean it was very much a cooperative effort, but Mike was very much the head of it. Eden didn't consult his Cabinet. He consulted some individual ministers; one of them, who was Minister of Defence, Walter Monckton, wouldn't go along with this and, two weeks before, he resigned ostensibly on grounds of ill health and took a less responsible and less arduous Cabinet post.

Mike kept his head through this, he felt his way pragmatically and he proposed something that accomplished a wide range of purposes. It did prevent a destruction of the prestige of the UN; and it did save Egypt; it did save the British government from an untenable position that could have led to almost anything because there was no future ahead for the British government.

Rab Butler, whom I knew and whom I've seen often since— Eden's prestige in foreign policy was very high and Rab Butler didn't oppose it. He was one of the few who was consulted, but very quickly he realized it was a boo-boo, and he helped us get Britain to back out. He became acting prime minister when Eden couldn't carry on, and he played a very useful part in getting Britain out. He said to me afterward, "I couldn't really have opposed this openly, could I?" Well, if he had, you know, he would have ended up as prime minister. He didn't and so Macmillan ended up as prime minister.

As soon as he was appointed UNEF commander, General Burns went to work assembling the international force. He visited Cairo before coming to New York and Nasser told him that it would be better if there were no Canadian troops in UNEF. However, the Canadian government had already offered to contribute an infantry battalion group, which would be a self-contained military unit with its own service detachments. Lester

Pearson knew that there would be trouble when Ottawa announced that the infantry battalion would be the Queen's Own Rifles.[1] *"Here we were," he wrote in his memoirs, "sending in the Queen's Own, wearing essentially a British uniform with UN badges. The Egyptians had just been fighting the Queen's Own."*

When he mentioned this to the Minister of Defence, Ralph Campney, his reaction was so violent that Pearson did not pursue the matter. However, the Egyptians would not have the battalion and no one, not Dag Hammarskjöld, nor the Indians, could get them to change their minds. The Canadians provided the support troops for UNEF, which were essential, and, in the end, Tommy Burns found that he did not need the Queen's Own Rifles. The Canadian aircraft carrier, HMCS Magnificent, *carried the men and all the equipment to the Middle East and became known as "Burns' Truck Wagon," a take-off of Burns' Chuckwagon in the Calgary Stampede.*

GENERAL E. L. M. BURNS

I had two trips to Egypt to see what arrangements could or should be made. At that time I discovered that there was a desire not to have any Canadians in the force with the exception, perhaps, of some administrative troops. Nasser put this forward to me. He said, "We don't object to Canadians as such, and we know what Mr. Pearson has done to get this arrangement for bringing the hostilities to an end. This has been to our advantage. But after all, they will be wearing uniforms like the British; they still have allegiance to the same Queen as the British; and they will be regarded by our people as British troops and there might be

---

[1]The problem with the Queen's Own Rifles was that the unit had been earmarked for the United Nations (stand-by force), and the military brass, represented by the defense minister, Ralph Campney, simply assumed that therefore it was part of the United Nations Emergency Force, and nothing could persuade them to the contrary. The battalion was moved to Halifax and billeted on the aircraft carrier, HMCS *Magnificent*, which was to carry the contingent, together with equipment, to the Middle East. After two weeks and much chagrin, the Queen's Own were deboarded and sent home. The Canadian regiment was affiliated with the Queen's Royal Regiment, West Surreys, and it is not at all certain that this outfit was engaged in the Suez campaign. However, it would have been diplomatic license for Lester Pearson to say that the Egyptians had fought against the Queen's Own Rifles because, even if they had not, they felt that they had.

incidents where they would be attacked, and we don't want to have that happen."

This was the line that he gave. I mentioned at the time that if no Canadians were allowed on the force, I couldn't continue as commander; and he said, "We're sorry about that; we're perfectly willing to have you as commander, but these other things make it difficult for us to accept Canadian troops on the force." And that wasn't really settled until Hammarskjöld went out there, I think around November 14, and fought it out with President Nasser. Hammarskjöld told me afterward that he said, "Well, if you say the Canadians won't come, then the Scandinavians aren't going to come, and then where's your force going to be?"

At any rate, they agreed at first that Canadians would have air transport and administrative troops of various kinds. We found afterward we didn't need the infantry battalion, the Queen's Own, which so much has been made of. But later on we did have some Canadian combatant troops in the shape of a reconnaissance squadron, an armored reconnaissance squadron, which usually operated in the Sinai.

The first troops, the Norwegians and Danes, arrived on November 18 or thereabouts, which was pretty quick considering that there was no pre-organiztion at all. Then they continued to build up and the last to come were the Brazilians and this Canadian reconnaissance squadron, which was after the New Year.

ESCOTT REID

I got a telegram [from Pearson] about noon. My secretary phoned for an appointment and Nehru gave me an appointment right away. He always did that. I was over to see him about twelve-thirty. I told him of Pearson's request that he ask the Indian ambassador in Cairo to talk to Nasser about this [the Egyptian objections to a Canadian contingent]. He said, "We already have." He was more up to date than I. I didn't know anything about this problem until I got the cable from Pearson in New York. Nehru knew about it. He said that Krishna Menon had been in touch with him about this and they had already talked to Nasser, and then he explained the difficulty. I said to him that it ought to be possible for Nasser to distinguish between Canadian policy and British policy, and gave examples of how we differed from the British, and Nehru said, "You don't need to persuade me of that. I know about that. I don't know whether it will do any good or not but I will certainly ask our people in Cairo to talk to Nasser again," which he did. But we should not have considered sending the Queen's Own Rifles to Egypt. We should have thought of some other unit.

GENERAL E. L. M. BURNS

The first thing that we did was to make an arrangement that the Egyptians would stay where they were and the United Nations troops would take up a position in front of them when the British withdrew down the Canal. They continued to withdraw in steps and we moved up. The Egyptians, except for some unauthorized terrorists or guerrillas, stayed where they were, and eventually the withdrawal from Port Said took place about Christmastime. The British were out, and then with a great deal of fanfare the Egyptians moved into Port Said. They were very anxious to get us out of there. I don't know who they thought they would impress with the idea that it was due to their valor that they had recaptured the [city].

There were two main roads [to the Egyptian-Israeli border]. The Yugoslav armored reconnaissance battalion had just arrived, and they were moved in opposite the Israelis. The Israelis moved back forty or fifty kilometers, say about a quarter of the way back toward the border, and the Yugoslavs moved in, and thereafter there was a series of moves back. I would meet General Dayan or some of his officers and they would swear they were going to leave by such and such a date and we would then move up our forces to be in between them and the Egyptians, with the exception of some parties that were mainly for collecting the dead and burying them.

The Israelis weren't actually hostile, but they kept us at arm's length. They suggested at one time that we should let our people go up to Tel Aviv and Jerusalem on leave; but Hammarskjöld felt that since they wouldn't allow us to establish a force on their soil, we shouldn't send our leave people there, so we never did. The Israelis were at first very dubious that it [UNEF] could achieve

what it was supposed to—that is, to prevent any hostilities
arising—but after a while when we got settled down in Gaza and
troops were in position and patrolling and an understanding
reached with the Egyptians to control any people that might be
wanting to infiltrate, as the then expression was—that is, terrorists going across the border and shooting up the other side—
they saw that the thing was working and for ten years it did
work.

*Not only did the Israelis dislike, as General Burns put it in an
understatement, giving up the territory they had won to the United
Nations Emergency Force, but so did the British and the French. In
retrospect, it would seem that the withdrawal of the allies or accomplices
was not achieved without a great deal of pressure from the United States.
Hugh Thomas says that Britain was forced to retire by what he describes
as "remorseless U. S. pressure and threats to cut us off from oil," and
asserts that "no time since the 1780s has been quite so humiliating [for the
British] as the weeks following Suez."*

*When Lester Pearson returned to Ottawa, he found himself faced, as he
said, with a very difficult Parliamentary situation, which was largely
unexpected since there had seemed to be general support for the action he
had taken in the beginning. In fact, Prime Minister St. Laurent, on the
basis of private discussions with Opposition leaders, did not think there
would be any serious division in the House of Commons over the Suez
policy. But he was wrong: there was angry and bitter denunciation. The
Conservative attack was led by Howard Green, who said that it was
aimed not so much at Pearson as at St. Laurent. However, in his memoirs
Pearson recalled that "Green accused us of being the 'chore boy' of the
United States, of being a better friend to Nasser than to Britain and
France, and claimed that our government, by its actions in the Suez crisis,
had made this month of November 1956 the most disgraceful period for
Canada in the history of this nation." It was high time, Green went on,
that Canada had a government that would not knife its best friends in the
back.*

*The Suez Affair did have an effect on the 1957 election, which brought
the Conservatives to power, and Howard Green became external affairs
minister in 1959.*

HOWARD GREEN

We thought that Canada certainly should not have jumped in to criticize Britain and France. Of course there is the fact that these are our two mother countries and, as I said, they were under great stress and had been provoked very badly, and also, in the House, the prime minister, Mr. St. Laurent, took what I thought was a very unfortunate course. He spoke of the "Supermen of Europe," referring to the leaders of Britain and France in a very slurring way. It was really a nasty statement about Britain and France and we were very annoyed at his attitude, which he maintained actually throughout, and I criticized him very bitterly in my speech. I was reading it over recently, and if I had to do it again, I would make the same speech. It was a very, very sad situation, and we were very critical. As I said, we thought that Canada should at least have kept out of attacking Britain and France.

Pearson didn't take a very active part in the House. We were mainly criticizing the prime minister. Pearson, of course, was involved at the United Nations. I had the feeling that as a result of the criticism in the House and the criticism across the country, which was very strong, even by some of the Liberal press, that the government moved at the United Nations to have them set up an Emergency Force for this area, that our action in attacking them was one of the reasons they did this. They had to do something to soften the criticism in Canada. One reason they lost the 1957 election, certainly in parts of the country like Vancouver, one of the reasons was what they did in the Suez Crisis.

PAUL MARTIN

Oh, I'm sure Suez hurt in some places. It would help in other places. And it did hurt us in many places in the Atlantic Provinces; I'm sure in some parts of Ontario, in some parts of British Columbia. But these things balance off. I don't think that was the reason for our defeat. I think we'd been defeated then because we'd been there a long time; we had made some awful blunders on the pipeline, on a lot of other things.

I took part in that election all over the country, and I can't recall at any time ever being questioned or heckled over Suez, and I went all through the Maritimes. But I do know that in the Maritimes there was a strong feeling which people opposed to the government were happy to use as an excuse for their continued opposition.

As Pearson noted, any feeling of exaltation or conceit or euphoria that he might have had over the diplomatic initiative he had taken at the United Nations in setting up the first peace-keeping force was dissipated, as he put it, "by the vigor of the assaults on my conduct, my wisdom, my rectitude, my integrity, my everything else by an embattled Conservative Opposition." However, his Suez action was criticized not only by political foes at home but by some of his friends and colleagues abroad, notably Dean Acheson, with whom he had had a mixed relationship. They were friends but, as Geoffrey Pearson said, they were wary of each other and had had a number of quite important public disagreements. Geoffrey characterized Acheson as a man who never hid his views and did not mince words; he had written about certain aspects of politics, especially on Korea, which puzzled and hurt his father.

By 1956 Dean Acheson had been out of office for some years but he took a keen interest in international affairs and, according to his son-in-law, Bill Bundy, was critical of what Pearson had done over Suez.

WILLIAM P. BUNDY

During the Suez Crisis of 1956–57, Pearson did a very effective job, in most people's judgment, in putting the thing together again, and I guess that was the principal reason he was awarded the Nobel Prize. Acheson's view was very much that the United States had been excessively negative and moralistic; he would have liked to see the Suez expedition carried through. His viewpoint was really very close to that of Salisbury or Eden. He was very strong privately; I don't think he ever wrote particularly on this, but he felt that the British had been right to attempt the Suez business and that it should have been carried through. And he felt that Dulles and Eisenhower were very legalistic in their whole approach to the thing.

And he felt that along the way—now this had nothing to do particularly with Pearson—that Dulles had misled the British. This is a familiar litany on the British side, and Acheson felt that way about it and felt in roughly the same way that he had in '52, that Mike was being a little woolly and not paying enough attention to the power aspect of the situation, and to the need to deal with a situation in firmness. He didn't think that Mike Pearson was a man you could really count on in a tough, nasty decision or negotiation. That may sound strong, but I think that's a fair summation of where he came out in the end.

You will find [this expressed] in Acheson's contribution to the volume that Arnold Heeney and Livingston Merchant edited on Canadian–US relations. The title of Acheson's essay, "Canada: Stern Daughter of the Voice of God," was typical of his feeling that Canadians tended to be moral at other people's expense.

Then there was the suicide of Herbert Norman, the Canadian ambassador to Egypt, which was probably the worst blow that Lester Pearson suffered in the aftermath of Suez. Although Norman had only recently come to Cairo, he played an important part in the negotiations over the Canadian participation in the United Nations Emergency Force. The ambassador had tried to blunt the sharp reaction of the Egyptians to the prospect of the Queen's Own Rifles of Canada being stationed on the canal, and succeeded in working out a compromise formula whereby the question of Canadian ground troops was left open till the UNEF commander could assess his needs on the armistice line. When General Burns decided that he did not need any more infantry, Norman on December 4, 1956, telegraphed from Cairo that it was now the general's opinion that some other type of contribution from Canada would result in both a better-organized and more effective force (the other type of contribution turned out to be the Canadian reconnaissance squadron).

It was in 1951 that E. Herbert Norman's name came up for the first time in the hearings of the U. S. Senate's internal security subcommittee, the notorious Un-American Activities Committee, where there were charges that he had been a Communist as a student. At the time Norman was the chief of the Far Eastern Division at External Affairs; at his request, he was subjected to a thorough security check by the RCMP and was cleared of all charges, according to a press release. However, it was not felt wise to post him to an area of sensitivity in the United States, and so in 1953 Herbert Norman, who spoke Japanese fluently and was an acknowledged expert on Japan, was appointed Canadian high commissioner to New Zealand. In 1956 he was sent to Cairo as ambassador to

Egypt. On March 12, 1957, the allegations that he was a Communist were repeated in the Un-American Activities Committee. In Ottawa an angry external affairs minister said that the government would be making strong protests on this matter to Washington, and added that he had the fullest confidence in the ambassador. On April 4 1957, Norman leaped from the roof of a nine-story building in Cairo to his death.

The Canadian Embassy in Cairo put out a statement saying that Norman had committed suicide because his spirit had been broken by the revival of old charges of Communist association in the past. However, according to a report in the Montreal Gazette of March 23, 1967, the Central Intelligence Agency had a file on Norman which contained a dispatch from what was described as a most reliable source. This dispatch said that on the night before the ambassador plunged to his death, he had dinner with a doctor and told him that he was afraid that Prime Minister St. Laurent was not standing behind him and that a Royal Commission of Inquiry would be appointed. If he were called to give testimony before this commission, Norman said that he would have to implicate sixty or seventy Americans and Canadians and that he could not face up to this and that he was going to destroy himself.

As might be expected, when Norman committed suicide, there was an angry outburst in the Canadian Parliament, with MPs denouncing the U. S. Senate subcommittee and demanding that Canada stop sharing its security secrets with the United States. On April 5, 1957, the Toronto Daily Star had headlines crying out that more Canadians were being investigated in Washington and that Pearson was on the list. His name had come up before in the testimony of Elizabeth Bentley.

GEOFFREY PEARSON

I remember it as a very important event for him and one which gave him great anguish, I think more anguish than anything that could ever have happened to him up to that point because he felt responsible in some way for Norman's death. Norman was an old friend, and I think he regretted that he hadn't done more to reassure Herbert Norman when, in fact, I think he probably did everything he could. He had written him the week before he died. I have never seen that letter, but I believe he wrote him after the revelations just in order to tell him that he didn't believe a word of any of this and Herbert Norman should not pay any attention to it, that he himself certainly wouldn't. So he was, as you can imagine, very deeply affected by the suicide.

A lot of Americans thought Canadians were dupes of Communists then. But that never bothered him because he didn't agree with American views on a number of questions involving the Soviet Union or China. He never felt that way, that you had to be aggressive in order to counter danger. He believed the Soviet Union was a danger, but he didn't think it was a matter of threatening a third world war in order to counter the danger. That's where he disagreed with American policy, over tactics, and he didn't think that China was necessarily a part of some kind of world conspiracy with the Russians. He thought of China as being a separate problem.

By the way, he was influenced in that regard by Herbert Norman, who was a scholar of Japan, of course, but also in that sense a man who understood Asia. There were Canadian diplomats who had been born in China; Herbert Norman was born in Japan; people like that usually were sons of missionaries, Methodist missionaries, and this is where there was a kind of Methodist fellowship, my father's father having been a Methodist minister. They all knew each other. I don't think he knew the Norman family because they literally spent their whole life in Japan, but there were a number of families who had been in China: Endicott, in particular, the famous Toronto family, one or two of whom became Communists.

Anyway that family was known to my father very well, and there's a good deal of correspondence with that family in his file. So somebody like Elizabeth Bentley could have made a connection through this very innocent group of Methodists and Christian missionaries and churchmen who spent long years in China and who were sympathetic to the aims of the Chinese revolution, and through them, I think, my father had a different view of China. So it was easy to take that one step further and say he was also a dupe or he was even connected to some kind of conspiracy. It didn't bother him because it was so absurd.

What bothered him was that the Americans should sink to these depths or take these charges seriously; that a man like Norman should be, in effect, harried to death because Norman had been associated with a small group in the Thirties, whether you call it Communist or not, it was subsequently said to be Communist. Norman knew this. He'd told my father; he'd told anybody who asked him that he was afraid that it would make his future service to the government of no value because of American suspicions. But I don't think my father ever guessed or foresaw that this might lead to the ultimate act of taking his life. However, it was a good example of my father's resilience. He was deeply affected, but he was able to put it aside.

PAUL MARTIN

The best account I ever received about Norman was from the prime minister of New Zealand. I was there in 1956. Norman had been our high commissioner in New Zealand. And Mr. Holland, the conservative-minded prime minister of that country, had been a great friend of Norman's, and told me of many hours of conversation that he'd had with him. Now, Holland was not the kind of man that would go off the deep end. He certainly wasn't a Communist. He disliked Communists. And he put Norman's situation in the finest perspective that I have ever experienced anybody to do. Norman was a brilliant officer, he'd been a brilliant student. As a young man he may have had ideas, as so many have, about the nature of society. But I'm satisfied from what Mr. Holland told me and what others told me that Norman was much more sinned against than sinful. And I always admired Pearson for his defense of Norman. You know, it's so easy to accuse a man, particularly at that period, the McCarthy period, and so on. And I don't know of anything that ever caused me to have greater admiration for Pearson than the way he defended Norman.

However, there were others who felt that Lester Pearson had let Norman down, among them J. M. Macdonnell, the Conservative MP and George Bain of the Toronto Globe and Mail. *In the House of Commons, Macdonnell read extracts from Bain's article which charged that the protest note was largely a sham, meant to impress Canadians before an election, and that the government was afraid that standing up for an official accused of communism would not win it any marks in some parts of Canada, notably the province of Quebec. Bain wrote: "I have been trying for a week to get from the Department of External Affairs the answers to the specific allegations which were made against Mr. Norman by the United States investigators. This has produced nothing except reasons why it is impossible to do so, none of them particularly convincing." One of the reasons given was that it was a well-established policy not to disclose information on security cases. But the man was dead, and so that policy should not apply. Bain did not believe that the confidence that the government expressed in Norman in 1951 was unfounded, and he felt that its refusal to clear his name was an example of the worst sort of gutlessness.*

The Japanese were shocked and dismayed by the news of the ambassador's suicide, according to Dr. N. A. M. "Larry" Mackenzie, president of the University of British Columbia, who happened to be in Tokyo at the time. Herbert Norman, who had been born in Japan and had grown up speaking Japanese, was such an authority on the Japanese language and Japanese history that he was regarded as one of them by many prominent Japanese. He had absorbed so much Japanese culture that Dr. Mackenzie felt that, when faced with this agonizing situation, he had decided on hara-kiri as the honorable way out. Only the method of killing himself was different.

Another blow for Mike Pearson was the defeat of the St. Laurent government in the 1957 election. The Suez policy, for which the external affairs minister was of course responsible, played a part, if only a minor one, in the campaign, but Pearson somehow escaped all blame and seemed to suffer less from this extraordinary political reversal than some of his Cabinet colleagues. It was the first time that the Liberals had been out of power for twenty-two years. Several ministers had lost their seats, including the finance minister, Walter Harris, who had been regarded as the likely successor to the aging St. Laurent, and Pearson must have realized that his chances of becoming leader of the Liberal Party, and eventually prime minister of Canada, had been improved by the 1957 election results. Then there were the jobs outside of government in international organizations and academic institutions which he knew were available. So, it was with a genial acceptance of fate and a shrug of the shoulders that he moved from the secretary of state's ministerial suite in the East Block to a small office in the basement of the Parliament Buildings' Centre Block.

On October 14 1957, Pearson was in his basement office when he was rung up by an excited Canadian Press reporter with the news that he had been awarded the Nobel Peace Prize: it was the day that the Queen opened Parliament.[2] The timing could not have been better from the point of view of his political future because the announcement came just after Louis St. Laurent had issued a statement that he was resigning and preparations were being made for a leadership convention. Now he was certain to be chosen leader; in fact, it would be difficult, if not impossible, for him, as the first and only Canadian to be honored with a Nobel Peace Prize, to refuse his party's highest office. He would be told that it was his duty, and Lester B. Pearson had been brought up to do his duty.

Who had recommended him for the Nobel Peace Prize? Nobody knew for sure but Paul Martin, whom Pearson was to appoint external affairs minister, had an educated guess that it was Dag Hammarskjöld. The UN secretary-general, Martin said, had a high regard for Pearson. The admiration was mutual: the external affairs minister was lavish in his praise of Hammarskjöld in the Canadian House of Commons. At the time of the formation of the United Nations Emergency Force, Pearson wrote to a friend: "Thank God we have Dag Hammarskjöld as Secretary General. He has really done magnificent work under conditions of almost unbelievable pressure. I have been very close to him in the last week, and I know." They had worked as a team during the Suez Crisis, but they could not have both got the Nobel Peace Prize because Hammarskjöld, as secretary-general of the United Nations, was barred from receiving the award.

---

[2]For a fuller account of his receiving this award, see *Lester Pearson and the Dream of Unity.*

8 The American Dilemma: Political

SHORTLY BEFORE THE 1957 election was called, Lester Pearson spoke to a meeting of American publishers in New York on the subject of Canadian-American relations. He said that these relations, already very close, were getting closer still, and with the increasing points of contact between the two countries, there was the potential danger of increasing points of friction. Robert Fowler, a Montreal businessman and friend of Pearson's, was at the meeting and described the reaction of the American publishers as being "very odd"; they appeared to be hurt by the speech and seemed to regard it as an unfriendly statement by the Canadian external affairs minister. The reason for this, Fowler asserted, was that it disturbed the American view of Canada as a holiday place for hunting and fishing, and of Canadians as good guys like themselves whom they could take for granted, if they ever thought about them at all. This misconception was one of the problems of Canadian-American relations, Fowler said.

Pearson told the assembled American publishers that Canadian-American relations should not be regarded as automatic. "We have a different constitution," he said. "We have a different parliamentary system to yours. We have a different culture. We have a different population mix and a different language mix." Actually, there was really nothing new in what the external affairs minister was saying: he had said the same things some six years before; only that was in Canada. He had told a joint meeting of the Empire and Canadian clubs in Toronto:

"The days of relatively easy and automatic political relations with our neighbor are, I think, over. They are over because on our side, we are more important in the continental and international scheme of things, and we loom more largely now as an important element in United States and free world plans for defence and development. They are over also because the United States is the dominating world power on the side of freedom. Our preoccupation is no longer whether the United States will discharge her international responsibilities, but how she will do it and whether the rest of us will be involved."

The 1951 speech created much controversy, Pearson said in his memoirs, largely because it happened to have been delivered on the same day (April 10, 1951) that President Truman fired General MacArthur. It would probably have passed unnoticed but for this, and was yet another example of Pearson's extraordinary sense of timing.

GEOFFREY PEARSON

I think the first example of abandoning quiet diplomacy was in 1951 when he spoke in Canada about our relations with the United States, and said that there might be occasions when Canadians would have to differ with the Americans on important issues. This was as a result of their disagreement on Korea, and that speech stimulated a good deal of comment and got a lot of letters from both Canadians and Americans who were surprised that a Canadian statesman would suggest that on important issues Canada would differ with the United States.

There's been quite a change in climate since then. That was the beginning, I think, of the view that one had to speak up occasionally because American public opinion simply tended to ignore the views of Canada, and unless one spoke up they would never know what they were. He had a great faith in American democracy, but he felt you had to reach Americans sometimes; otherwise, they just assumed too much and you had, therefore, to speak out in a friendly way. This was after you tried to reach agreement privately, but if you couldn't and the issue was important enough, then it might well be that a public statement was necessary.

That speech in 1951 was followed by a famous speech on Vietnam many years later, [all of which] points to the role that

Canada played in the Fifties and to some extent later where we had influence in Washington but also we had the respect of countries in Asia and Africa. And we certainly did think that we were the country to persuade the Americans to do this or that. We had credit, in other words. Diplomats attach a lot of importance to credit. If you run out of credit, you might as well stop trying to be a diplomat. No matter what you say, nobody will believe you.

We had credit and he kept that kind of credit in Washington I think almost until the end, even with Mr. Dulles. But he felt that to gain the trust of the Americans you had to speak to them frankly in private and let them know what you thought, and he didn't accept their prescriptions always: Mr. Acheson on Korea, Mr. Dulles on Formosa, President Johnson on Vietnam; there were serious differences on these. The Americans never felt, I don't think, that he was untrustworthy. They trusted him even though they disagreed with him. Although I think Acheson over Korea came close to wondering whether he was speaking for Canada. But on the whole he maintained this trust.

So it was a very diplomatic card, and it may have had some effect in moderating American policy, especially in Asia. It always seemed to be applied in Asia. It was much less appropriate in Europe because the Europeans didn't need anyone to speak for them: they could tell the Americans what they thought. The British were always telling the Americans what they thought. In Asia, though, the Americans didn't have many friends or allies. They couldn't talk to China; they didn't trust India; and it was really only a country like Canada or Britain and maybe one or two others who could talk to them. So it was an important role. It might have prevented violence in Asia. A war with China was very close on several occasions.

After delivering the 1951 speech, Mike Pearson wrote a personal letter of explanation to his friend, Hume Wrong, then the ambassador in Washington, which he quotes in his memoirs. He said that Canadian anxiety over the development of American policy, especially in regard to the Far East, had its origin in "our feeling of dependence on the United States and frustration over the fact that we can't escape this no matter how hard we try." He said that he did not mind the hostile and indeed abusive mail that he had received from the Americans since making that speech.

What worried him was the extravagant praise from Canada because it showed "how easy it would be to work up a strong anti-American feeling in this country at this time." This was why, having said his piece, he was going back to the usual platitudes about traditional Canadian-American relations. However, Pearson did give notice in this letter that "there will be times in the future when we will have to do what we avoided doing in recent months, namely, take our own line even at the risk of weakening that [Western] unity which it is our first objective to preserve."

Perhaps the best example of Canada acting on its own, or "taking our own line," as Pearson put it, was the so-called "Package Deal," which opened the doors of the United Nations at the end of 1955. It was a masterly diplomatic stroke of the greatest significance because it served to revitalize the world body, which had been too long a closed corporation of sixty members, fully two-thirds of whom were allies or client states of the United States. In fact, Washington had come to regard the international organization as an extension of Congress or, at least, of the Organization of American States. The man who put together the Package Deal and guided it through all the deliberations of the policy committees and the plenary sessions was Paul Martin, the minister of national health and welfare; he was in charge of the Canadian delegation to the Tenth General Assembly of the United Nations, in the absence of the minister of external affairs, Lester B. Pearson, who had been invited to visit the Soviet Union. It was as a result of the complications with regard to Pearson's Russian trip that Paul Martin got launched on the project, which took altogether three months to bring to a successful vote and final approval in the Security Council.

PAUL MARTIN

It had a very curious origin. At the commemorative meeting of the United Nations in San Francisco in June of 1955, Mike had made a speech. I didn't pay much attention to that speech at the time. I guess I was busy with my own departmental responsibilities. But I was going to the Assembly two months later, in September. He wouldn't be there, he was going to the Soviet Union and elsewhere, and I was taking over the delegation. But during the summer I was reading the proceedings of the commemorative meeting, and he made a very good speech. And one of the things that he said was, "Surely the time has come when we ought to do something about the membership problem." He'd said that before; I had said that in speeches too. It didn't make any special significance, but it just hung there.

Well, it happened that in September, just about the time that the Assembly was to open, he was to go to Europe and ultimately to the Soviet Union. He had received word just two days before I was to leave for New York that the Soviet Union was taking a different position on his use of a Canadian military plane to travel while there. He could go to the Soviet Union in a Canadian military plane, but he wouldn't be allowed to travel in that plane in the country. Well, this aggravated him. He wasn't going to go to the Soviet Union. He had accepted an invitation and this was one of the conditions. And he wanted to know if I would go down to New York a day ahead, and see Molotov and iron this thing out.

I went down a day ahead and saw Molotov. Molotov was the foreign minister at that time. He was going to be in the Soviet Union three weeks later when Mike came. I told him about the problem, and Molotov was very impatient that he would have to be concerned with that kind of a situation. I said, "Well, I'm sorry, but Mr. Pearson said that unless this is arranged, he will not be going to visit the Soviet Union."

Well, that didn't make much of an impression on Molotov, but [Arkady A.] Sobolev, who was the Soviet ambassador at the time and a very good friend of mine and Pearson's, I think he wanted to help. He said, "Well, Mr. Molotov, would you put this in my hands and let me see what I can do?" And Molotov was very happy to have that done; he wanted to get rid of it. So Sobolev undertook to look into the matter, and he left us.

Then I started to go out, and Mr. Molotov said, "Oh, would you not like to sit down and let's discuss the problems of the Assembly?" Well, why not. This was a good opportunity with the Soviet Union foreign minister. He asked me how I saw the Assembly developing, what would be the issues, and so on. And with this speech of Mike's in San Francisco in my mind, his suggestion that we ought to do something about the members problem, I said, "We'll have the old questions on the agenda, but maybe this is the time to do something about the unresolved membership of so many countries."

To my great surprise, he said, "Yes, I think this is a good time; and you, Canada, you, Mr. Martin, you ought to take the initiative." Well, I couldn't believe my ears, and I said, "We have been thinking about this." By that I meant that Pearson had been thinking about it and he expressed this in San Francisco. "Well," he said, "we would be very interested in working with you and in moving this along because the time has come, as you say." Now that's how the idea of doing something developed.

I called Pearson at once and told him about the airplane business. I knew that that was the first thing on his mind, and I said, "I'm sure that Sobolev will work this out," as he did. Mike was in England when he got word that he would be allowed to take the plane into the Soviet Union. As a result of his difficulty with the plane, I had been able to make an arrangement with the foreign minister of the Soviet Union to move ahead successfully on the membership question.

Now that's a long story. It took the whole period of the Assembly that autumn to bring about a solution of the problem, when sixteen new members did come in. That decision was made, of course, by the Security Council, but it was made as a result of the emphatic vote in the General Assembly that the problem be resolved. Countries like Italy, Bulgaria, Austria, and Ireland are now members of the United Nations because of that initiative, and that unexpected agreement with Mr. Molotov on the day I called to see him about Mike's plane.

For five years, membership at the United Nations had been frozen by the Cold War. Every time a state wanted to join, its application was rejected either by the "automatic majority" of the United States or by the Soviet veto. It was an international game of tit-for-tat: the Americans would not let in any Communist country, so the Russians barred any Western democracy or U. S. client state. The situation was grotesque, with more than half the world excluded from the international organization and more than a third of the membership made up of Latin American countries that were the least likely to provide leadership; the Latino diplomats were embarrassed and longed for the anonymity that universality would give them. The only way to break the deadlock was by a trade-off of so many Soviet satellites for so many Western nations or emerging countries.

Paul Martin put together the Package Deal, which included five Soviet Bloc countries, Albania, Bulgaria, Hungary, Rumania, and Outer Mongolia (Mongolian People's Republic) and thirteen others — Austria, Cambodia, Ceylon, Finland, Ireland, Italy, Japan, Jordan, Laos, Libya, Nepal, Portugal, and Spain. These were all the countries that had applied for membership in the UN about which "no problem of unification arises," to quote the resolution. Thus, North and South Korea, and North and South Vietnam were excluded, and so, really, was Communist China although the argument there was that it was not a question of membership — China was one of the five permanent members of the Security Council — but a question of credentials.

Just as in the case of other diplomatic achievements, it was the performance that counted more than the proposal, the ability to get the largest measure of agreement, if not consensus. Paul Martin showed himself to be a skillful manipulator in pressing the Package Deal to its final successful conclusion. He knew that there was a substantial majority of the sixty member states in favor of opening the doors of the United Nations, and that was why he approached the General Assembly first. But he knew that he could not be in a hurry; he had to be patient and wait for the right time. He kept talking to delegations, letting out information where he thought it would do good, and keeping control of the situation. Martin got the overwhelming majority that he had expected for the Package Deal in the General Assembly, but he knew that the United States, which was being forced to go along with most of the proposal, would not agree to letting in Outer Mongolia.

The showdown came in the Security Council. Albania got through the first test, then the Chiang Kai-shek representative vetoed the application of the Mongolian People's Republic; Bulgaria, Hungary, and Rumania passed, but the Soviet Union vetoed the rest, and on a second vote, all the Communist states were rejected. So the Package Deal seemed to have failed. However, the next day, December 14, 1955, the Security Council met again at the request of the USSR — there had obviously been consultations. The Soviet delegate said that he wanted to withdraw the negative vote he had cast on the application of a number of states for membership and submitted a revised Package Deal — all those countries that had been in the original package deal except for Outer Mongolia and Japan, whose cases would be deferred to the next session. The American delegate immediately submitted an amendment to add Japan to the sixteen states in the new Package Deal, and this was promptly vetoed by the

Soviet Union. Even a quarter of a century later Henry Cabot Lodge was shocked by the Russian action: "It was preposterous," he said, "to rank Japan with Outer Mongolia; the Japanese observer was very upset." The new sixteen-member Package Deal was then quickly passed by the Security Council, and the doors of the United Nations were opened and have remained open since. Japan got in at the next session and Outer Mongolia a little later.

It was a remarkable diplomatic feat by Paul Martin because he had to overcome the opposition of not only the United States but the British and the French as well.

HENRY CABOT LODGE

The United States didn't like it [the Package Deal] but I'm 99 percent sure that we voted for it in the end. We didn't like the Package Deal but we did attach great importance to not having trouble with Canada. Dulles didn't like the Package Deal. I don't think Eisenhower cared very much. When the time came to vote, I remember I called Mr. Dulles on the telephone and he said to me, "The really important thing about the whole Package Deal is Canada, and it's worth much to us to have Canada's good will even if we do let in some countries that we don't like very much."

PAUL MARTIN

On one occasion Cabot Lodge called me at my hotel in the morning. This would be about a month before I made the actual proposal to the General Assembly. The whole membership deal was a three-month operation. It took every minute of one's day from the time that Molotov and I had first met and when he had agreed that this was the propitious moment to try and break the deadlock. But the Americans, as I said earlier, and the British and the French were very anxious to stop the initiative, and they brought every pressure that they could bring on me, on the Canadian government, and on the twenty-five countries who had associated themselves with us in the proposal.

Cabot called me one morning and he said that he had a very important message to convey to me. We met in the Security Council chamber early in the morning and nobody was present.

He said that he was well aware of Pearson's opposition to the American government under Eisenhower. I took exception to that at once. I said there was no basis for that remark. He went on and said that everyone in the administration knew of the reservations that not only Pearson had but some others in the Canadian government. I took exception to that as well, but I said, "What has this got to do with whatever you came to see me about?"

"Well," he said, "at this very moment your ambassador is being seen by Foster Dulles, the secretary of state, and we want this resolution to expand the membership, standing in Canada's name and put forward by you, to be withdrawn." I said, "As far as the Canadian government is concerned, there is no hope of withdrawal. We are proposing something that we strongly believe in."

It is true that, as matters turned out, Foster Dulles, at about that very moment, was seeing George Glazebrook, our minister in Washington. The ambassador, Arnold Heeney, was out of town. Foster Dulles told George Glazebrook, as Cabot Lodge was telling me, that the Americans were very unhappy with our initiative and that if we did not withdraw it, there was, not too well articulated, but there was the hint that Americans could very well stop buying Canadian oil and gas.

Mr. St. Laurent phoned me at once, after my interview, because he received word at once from George Glazebrook, and I told Mr. St. Laurent, "I know what you are calling about." "Well," he said, "you know, this is a very serious matter." I said, "Of course, it's very serious." And he said if Americans didn't buy Canadian oil, this would be a very serious thing.

"Well," I said, "I don't believe that the American government is behind this idea; this is an idea, if it was stated in those terms, of Foster Dulles himself. I have known Foster Dulles a long time. I know his methods. In any event, why are you calling me?"

"Oh well," he said, "I just thought I'd tell you how important this matter is to Canada." "Well," I said, "if you're suggesting that we should withdraw the motion, you then would have to get a new minister of national health and welfare." "No," he said, "I'm not suggesting that at all. I'm just indicating to you my concern over the situation."

That was the reason that Cabot Lodge came to see me. It was an unsatisfactory intervention by him. I've since discussed it with him several times. I'm sure that he was asked to do this. But I was right in concluding that, while Eisenhower didn't like what we were doing, Eisenhower was not a party to any reprisal or any threat of reprisal.

It was in June 1955, at the tenth anniversary commemorative meeting of the United Nations in San Francisco, that Molotov invited Pearson to pay an official visit to the Soviet Union. Prime Minister St. Laurent agreed, and at the end of September the external affairs minister and his party, which included Maryon, left Ottawa. The first stop was London, where Pearson had a private talk and lunch with Anthony Eden, who had just become prime minister. Then they flew to Paris, where their son Geoffrey was posted, and the Pearsons had a brief family reunion, the most important part of which was getting better acquainted with their first grandchild. On October 4, 1955, they flew from Paris to Berlin, where they spent the night, and the next day they took on a Russian pilot and navigator and were off again on the final leg of their journey to Moscow.

The visit to the Soviet Union was another example of "taking our own line," for, while there was no official objection from Washington, it could not escape the United States' attention that Pearson was the first Western foreign minister to be officially invited to Moscow since the war. It was a rare opportunity to size up what was happening in the USSR since the death of Stalin, and could not be missed, but the Americans were aware that the Russians would benefit from this trip because it would help to break down the barriers of the Cold War and make possible what Paul Martin was doing in opening the doors of the United Nations. Soviet-Canadian relations, which had been strained by the Gouzenko spy scandal, were improving, and there had been an exchange of ambassadors recently. Among those who accompanied the external affairs minister were John Holmes, who had been chargé d'affaires in Moscow in the late Forties during the awkward days of the Gouzenko Affair; George Ignatieff, who spoke Russian; and Mitchell Sharp, who was associate deputy minister of trade and commerce. The latter went along because Pearson, who was ever sensitive to American criticism, wanted the trip to be more than just a good-will junket.

MITCHELL SHARP

Mr. Pearson felt that there should be something concrete that would be accomplished during this visit. So he put to the civil servants the question of whether we could have a trade agreement between the Soviet Union and Canada, because up till that time the Soviet Union was being treated as a country outside of most-favored-nation treatment. We met as a group, the top civil servants, and we came to the conclusion that an agreement was possible; indeed, that we probably could get an agreement with the Soviet Union in which we got some concrete advantages by way of access for some of our goods, particularly wheat, into the Soviet Union in return for granting them most-favored-nation treatment; that is, the same treatment as is accorded to the United States. This proposition was put up to the Cabinet, and it was agreed. So I was sent along on the mission as the second-ranking person to try to negotiate a trade agreement.

There was room for a number of reporters on the government's C-5 plane that took Pearson to Moscow, and a lot of them wanted to go along on this historic trip, and many of them did. As John Holmes said, Pearson appreciated hospitality and was naturally outgoing and friendly, but he had to be careful what he said lest his remarks be taken out of context and he be made to sound like a pinko, as Holmes put it. A particular menace was a CBC correspondent with a portable tape recorder, which was quite new then. Every time Pearson was about to say something genial, he found a microphone pushed under his nose. "For heaven's sake," he said to Holmes, "keep that fellow away from me, if you can." That fellow was René Lévesque, who left broadcasting for politics and ultimately became the separatist premier of Quebec.

It was an extraordinary time to visit Moscow because the Soviet leadership was in a state of transition. After Stalin's death on the night of March 5, 1953, a group of top members of the Communist Party's Politburo held power: Malenkov was premier; Molotov, foreign minister; and the other members of the Big Five, as they were called, were Kaganovich, Bulganin, and Khrushchev. However, when Pearson arrived in the Russian capital, he found that only three of them were in the Kremlin; Bulganin and Khrushchev were in the Crimea, evidently plotting to take over the leadership. Although Malenkov had been demoted to deputy premier, Pearson found him, as he said in his memoirs, witty, intelligent, and confident, and much more interesting than the dour Molotov; he described Kaganovich as "certainly an engaging old pirate."

At the end of the visit, word was received that Mr. Khrushchev wanted

*to see the Canadian external affairs minister. So the C-5 flew south, first
to Stalingrad where Pearson laid a wreath on the monument to the Red
Army troops who died in the defense of the Volga city, then on to
Sebastopol, a tour of the Balaclava battlefield, and the drive along the
spectacular Crimean coast to Yalta. George Ignatieff accompanied Pearson
to the Yousopoff Palace for the meeting with Khrushchev and Bulganin.*

GEORGE IGNATIEFF

It was a fascinating evening. Mr. Khrushchev was unusually
frank, although he hadn't taken office yet but was obviously
making preparations, with the aid of the military and police
power, which one had to have, to take over the leadership in
Moscow. He was down there with Bulganin making all these
arrangements—and the strange thing was that the leaders in
Moscow seemed quite compliant. Although Mr. Malenkov didn't
lose his head, he certainly lost his whole position and was sent to
look after some power station in Siberia. The conversation lasted
from half-past seven until well past midnight; it went on before
dinner, during dinner, and after dinner, and proved to be a very
long and arduous performance [for Mike].

From the moment we met him, Mr. Khrushchev started off
with the challenge that Canada belonged to an aggressive military
alliance and "I advise you to get out of it." There was a lot of
aggressive banter, but he had two subjects that he wanted to deal
with seriously, and that was NATO and his own intentions [when
he came to power]. First of all, he said that it was inconceivable
that the United States and the Soviet Union should go to war, that
war was out of the question in the nuclear age because its consequences were unpredictable, that the capitalist system as represented by the United States and the so-called Communist system
could and should compete on the basis of peaceful coexistence,
which meant competition.

He said, "We will show that we can outproduce you, that we
can satisfy consumer needs, that we can plan better," and so on.
But then, on the military side he said, "We have no fears of the
United States as such, we don't expect or envisage war, but we do
fear the combination of American technology, industrial leadership, and German militarism." He said, "We have been invaded,

don't forget, by Germany, and we lost twenty million as a consequence of the war and the occupation. We can deal with the Germans alone but what you and NATO are facing us with is in effect a German-American military alliance. Now, if you want to, if you want to make for an assurance that there should be no war, let us into NATO. We'll become members and make this collective, and then we won't have anything to fear. You can then make it clear that there'll be no war. But," he said, "as long as you insist on a American-German alliance, we will continue our military preparations." And he said, "The cost of this has its risks for Canada because make no mistake that in the two world wars Canada has not been occupied or directly attacked. I know that you participated, but if there were to be a war resulting from this American-German military combination, Canada would not escape the fearful consequences."

That was one line. The other line was that, internally, what he called the reign of terror, which had continued since, as he put it, the time of Ivan the Terrible, there were no exceptions for any of the Soviet leaders, whether it be Lenin or Stalin, had to end. It had been terrible in its consequences for the Soviet Union. There was a sense of distrust, there was fear, and that he was going to end. This was before the secret report on Stalin to the Communist [Party conference in Moscow].

GEOFFREY PEARSON

My father didn't know the Russians; he didn't like the Soviet Union. He liked them personally but not as a country. He never lived there; he only went there once and that was in 1955 for a short time, the famous meeting with Khrushchev. He liked them individually; he quite liked their direct ways, but he shared the general Western view that the Russians were out to conquer the world. I think he genuinely believed that. It was, therefore, very hard for him to be on anything but difficult terms with them.

It didn't affect his personal relations with somebody like Vyshinsky. They got along all right. He never used vituperative language. He never at the UN criticized people directly, but he used strong language about Soviet imperialism. I don't think he ever said "the red menace" but he used that sort of language because he believed it. People forget now that statesmen then thought that the Soviet Union, if it hadn't been stopped, would have provoked a war. Some people still believe that, of course, but they all thought that then and it was the reason for NATO. So his relations with the Soviet Union were not neighborly; I don't think he thought of them as a neighbor.

There was no doubt that Lester Pearson regarded the United States as a neighbor, and a good neighbor, but this, in itself, did not make relations any easier. It was very difficult and very awkward to have to live beside a superpower, and every Canadian, the extenal affairs minister included, was aware of this—"like sleeping beside an elephant," as Prime Minister Pierre Trudeau was to say. Aside from the overwhelming effect that the United States had on the life and culture of its middle-power neighbor to the north, there was the extraordinary pull that it exerted on the Canadian population; it was like a magnet drawing hordes of people below the border. During the years between World Wars One and Two it was estimated that Canada lost some five to six million people, all to the United States.

As a professor of history, Pearson was concerned about this "brain drain," and as a diplomat and external affairs minister, he was determined to do something about it. At first Jean Fournier thought that he was joking. But he was quite serious about wanting to reverse this trend.

JEAN FOURNIER

Mr. Pearson said, "You are going to Boston as consul general." Well, as I have not the kind of face a diplomat is supposed to have—I certainly do not have a poker face—he saw that I was a little bit surprised, to say the least, and he went on to tell me, "You are the first French Canadian who will be consul general there." There had been consuls who were French Canadians but I was the first French Canadian consul general. He said, "One of your jobs there will be to try to persuade as many Franco-Americans as possible to come back to Quebec." There wasn't much I could say about that. I had no comeback. I just said yes.

Needless to say, whenever I tried to do that in New England, I was received with disbelief by these people, who said, "Look, we are now third-generation American and we are very attached to the United States; we have a very comfortable life and we don't necessarily want to go back to Quebec." So I didn't follow through with Mr. Pearson's wishes.

I had an uncle there and two or three cousins. They didn't take me very seriously when I suggested that they should cross the border. I was very impressed with the way they were strictly Americans. Oh, they had by no means forgotten Quebec—especially the older generation, who were the old French gentlemen type and very wonderful people—and culturally they were emotionally attached to Quebec. But the younger generation—those who were twenty and twenty-five—had almost ceased speaking French.

This was illustrated by what the parish priests told me: years before, they would have had, for example, four Masses on Sunday exclusively in French, and that particular time I'm speaking about [mid-Fifties] they had three in English and only one in French. The reason is that they didn't want to lose their young Franco-American parishioners.

By the mid-Fifties, Lester Pearson had become world-famous; he was probably the only Canadian statesman ever to be featured on a bubble gum card. Max Wershof said that his son Peter was collecting a series on the great men of history, and who should turn up but the likeness of his father's boss, the external affairs minister. There could have been no greater popular acclaim, and Pearson was in the company of such heroes as Julius Caesar, Napoleon, the Duke of Wellington, and George Washington. This was a couple of years before he was awarded the Nobel Peace Prize.

It was not surprising that the international community should have been shocked when Pearson gave up his portfolio of external affairs as a result of the defeat of the St. Laurent government in the 1957 election. As the representative of Canada, he had been such a familiar and friendly figure on the diplomatic scene for so long that it was difficult to realize that he would no longer be around. As Louis Audette was told by several heads of delegations at UN and NATO meetings that he attended after his resignation, "It's all very well for you Canadians, you people still have him, but what are we going to do without him?" Temp Feaver, who was ambassador in Copenhagen at the time, wrote Pearson that Prime Minister Hansen of Denmark had offered him the post of foreign minister of

Denmark: all Mike had to do was become a Danish citizen and he would be appointed the next day. Pearson replied, in a Dear Temp letter, "I accept with great pleasure, provided I don't have to learn Danish, change my citizenship, or cease living in Canada."

The 1957 election pointed up for Pearson the fact that Canadian-American relations were complicated by domestic politics: the Democratic Party in the United States was considered to be closer to the Liberal Party in Canada, while the Republicans were more akin to the Conservatives.

Certainly, Prime Minister Diefenbaker got along well with President Eisenhower; the Conservative chief had the highest regard for Ike, whom he admired almost as much as he did Winston Churchill. However, it was quite the opposite with President Kennedy, whom the Canadian prime minister disliked from the moment he met him in the White House. They were very different people, the poor farm boy and the rich man's son, the prairie populist and the Harvard-educated intellectual, and there was a generation gap: Diefenbaker and Eisenhower were about the same age, whereas Kennedy was young enough to have been either man's son.

All of this would not have mattered so much had it not been for the president's high-handed manner in pushing Canada to join the Organization of American States (OAS) and the Alliance for Progress. Prime Minister Diefenbaker resisted and was further incensed by American attempts to prevent Canada from trading with Communist China and Cuba. On the subject of the OAS, Diefenbaker noted in his memoirs, "This was the first of a number of occasions on which I had to explain to President Kennedy that Canada was not Massachusetts or even Boston." The antipathy and contempt were mutual, and relations deteriorated to the extent that Kennedy made no secret of his desire to get rid of the Conservative government. "Our independence was not without price," Diefenbaker noted.

It would have been difficult for Pearson not to have become embroiled in this feud, and, as Opposition leader, he advocated Canada joining the OAS at a time when it looked as if he was taking orders from Kennedy. The fact that he did not do anything about this as prime minister was duly recorded in Diefenbaker's memoirs. Then there was the dinner party that President Kennedy gave for the Nobel Prize winners: Pearson was invited and attended, which annoyed the Conservative Prime Minister. And there was the occasion when the president consulted Pearson. John Matheson knew about this because it had delayed his taking his seat in the House of Commons: he had been elected the Liberal member for Leeds at

a by-election on May 29, 1961, and he was to be introduced by Pearson,
but at the last minute it was postponed for a week.

JOHN MATHESON

What happened was that Pearson was asked by President Kennedy to go and have a visit with him, and he was quite alarmed at
this invitation because he said, "Oh, I can't possibly do that; I'll be
subject to all kinds of criticisms. Mr. Diefenbaker will regard this
as a most untoward step on my part, the leader of the Opposition,
to go to discuss anything with the president of the United States."
But according to my information—that is, Mary Macdonald—
the new president was planning a trip to see Mr. Khrushchev, and
he was becoming very well briefed, and his advisers had said,
"You must under all circumstances talk matters over with Mike
Pearson. His background in the UN and so on and his knowledge
in this thing is absolutely necessary."

So I was told that Mr. Pearson, who turned down this suggestion, was phoned by Kennedy and he said, "Do you have a degree
from Harvard?" and Mike said, "Yes." "Do you have one from
MIT?" And Mike said, "Yes." "Do you have one from Boston
University?" And he said, "No, I don't." "Well," Kennedy said,
"you're going to, and when you do there'll be a car waiting for
you, and I do need you for a weekend. I need your guidance and
advice. This is a matter affecting the security of the free world and
I want all the help I can get, and I think I can fairly ask for it," and
how could he turn him down?

In 1962 Charles Ritchie was appointed ambassador to Washington, and
he recalled what a rough time he had representing the Diefenbaker
government.

CHARLES RITCHIE

Shortly after I arrived in Washington, I was really attacked by
Dean Rusk as a Canadian ambassador at some social occasion. I
hadn't even presented my letters of credence.[1] I remember Walter

[1] When Charles Ritchie presented his letters of credence to President Kennedy, the
atmosphere was so chilly that there were long pauses in the conversation. Toward the
end of the interview Kennedy suddenly said, "Shhh ..." and Ritchie thought, "My

Lippman, who was a great friend of mine, was there and he said afterward, "I've never heard a secretary of state speak to a foreign representative like that." Afterward Rusk and I were on very good terms, I think, but it was a most extraordinary outburst and was symptomatic of the really unpleasant atmosphere which the Americans had created.

It was a very tricky time, and it was brought home to one in so many small ways that the word was that the White House was not on good terms with the Canadian government and the Canadian prime minister, and it percolated through to other departments. Even if you were doing some rather minor piece of business, you were soon aware that a sort of general signal had gone out: "Those Canadians, don't give them an inch on anything." A most interesting study of the way power worked in Washington at that time.

As Charles Ritchie indicated, there was nothing very subtle about the Democratic administration's opposition to the Conservative government. Bruce Hutchison, the West Coast journalist who was a friend of the Bundys, said that Jack Kennedy made no secret of the disdain in which he held Prime Minister John Diefenbaker.

The breaking point came over the Cuban missile crisis, and the length of time it took the Canadian government to put the country and the armed forces on the alert. There was a breakdown in communications: Gordon Churchill, one of Diefenbaker's close associates, said that Ottawa was not informed as early as the British were that the Russians were installing offensive missiles with nuclear warheads in Cuba, despite the fact that Canadian forces were an integral part of the defense organization of North America, NORAD. Then Prime Minister Harold Macmillan urged Diefenbaker not to take any additional provocative action because his sources in Moscow had warned that war hung in the balance. There was resentment among the Cabinet ministers at the shabby way Canada was taken for granted and expected to say, "Ready, aye, ready." On October 24, 1962, a couple of days after the crisis began, Diefenbaker did

God, am I going to be shooed out of the White House? This will be the first time that's ever happened to any ambassador. It's not the way I intended to go down in history." It was the president's daughter, Caroline, coming through the French windows from the lawn with her pet donkey.

put the country on a state of alert, but the prime minister asserted that President Kennedy had wanted him to declare a state of emergency, which he refused to do. He was incensed at this demand since the president had no intention of declaring a state of emergency in the United States.

As a result of the Cuban crisis, the difference between Howard Green, the external affairs minister, and Douglas Harkness, the defense minister, came out in the open. Green was opposed to the acquisition of nuclear weapons because of the strong stand that he had taken on behalf of Canada at the United Nations against nuclear testing, which was one of the great issues of the day. Harkness, on his part, was insistent that the nuclear warheads be acquired because the crisis had shown that the main weapons for the defense of the country—the CF-101 Voodoo planes, and the BOMARC missiles—were essentially unarmed.

On January 3, 1963, General Lauris Norstad, the retiring NATO commander, visited Ottawa, and said at an airport news conference that Canada would not be fulfilling her commitments if she did not acquire nuclear warheads. Ostensibly, Norstad was paying a farewell call, but Diefenbaker believed that he had come to Canada "at the behest of President Kennedy" to prepare the way "for Pearson's conversion to the United States nuclear policy."

On January 12, 1963, Mike Pearson reversed a long-standing Liberal policy when he told a party meeting in Scarborough, Ontario, that the Canadian government should live up to its commitments and accept nuclear weapons. The speech came as a shock to Walter Gordon, who was his closest adviser at the time, and so appalled Pierre Trudeau, then professor of law at the University of Montreal, that he wrote a scathing article for Cité libre in which he called Pearson "the unfrocked pope of peace." On January 14, 1963, the American ambassador in Ottawa, Walton Butterworth, was alleged to have written to the Liberal leader congratulating him on the "excellent and logical" speech he had made and saying how much the United States government appreciated it, and that it would be "quite evident to the electorate" that the Conservatives were "unfit to continue governing this country."

Several copies of this letter were mailed to various persons in Canada, and the one that Diefenbaker received, just a few days before the 1963 election, was postmarked Acton, England. Little or no use was made of the letter during the campaign since it could not be confirmed. Walton Butterworth angrily and repeatedly denied it, while Lester Pearson said that he had never received the letter and that it was obviously a forgery.

Gordon Churchill tried to solve the mystery of the letter but could not, and wondered whether the CIA had "concocted" it. Colin Cameron, the NDP member, suggested that the letter might have been written for the purpose of raising money during the election campaign, that it could be shown to American subsidiaries as proof that the Liberal Party had the blessing of the Kennedy administration. Alvin Hamilton, who was Diefenbaker's agriculture minister, claimed that American companies "somehow got the message that under no circumstances could they contribute to the Conservative Party." In retrospect, Hamilton said, it came as a shock to him to discover that what was said in the negotiations with the Americans on the nuclear warheads would appear in the newspapers the next day; he did not know, at the time, that Ambassador Butterworth was briefing a select group of Canadian reporters in the basement of the U. S. Embassy in Ottawa.

While there were doubts as to the authenticity of the Butterworth letter and its intervention in Canadian affairs, there could be none with regard to the unprecedented State Department press release of January 30, 1963. It sought to correct statements that Prime Minister Diefenbaker had made in the House of Commons. The press release said that the discussions on nuclear weapons were exploratory in nature and "the Canadian government has not yet proposed any arrangement sufficiently practical to contribute effectively to North American defense." There was no question, the State Department said, "of the appropriateness of nuclear weapons for Canadian forces in fulfilling their NATO or NORAD obligations." The Washington announcement ended by denying an argument that Diefenbaker and Howard Green had used: "The provision of nuclear weapons to Canadian forces would not involve an expansion of independent nuclear capability, or an increase in the 'nuclear club.'"

The State Department press release amounted to interference in Canadian affairs, and even Lester Pearson and the Liberals denounced it as such.

DEAN RUSK

As I remember, the statement had to do with the United States view on the particular matter. The United States view was our business, and if somebody else misrepresented it, we had every right to clarify it. But you know, I can't imagine that the United States has the slightest capacity to tell the people in Canada how to vote. I think the idea that we sort of intervened in elections is inaccurate and if we had tried, it would have been futile. People across the border don't let us campaign about who is going to be elected.

CHARLES RITCHIE

You see, when you make a statement like the famous press statement by Rusk, it's perfectly intellectually defensible and Rusk was very good at defending things intellectually, so that it was correcting a misleading account, but it also had the effect of doing a bit of harm to the Diefenbaker government that certainly added relish to the occasion even if it wasn't its first motive. One way of interpreting it was that it was a deliberate attempt to influence Canadian internal politics for a change. I don't know if that's the right way of interpreting it or where the actual responsibility lay. I believe myself that it lay in the White House, but I wouldn't want to spell out why I think that, but I believe it did rather than the State Department.

On February 5, 1963, less than a week after the State Department press release, the Diefenbaker government fell (the Conservatives were defeated in the House of Commons by one hundred and forty-two votes to one hundred and eleven); Parliament was dissolved the next day and an election called for April 8.[2] There was no doubt that Jack Kennedy was delighted at the turn of events, but there were charges that he was taking part in the election, and that he had a man directing the Liberal Party's campaign. That man was Lou Harris, the pollster, who had helped Kennedy a great deal in the 1960 presidential election campaign and was now helping Pearson. The excuse that Walter Gordon gave for hiring Harris was that there was no one in Canada who could do the public opinion surveys that he wanted. Gordon was the Liberal Party's campaign chairman. The questions and the questioning were done by Canadians, he said, but Lou Harris interpreted the results. The American pollster was kept under wraps as much as possible, and Keith Davey, who worked for Gordon as campaign director, remembered the only

[2]For a full account of the fall of the Diefenbaker government, see *Diefenbaker: Leadership Lost 1962-67* (Toronto: University of Toronto Press, 1976).

"covert operation" in which he was involved was when he was at the Toronto airport with Lou Harris and could not avoid meeting a Tory friend, Frank McGee; he introduced Harris by his middle name, thus keeping his identity a secret.

(It was ironic that Walter Gordon should have been regarded as the great hope of the Americans during the 1963 election campaign—Lou Harris was reported to have told the Kennedy crowd on Newsweek Magazine *that Gordon had a mind like a steel trap—because when he became finance minister in the Pearson government a short time later he was to carry on a campaign against American ownership of Canadian industry.)*

Then, there was the telephone call that President Kennedy was supposed to have made to Lester Pearson during the election campaign. But did he make it? Or was it made by someone in the White House on his behalf? Dick O'Hagan, who was the Liberal leader's press secretary, remembered taking the call at the Legion Hall in Edmonton: the telephone was in the bar, and the noise was so great, he had difficulty hearing. At first the caller refused to speak to him, but O'Hagan insisted that Pearson was not available because he was addressing a meeting in the auditorium next to the bar. The caller finally came on the line and, according to O'Hagan, was Max Freedman, a Winnipeg journalist who was a friend of the Kennedys.

RICHARD O'HAGAN

Whether Max Freedman was conveying a message from Kennedy or whether Mr. Pearson ever talked to Kennedy, I literally don't know. He may have, but I don't know that. He talked later to Freedman. I know he talked to Freedman; of that I am perfectly satisfied. Now, whether Freedman was able to hand him over to Mr. Kennedy at the White House or whether they actually... I just don't know.

Bruce Hutchison's account of this incident was that the person who called said that he had been instructed or authorized to say that if President Kennedy could do anything to help Mr. Pearson by issuing some kind of a statement, he would do so. Which, according to Hutchison, horrified Mike who said, "For God's sake, tell the president not to say anything. I don't want any help from him. This would be awful." Max Freedman, who retired to Winnipeg, could not remember the call that he was supposed to have made. He did say that he had advised Kennedy to call Pearson about a foreign policy issue, and that Kennedy had spoken to him, but that was during the 1960 United States election campaign. However, he could not remember making a telephone call from the White House or on behalf of President Kennedy, but he pointed out that he had had a heart attack in mid-April 1963 which left him with a loss of memory.

There was no way that Pearson could prevent Kennedy from praising him or denigrating that "son of a bitch" Diefenbaker. The American press, taking its cue from the White House, mounted a campaign against the Conservative government, and border radio stations broadcast editorials denouncing Diefenbaker; while Newsweek Magazine, which had a large circulation in Canada, had a cover picture of the prime minister that made him look demented. Alvin Hamilton believed that the American intervention was coordinated and directed by the United States Embassy and the United States consulates across the country; in retrospect, he wondered whether the CIA had not been very active in Canada during the 1963 election. Howard Green said that an American agent or a CIA man had attended a couple of his election meetings in British Columbia.

HOWARD GREEN

I was at a coffee party in Cranbrook, and a chap appeared at this coffee party one morning, and couldn't explain where he came from or where he was going to, or just who he was. I don't know whether he was a CIA agent or not, but he certainly was a most peculiar visitor at a coffee party. I had a young American Foreign Service officer go to one of my meetings in my own [Vancouver] riding and ask for a copy of my speech. I just spoke from notes and I didn't have a copy, but I would have been very annoyed if one of our young secretaries had gone to an American meeting and gone to the minister and asked him to give him a copy of his speech. Two or three things like that in my own experience.

DEAN RUSK

If anybody suggests that the CIA was given a mission to go up there and destabilize the Diefenbaker government, that's nonsense.

Lester Pearson won the 1963 election but did not get a majority, despite the fact that the Diefenbaker government had collapsed and despite the support Pearson got from business and the press and the Canadian establishment generally, as well as the American administration. The Liberals had only one hundred and twenty-nine of the two hundred and sixty-five seats in the House of Commons. It was not the greatest triumph. On April 22, 1963, Pearson was sworn in as prime minister of Canada. One of his first acts as head of government was to visit President Kennedy at his Hyannisport home in Massachusetts. It was, by all accounts, a love feast. Charles Ritchie was one of the officials who attended this get-together; so was Walton Butterworth.

CHARLES RITCHIE

I went to Hyannisport with Pearson for a meeting with Kennedy, and the honeymoon was on and everything which had been sour was sweet. I don't know what was the exact achievement at Hyannisport; that remains to be evaluated, but they had a very long, intimate talk together. There were a small group of officials present. Walt Butterworth, the American ambassador, played an interesting part in all this because Walt was an old friend of Mike's dating back to long before Mike had been in politics at all. Walt was really Dean Acheson's man and also very close to the Kennedy family because he had served in the American Embassy in London with Joe Kennedy, and he was a very amusing and likable but very overbearing and arrogant man. It was very curious that in difficult times with the United States, Mike was always available to Walt. I don't think Walt had much influence. This is always a most puzzling thing with ambassadors. They may have access on personal terms, but it doesn't necessarily mean it will change policy. In later years when Walt was still here, he saw Mike a lot but didn't really make Mike tow any particular American line.

The Canadian-American honeymoon lasted for a couple of months—until the United States imposed the so-called Interest Equalization Tax, which had a devastating effect on the Canadian economy. The reason for the tax was a serious balance-of-payments problem: there were just too many American dollars being spread around and, after some prodding by European governments and the Organization for Economic Cooperation and Development (OECD), the Kennedy administration decided to levy a tax of 15 percent on the export of all capital from the United States. Lou Rasminsky, governor of the Bank of Canada at the time, said that he did not think that the United States action was in retaliation for Walter Gordon's first budget, which had so many anti-American features. However, he did say that after he had been able to negotiate an exemption, George Ball, one of Kennedy's advisers, said, "You know, your last budget hasn't made it any easier for us to agree to what we have just done."

It was a case, Rasminsky said, of the Americans not taking into account the special position of Canada in imposing the tax. The way it worked was as follows: if Ontario Hydro, for example, were to issue a bond with a face value of one thousand dollars and an interest rate of 8 percent in the New York market, the American purchaser would have to pay one thousand dollars plus 15 percent, or one thousand one hundred and fifty dollars, for that bond. This would mean that the effective yield would be something like 7 percent, and there would be no buyers. For Ontario Hydro to sell that bond, the interest rate in Canada would have to go up by a whole point, and the Canadian monetary policy would therefore be thrown into reverse. As soon as the Interest Equalization Tax was announced in Washington on July 18, 1963, all hell broke loose in the Canadian markets. Bond prices dropped; the 4-1/2s of 1938, which was a kind of bellwether long-term issue, fell by three to three and a half points in a single day. The exchange rate suffered sharp losses, and Walter Gordon, the finance minister, was faced with the prospect of having to devalue the Canadian dollar again.

Lou Rasminsky was salmon fishing on the Gaspé peninsula when he first heard of the equalization tax. He hurried back to Ottawa to find, as he put it, people in a state of very profound depression. There was a meeting in the minister's office on Saturday morning, July 20, at which arrangements were made for him to meet with Douglas Dillon, the secretary of the treasury, and Bob Roosa, the under-secretary, in Washington.

LOUIS RASMINSKY

I went down with Wyn Plumptre, and we were joined by Charles Ritchie, then our ambassador in Washington. We were down there within about an hour and a half of the appointment being made, because the Jet Star was on the tarmac and I guess we phoned our wives to bring us a clean shirt for the next day. So we walked into Dillon's office much before he expected us. Well, he greeted us very warmly and then he said how soon we had got down there. I said that the Jet Star was on the tarmac and proceeded to say what a wonderful aircraft the Jet Star was. Dillon let me go on and then he said, "Oh yes, I know about the Jet Star, we used to have many of them in the United States government, but we sold them. We couldn't afford it." So, this was the beginning of the negotiation.

Dillon started, as I recall, by expressing surprise at the strength of the reaction in the markets. Dillon was a market man and he followed what was going on in markets. I agreed that the market reaction had been very strong, but I argued that there was a real basis for it because the American action in imposing this tax on us really did put our balance of payments into an untenable position and confronted us with this very difficult choice of either getting up the domestic level of interest rates, which was contrary to the requirements of the domestic economy, or trying to deal directly with the balance-of-payments situation through import restrictions, or through exchange adjustment of some sort, including the possibility of a floating exchange rate.

Then I had to make the argument why the United States was making a mistake in its own interests in this policy; why it was misconceiving the problem. The argument ran this way: that it was wrong for the United States to consider their payments position with Canada as imposing any burden on them. It was true that the United States was a large net exporter of capital to Canada. However, their net export of goods and services to Canada were even larger than their net export of capital to Canada. Or, if you want to look at that the other way, in order to pay for our current account deficit with the United States, we had to use, not only all the capital that we imported from the United States, but all the money that we earned in third countries as well, such as Britain or continental Europe with which we had an export surplus, and all the capital that we imported from those countries. So that in fact, if you look, not at the capital account alone, but at the whole balance of payments, the United States gained foreign exchange as a result of the totality of its transactions with Canada.

I developed this at greater length than I've done now. I also pointed out various ways in which Canada had been helpful to the United States in trying to manage and her attempts to manage her own exchange problems. I'll mention one. Part of the American problem at the time was their short-term liabilities to foreigners, which were a claim on gold because they were at this time, theoretically, on a gold convertible standard. Anybody holding a short-term claim in the United States, certainly any central bank or treasury, was under their law free to go and ask for gold. The total of these short-term liabilities was far in excess of their total of gold holdings, so they were always very concerned about their gold position.

Well, we had never made any claims on the United States for gold when we were accumulating reserves, and, in fact, we allowed the proportion of gold in our reserve to run down from about 50 or 60 percent to about 15 percent. We did this without any discussion with the United States, but we knew in the situation that they were in that for us to claim gold from them would be a burdensome thing so far as they were concerned.

Dillon said that I'd made a very strong case and had raised some matters that they perhaps hadn't paid as much attention to as they might have. He was concerned, however, with anything that was discriminatory against other countries. He was concerned with making a special exception for Canada that wouldn't be applied elsewhere. Roosa took that up and he said, "You don't want to increase your exchange reserves; tell us how much you need to borrow in the United States, and we will give you a quota for whatever amount you think is reasonable."

On the face of it, that was a rather forthcoming suggestion, but I said that I didn't really think that that would meet our case for two reasons. One, the principal Canadian borrowers in the United States were provinces, and, two, the government of Canada would be in a position of having to dole out a limited amount of access to the American capital market among the provinces. The constitutional situation and the broad political situation in Canada were such that that was a very, very difficult, perhaps even impossible, position for the government to be in. Wyn put in a very useful remark that the difficulty with a quota—the announcement of a quota—was that people would rush to get in under the wire. It might be counterproductive. We had a good deal of further discussion about this.

Finally they said that the case had been made intellectually in their opinion, but they felt that they had to have some protection against overborrowing. They made the point that has some validity to it: that the only influence was not the difference in interest rates. It isn't only because they can get the money a little cheaper in the United States market than they can get it in Canada, but there's also the question of size. In some cases they need such large gobs of money that they can't get it anywhere but in New York. They also made the point that if they gave free access to Canada, third countries might do their borrowing in Canada, and push Canadian borrowers in the United States. So they'd be chasing the devil around a stump.

I acknowledged that there was real substance to these points. I did think that the interest rates were a major influence but one couldn't say that they were the only influence. Insofar as the second point was concerned, I said that I was sure that we could manage that. I knew that really all I would have to do would be to tell the Canadian underwriters that we didn't want them to place any foreign issues in Canada, and that would look after that. I said that I thought the way we should proceed would be to give a complete exemption to Canada, as this would be the only thing that would really convince people that our basic position was viable. To relieve them of their fears of overborrowing by Canadians, I thought we would agree that if our reserves went up very materially, the two governments would have something to talk about.

That is the way the thing came out in the end. An agreement was drafted which gave us exemption and which indicated that it was the expectation and desire of the Canadian authorities that the amounts borrowed in the United States would not result in any appreciable increase in Canadian exchange reserves from their existing level.

The agreement took seven or eight hours of intense negotiation, spread over Saturday night and Sunday morning, and afterward Lou Rasminsky was exhausted but exhilarated by success. Walter Gordon was greatly relieved, and Prime Minister Pearson expressed his thanks to the governor

British statesman
Malcolm MacDonald,
who was high
commissioner to Canada
during World War Two.
(*Photo by Julie Hamilton,
courtesy Malcolm
MacDonald*)

Sir Alex Douglas Home (Lord Home), prime minister of Britain in 1963–64,
inspects pipers during his visit to Ottawa in February 1964. (*Public Archives
Canada PA 113494*)

Canadian diplomat Arnold Smith in August 1965, when he was secretary-general of the Commonwealth. (*Public Archives Canada PA 113499*)

Canadian diplomat Charles Ritchie in 1952. After serving as a representative to the UN for four years he was appointed ambassador to the United States in 1962. (*Public Archives Canada PA 113491*)

Prime Minister Pearson meets with President Lyndon Johnson at the White House during a January 1964 conference that ended with the signing of the final agreements for development of the Columbia River Basin. (*Wide World Photo*)

William P. Bundy, now editor of *Foreign Affairs* Magazine, was U.S. Assistant Secretary of State for East Asian and Pacific Affairs, 1964–69. (*Photo by Jean Raeburn, N.Y.*)

Walter Gordon (center) with Patrick Watson (left) and Laurier Lapierre during an interview for the CBC TV show, "This Hour Has Seven Days," in May 1966. (*Public Archives Canada PA 113492*)

Léo Cadieu (left) with Pearson and Paul Hellyer outside Government House, where Cadieu was being sworn in as Minister of Defence, September 1967. (*Public Archives Canada PA 113497*)

In December 1968 Mitchell Sharp and Louis Rasminsky, attended a ceremony at Government House, where Rasminsky, governor of the Bank of Canada at the time, received an award. (*Public Archives Canada PA 113498*)

Canadian diplomat Chester Ronning, envoy to China, 1945–51, with Peter Stursberg (center) and Chinese guide, at the Shanghai Industrial Exhibition during a visit to the People's Republic of China, May 1971. (*Courtesy Peter Stursberg*)

Son Geoffrey Pearson, Maryon Pearson, Lester Pearson, and daughter Patricia Hannah, taken at the prime minister's residence in April 1967. (*Capital Press Photo, courtesy Geoffrey Pearson*)

of the Bank of Canada in the House of Commons. Rasminsky doubted if the agreement were due to any particular skill of negotiation on his part. The trouble with Canadian-American relations, he said, was that the United States was so important "that it's always on our mind," whereas Canada was only one of American concerns and was seldom on their minds. The trick was to get the top people of the United States to concentrate on the Canadian problem for a short time, and that was how the agreement was reached.

9 Vietnam War: the Speech

AMONG THE INTERNATIONAL *issues that the new Pearson government inherited from its predecessor in office were the Columbia River power and water project and disarmament. They were in the nature of unfinished business, although a Columbia River treaty had been worked out by one of Diefenbaker's ministers, Davie Fulton, after protracted negotiations, except for agreement on price; but disarmament was certainly an ongoing affair. In fact, the disarmament conference, whether held in Geneva or elsewhere, had become a permanent feature of the diplomatic scene: the delegates came and went like members of a Greek chorus crying doom and havoc, and the negotiating committees varied in size, expanding and even contracting as if trying to find the magic number for success but failing to do so. There were peripheral agreements reached, such as a hot line connecting the heads of the two superpowers and a nuclear test ban treaty, but in all this time, in the quarter-century since the war, the world's armaments had not been reduced by a single rifle.*

Before tackling disarmament Paul Martin, whom Lester Pearson made his external affairs minister, had to arrange for some important rearmament. He had to negotiate with the Americans for the storage of nuclear warheads on Canadian soil, which was the fulfillment of a Liberal election promise. Perhaps because they did not want to appear to be too closely tied to the Kennedy administration, Martin and his officials took their time about reaching an agreement. It was really just a technical arrangement, there was no policy involved, but they took six months

194

before they were ready to sign, which was a matter of some annoyance to the U. S. representatives.

There was no doubt that Howard Green, the Conservative external affairs minister, had seen disarmament as the main international issue. He was very much against above-ground nuclear tests, which were being conducted by both the Americans and the Russians at the time, because, he said, Canada was in one of the worst fall-out zones in the world. Beyond that, there was the danger of nuclear war itself, and Green was certain that, in the event of another holocaust, Canada would be the main battleground. It had been the Conservative external affairs minister who appointed General E. L. M. Burns, the commander of the United Nations Emergency Force, to be the government's adviser on disarmament and its chief negotiator, at the end of 1959. Howard Green had a great admiration for General Burns and felt that he did a magnificent job.

As for Canadian policy on disarmament, General Burns found that everyone in Parliament and in the country was in favor of reducing the number of weapons in the world: it was like motherhood. When he was appointed disarmament adviser, he submitted a draft of what he though Canadian policy should be, and eventually got the approval of Prime Minister Diefenbaker and the Conservative Cabinet. Generally speaking, the principles of this policy were that Canada was in favor of all measures of disarmament but that "we shouldn't give things up, or NATO shouldn't give things up, if the Soviet Union did not make a fair response."

When Pearson became prime minister, General Burns was continued in office as the government's disarmament adviser and negotiator.

GENERAL E. L. M. BURNS

I remember meeting him in London shortly after the government under him had been formed. He had become prime minister. He was there on some mission to see the British and I came over from Geneva to see him on instructions. He told me that the policies on disarmament were going to be continued just the same as they had been under Mr. Green. He said, "We're just as much in favor of disarmament, although we're not as optimistic as Howard."

I think this probably goes back to his experiences with the disarmament meetings under the League of Nations in 1932 and prior to that the London Conference on naval disarmament. The question at that time apparently was whether a weapon is offensive or defensive, and Mr. Pearson was at one of the meetings of the more junior members of the delegations at the very famous Bavaria Restaurant in Geneva and solved the matter by saying, "The calibers don't matter; if you're in front of it, it's offensive and if you're behind it, it's defensive."

HOWARD GREEN

In my first year [as external affairs minister] our main resolution before the General Assembly that year had to do with collecting information about radiation, strengthening the [United Nations] committee that was doing this sort of work. We got a resolution through to that effect. Then that led on to the testing and then to the question of the spread of nuclear weapons and so on—and to disarmament, although nobody expected total disarmament. It was really a question of cutting down on armaments, reducing armaments, and not getting more damaging armaments, which, by the way, has been going on ever since and is still going on today. I mean they're getting worse and worse all the time. So, as I saw it, this was the main problem for Canada in foreign affairs, and we concentrated on that very strongly. We were very fortunate in having General Burns as our adviser on this nuclear question.

The United States had a great deal of difficulty coming up with an agreed disarmament policy. There were so many contending interests, such as the Pentagon, the Senate, and the State Department, that the president himself had to be careful what he said. Howard Green recalled that after a meeting in the White House, President Kennedy accompanied him to the cloakroom and as he was putting on his coat and was about to leave, he whispered in his ear, "I want you to know, Mr. Green, that I'm going to do all I can on the question of disarmament." The external affairs minister wondered whether Kennedy was afraid to say this to him in the room where they had been talking in case it was bugged. Henry Cabot Lodge complained that, at a disarmament conference he attended in London, there was more disagreement within the United States delegation than with the Russians.

HENRY CABOT LODGE

I gradually concluded that we in the U. S. government were not well organized. At the end of each day we would meet at the American Embassy and have arguments between those of us who represented the State Department and those of us who represented the Atomic Energy Commission and those of us who represented the Pentagon. I told President Eisenhower, when I got back to Washington, that the U. S. government wasn't effectively organized at the disarmament talks. He appointed Harold Stassen to pull that whole thing together and Stassen did an excellent job and pulled it together and laid the foundation for the Disarmament and Arms Control agency, which [Paul] Warnke is the head of now. The result of Stassen's work was that today we do get a U. S. point of view. It's good for *us* to have a U. S. point of view and it's good for *other* countries to know what the U. S. point of view is.

The conference that Henry Cabot Lodge attended in the early Fifties was between Britain, France, the United States, and the Soviet Union, and its purpose was to revive the disarmament talks that had been suspended during the Korean War. There was a debate in the United Nations General Assembly, when Lester Pearson was president, on resuming the work of the disarmament committee or subcommittee, and, after some argument and delay, this was done in 1953, except that the subcommittee, instead of consisting of the Big Four, had five members, Britain, France, the United States, the USSR and Canada.

But what was Canada doing in such august company? The reporters covering the United Nations were told that Canada was included as a nuclear power, at the time the only other nuclear power outside the Big Four—the Canadians had chosen not to make the bomb although they had the capacity to do so. However, Paul Martin, who was the Canadian representative at these disarmament talks, maintained that Canada was there representing "the nations who were not in the Big Four"; it was Brazil, he said, who proposed Canada as the representative of the rest of the United Nations members (non-Communist), and there was general support for this. The fact that Canada was compromised by being a member of NATO was not taken into consideration by either Martin or Pearson, who seemed anxious to be recognized as belonging to the nuclear club.

This disarmament committee was a Cold War charade. There was never really any intention of negotiating, and its meetings were a propaganda exercise, meant to impress a war-weary world that something was being done about the awful array of nuclear weapons. The United States seemed to suffer from the illusion that progress could be made toward disarmament by a majority vote, and Lodge argued that, in any case, the support of the British, French, and Canadian delegates for the United States proposals made the Americans out to be the good guys, whereas Soviet opposition to the majority view made the Russians out to be the bad guys; but that did not work because the four were constantly talking to the one, which made the Soviet delegate look like the most important person at the conference table. What was extraordinary was that this exercise in complete futility went on for three years until even an optimist like Paul Martin was to say that it had become "ridiculous to keep on going this way."

So the committee of five reported failure to the General Assembly, and, after a decent interval of a couple of years, the United Nations doubled the number of participants and moved the venue of the disarmament talks from the United Nations headquarters in New York to Geneva. The committee of ten was a much more realistic negotiating group because it represented the opposing alliances: there were five from the North Atlantic Treaty Organization and five from the Warsaw Pact; Canada continued as a member of the committee, only now the Canadian delegate sat opposite the delegate of Rumania or Bulgaria at the conference table. However, this enlarged committee representing the two great military blocs did not last for long; it broke up, according to General Burns, in July of 1960 "because of disagreements arising, nominally at any rate, out of the U-2 incident" (the American spy plane that was shot down over the Soviet Union).

For a while there was sort of a hiatus, as General Burns described it, but in 1962 the disarmament talks were started up again in Geneva. The committee was expanded to eighteen members by the simple expedient of adding eight neutral nations, including India and Egypt, to the ten representing NATO and the Warsaw Pact. The Asian-African group in the United Nations had long complained that the question of disarmament should not be left to the nuclear powers and their allies, that the people of the Third World should be allowed to have their say. It was evident that there was a certain cachet about taking part in the Geneva talks, and no nation would agree to being dropped from the negotiating committee.

However, the larger it grew, with more delegates wanting their say, the less chance there was of negotiating and the more it became a forum for moralizing and speech-making.

Still, the committee of eighteen was the most durable of all the disarmament committees; it met on and off throughout most of the Sixties, from 1962 till the end of 1968, when General Burns, who was well over seventy then, retired. In 1969 the committee was expanded again, to twenty-six members: there were so many more nations who wanted to join in the disarmament talks, but not the one country that counted: the People's Republic of China refused to participate. Later the committee was expanded still further, but by 1969 it had lost all meaning as a negotiating body, and, in any case, the United States and the Soviet Union had withdrawn the question of nuclear weapons from the Geneva agenda and transferred it to their own two-member Strategic Arms Limitation Talks (SALT). So, it could be said that the disarmament committee, after expanding from four members to twenty-six, had its bubble pricked and was reduced to the two representatives of the superpowers in the ultimate negotiating stance.

General Burns summed up what the disarmament talks achieved in the decade that he was adviser on disarmament and the chief Canadian negotiator.

GENERAL E.L.M. BURNS

First of all, there was the hot line established between the Americans and the Russians which was intended to avert any misunderstandings that occurred at various times, such as the Suez Crisis. That was in 1962. Then there was an agreement not to put nuclear weapons into outer space. That was proposed by Mr. Green and he got ahead of the Americans with it, and they were a little annoyed. I believe when he came back to Ottawa he was asked, "It is understood that the Americans weren't exactly pleased with some of your initiatives there," and he said, "We didn't go to Geneva to please the Americans."

Next, there was the partial nuclear test ban treaty; that is to say, tests were banned in the sea and in the atmosphere and in outer space, but not underground. That was in 1963. It was signed in Moscow in August 1963.

Lastly, the nonproliferation treaty, which was the main thing and which took a good deal of working out. That was eventually approved by the United Nations General Assembly in 1968, but it didn't come into effect until a certain number had signed, which I think was 1971. The nonproliferation treaty was intended to prevent there becoming an increased number of nuclear powers— that is, countries that had made the nuclear weapon and under their own authority could set it off and use it as a weapon of war. That has not happened up to the present time except in the case of India. There were the original five nuclear powers: United States, the Soviet Union, United Kingdom, France, and then China. They are the five permanent members of the Security Council, strangely enough. And then the Indians, who had been maneuvering to keep their option open during the discussion of the nonproliferation treaty and had been denouncing it as discriminatory, set off what they called a peaceful nuclear explosion. The trouble is that while all these minor steps were being taken, the great powers were building up their nuclear arsenals so that they are now bigger and better than ever.

Although Lester Pearson told General Burns that he and his government were just as much in favor of disarmament as his predecessors in office, he showed very little interest in the subject. This may have been due to his diplomatic sense that nothing much would come out of the Geneva talks; there was also the fact that he knew that disarmament would never cause him any trouble in Parliament. Whenever General Burns made a progress report, as he had to do on occasion, although he said that there was usually very little progress to report, no one criticized him. No member said, "This report is a lot of nonsense—you're getting nowhere." On one occasion, when he was in Ottawa, the prime minister asked to see him and told him that he had read his book, Megamurder. Pearson said that his wife Maryon was very disappointed in it because she thought that it was a murder mystery. Paul Martin came into the prime minister's office, and Pearson pulled his leg about his not having read the book. General Burns could not recall Prime Minister Pearson going into any great detail on the question of disarmament.

When Paul Martin became external affairs minister, he took the same attitude as the prime minister: he left matters in the hands of the government's adviser, General Burns, and spent little time at the disarmament talks.

PAUL MARTIN

It was my view that once the [disarmament] committee had begun, that we must continue [that there must be no pulling out]. I went to the Disarmament Committee twice myself in Tommy Burns's time and took part in the discussions. I moved at one time that the Foreign Ministers should attend and take part in the discussions at least once a year to show earnest and good faith, but we weren't able to succeed in that move. The Russians didn't want that. Tsarapkin was the representative of the Soviet Union at that time and I remember once he said to me, "You know perfectly well I can't support that." I said, "Why?" "Well," he said, "Gromyko doesn't like the food in Geneva."

As for the Columbia River project, it was unfinished business in the sense that while the treaty had been signed by the Diefenbaker government in 1961, it had not been ratified by Parliament. It was one of the opportunities that Lester Pearson seized on, when leader of the Opposition, to cut the Conservatives down, as he put it, since the treaty was opposed by the Social Credit government of British Columbia. At the Hyannis Port meeting in May of 1963, shortly after he was sworn in as prime minister, Pearson told President Kennedy that changes in the treaty would have to be made. This was one thing that disturbed Kennedy, according to Paul Martin, since the treaty had been ratified by the Senate of the United States; the president did not want to send it back to that body because there would be a protracted discussion that might result in no deal at all. The only way around would be to have a protocol to the treaty which could come into effect by executive order, and it was agreed that this was the method to be used.

There had been discussions on harnessing the Columbia ever since World War Two. It was recognized by all concerned that this river, while not the greatest in North America, had the greatest power potential because of a drop of almost three thousand feet from its source in the Rocky Mountains to the sea at Astoria, Oregon—there were estimates that the Columbia had the power potential of five times the St. Lawrence Seaway. Furthermore, the waters of this twelve-hundred-mile-long river needed to be controlled to prevent flooding in the spring and to provide a steady flow for the Grand Coulee Dam and other power purposes, as well as for irrigation; however, there was little storage space in the United States because of the high level of development, while there was little need for irrigation in British Columbia. So it was a joint Canadian-American problem.

When General A. G. L. McNaughton, the World War Two army commander, became Canadian chairman of the International Joint Commission in 1950, his first task was to overcome the impasse that had developed between the Canadian and American governments over the building of the St. Lawrence Seaway. After long-drawn-out negotiations, he was able to clear the obstacles away so that Lester Pearson, as external affairs minister, could reach an agreement with the United States on August 17, 1954, and construction could begin; it was a mutually satisfactory agreement, and the notes exchanged at the time made it clear that Canada would have the right to build an all-Canadian seaway when the need for parallel works arose. This pleased General McNaughton, who was a great fighter for Canadian rights, as he had shown as army commander.

Once the St. Lawrence Seaway project was settled, the general turned his attention to the Columbia River. For the optimum development of this waterway, he wanted all the major dams to be built in British Columbia, with the Americans footing the bill by paying for the downstream benefits that they would get from the storage and flood-control measures taken in the upper and Canadian part of the river. While the Americans agreed to the concept of being charged for the downstream benefits, they insisted on building the Libby Dam in Montana, which they had wanted to do for a long time. The Diefenbaker government, under the prodding of Premier W. A. C. Bennett of British Columbia who wanted to get on at all costs, agreed to the American proposition, much to General McNaughton's chagrin. Ernest Côté, who had left the foreign service to become assistant deputy minister of northern affairs and natural resources, took part in the negotiations on the Columbia River.

ERNEST CÔTÉ

With the Libby Dam being established in the U.S.A., we only got about, say, 85 percent of the optimum benefits. This is what hurt General McNaughton. He wanted 100 percent. He fell out with the government of the day on a couple of occasions, with both the Liberals and the Conservatives. On reflection, I think that if somebody had had the wisdom and the wit and the ability to persuade Premier Bennett to call one lake McNaughton Lake, that would have settled the issue. At least it would have been a balm for General McNaughton; it would have salved the wound, because there was a wound there. But eventually it worked out to be quite a satisfactory system. There are problems and concerns always. The issue always is: are we getting the best we can for Canada, under given circumstances? And as far as I could see, we did get the maximum benefits obtainable at the time from the Americans. If we had waited for twenty-five years, maybe we might have got more benefits, but in the meantime we would have wasted the benefits that could have accrued to British Columbia.

At one stage I think that General McNaughton wanted to use the Fraser River diversion as a possible [alternative]. This had been initially suggested by the British Columbians, but when they looked into it, it wasn't entirely feasible because of geological faults and other [factors], but I think that General McNaughton wanted to persist in using this Fraser River diversion as a bargaining club because he was intent on getting 100 percent of the optimum benefits.

While Prime Minister Pearson said in his memoirs that the treaty, in the form that the Diefenbaker government signed, was too favorable to the United States, Paul Martin put his emphasis on the fact that there was no agreement between Canada and British Columbia on the question of price. Pearson felt that there should be an alteration in the time schedule, that the construction of the Mica Creek dam or the Arrow Lakes dam — the two that were to be built in Canada — should be postponed, and that the price of downstream power should be established in the treaty before ratification. The prime minister knew that the Conservative government had suffered from the fact that British Columbia ministers had carried on the negotiations with the British Columbia government: Davie Fulton appeared to be more conciliatory in his dealings with his provincial counterparts, but Howard Green was less accommodating as far as Premier Bennett was concerned, possibly for domestic political reasons. Pearson, therefore, insisted that Paul Martin do the negotiating, not Arthur Laing, who was his senior minister from British Columbia.

There were charges that Canada had sold out, that the treaty, as revised, was "nothing short of a fiasco," and that it failed to procure any advantage whatsoever for the people of Canada.

PAUL MARTIN

What we negotiated with British Columbia was a *sine qua non*, something that Fulton or Diefenbaker or Howard Green had not done. There was no agreement whatsoever with British Columbia, the owner of the resource. My negotiation with British Columbia was almost as extensive as the negotiation with the United States afterward. However, after a lot of discussion, we finally got an agreement with British Columbia and negotiated with Mr. [R. W.] Bonner, Mr. Bennett, and Mr. [Ray] Williston, the minister of lands and forests, and we finally got an agreement as to what the price should be. That price on the basis of the value of the dollar at that time would provide for the building of all of the dams and the result would be perhaps the cheapest electric power open to any segment in Canada. That's one of the cheapest sources of electric power anywhere in the world, and that is still the case in spite of the inflated cost.

I think we made a good deal on the price; had we known that inflation was going to reach its present dimensions, we could have taken care of that; we didn't. But the dams are there; the great electric development that is taking place in British Columbia has been made possible by the Columbia agreement, as well as the Peace River project, which was a provincial project of its own.

I know there are those who say we sold water—valuable water—to the United States. Of course we did. But that water was on its way to the sea. Canada lost nothing. British Columbia lost nothing by making an agreement, a limited agreement, for a period with the United States. As a result it was able to build dams that are going to give British Columbia a preferred position in the market for the sale of electric energy. I know the NDP particularly complained about the sale of a resource. Of course it was the sale of a resource. But it was a resource that had been for years flowing into the sea lost to anyone, and I don't think the mighty Columbia is servicing Canada or British Columbia any less today because of that agreement. I think it was a good agreement.

ERNEST CÔTÉ

But, you know, everything that's renegotiated by hindsight can always be so much more readily realized and achieved and a better deal obtained. But in the circumstances of the day, this was a relatively new theory of downstream benefits and paying for same. If Canada had not entered into any negotiations with the Americans and had decided to do Mica Creek dam on its own, there would be no benefits in return to Canada. And the Americans would still get the water in a regulated fashion. The same thing with Arrow Lakes dam. They'd get the regulated water. Now, maybe not entirely regulated the way they'd want, but there'd be prevention of flood damage and they'd get a regular flow which then they could use. So, I mean, there's a time when you can do things.

In September 1964 Prime Minister Pearson and President Johnson attended a ceremony marking the formal ratification of the Columbia River Treaty at Great Falls, Montana. Afterward, Pearson took the presidential party, which included a number of American senators, on a helicopter tour of the Canadian side of this great project, and he was astonished at the earthy and intimate way in which Lyndon Johnson and the senators discussed domestic politics before a comparative stranger. The ratification ceremony was repeated in Vancouver where Premier Bennett joined them on the platform, and Pearson noted in his memoirs that "while I was the head of the Canadian government and Mr. Johnson was the head of the American government, in British Columbia, Mr. Bennett was the head of all he surveyed." Altogether, a good time seemed to be had by all, and Mike got along well with LBJ.

However, it was a very different matter at Camp David the following spring when President Johnson angrily denounced Prime Minister Pearson for calling on the United States to stop the bombing of North Vietnam in a speech he made at Temple University, Philadelphia. Pearson wrote in his diary about this meeting: "If there had not been a kind of 'et tu Brute' feeling about the assault, without any personal unpleasantness of any kind, I would have felt almost like Schuschnigg before Hitler at Berchtesgaden!"

At no time did Lester Pearson hide his concern about Vietnam, his feeling that this was a dangerous, if not disastrous, place for the Americans to take a stand against Asian communism. He told John Foster Dulles as much when the Republican secretary of state was considering some way of helping the French after their defeat at Dien Bien Phu; he got Prime Minister St. Laurent to pass on this warning to President Eisenhower. The reason for his concern about Vietnam, which became almost an obsession with him, was the experience of the Korean War: as his son Geoffrey said, he was afraid that it could be the spark that would set off World War Three, and he was not at ease until the armistice had been signed at Panmunjon. Furthermore, Pearson could not understand how the Americans, after all they had told him about the Korean War— that it was the wrong war in the wrong place at the wrong time and that never again would they fight on the Asian mainland—could become involved in Vietnam. He wondered aloud if they ever learned. At Hyannisport, just after he was sworn in as prime minister, Pearson cautioned President Kennedy about Vietnam, and after the assassination he spoke to President Johnson in the same vein.

PAUL MARTIN

Pearson thought that the [Vietnam] war was a tragedy. He had played a part, in the days of President Eisenhower when Foster Dulles was secretary of state, in inducing the American government not to get involved in Vietnam. Foster Dulles had been seriously thinking after Dien Bien Phu of doing something there to arrest Communist progress. Anthony Eden and Pearson thought that it would be very dangerous for the Americans to get in. I remember very well when Mr. St. Laurent called Eisenhower. I happened to be at 24 Sussex when he called Eisenhower, on Pearson's strong recommendation, to tell him how dangerous it would be to get into a conflict in faraway Asia. And Eisenhower gave Mr. St. Laurent the strongest assurance that that was not going to happen. And so I mention that incident simply to show that Pearson was opposed to that kind of an intervention in Vietnam from the beginning.

Of course, the Americans got into this almost clandestinely, quietly. When we were in opposition, I went to a meeting at Pearson's instance, at the Aspen [Colorado] Institute of Higher Learning. Bob McNamara and Walt Rostow were there. But they had no supporters. We thought—all of us who were at that meeting, and most of us were Americans—that the United States was getting into a very dangerous position. This was the period when Kennedy was sending in the so-called "military advisers," some fifteen or sixteen thousand. Well, I know Pearson at that time thought that it was a mistake for Kennedy to even do what he was being advised to do and that was when the thing really began. I don't want to argue that Kennedy was responsible for the tragedy, but he must accept a good bit of the responsibility. I think Eisenhower is clearly exempt from any of it.

When Lester Pearson went to Hyannis Port in May 1963 President Kennedy was obviously worried about Vietnam, as Pearson put it in his memoirs, and he quoted Kennedy as stating that Vietnam was "the very place that we should not like to be. But how do we get out of there?" Pearson does not say whether he gave the president any advice or offered any suggestions, but the impression is left that if Kennedy had lived, he would have got the United States out of Vietnam—or at least tried to do so.

WILLIAM P. BUNDY

That's a very tangled issue. I would think it a mistake for anybody to attempt to untangle anything on the basis of either that individual remark or other individual remarks by Kennedy in the spring and summer or fall of 1963.

We've had a considerable controversy in the United States on the question, triggered in the first instance by an article in *Life* by Kenneth O'Donnell about six or eight years ago, saying that Kennedy had told him in late May or June of '63, that he was going to see that we got out of Vietnam right after the 1964 election, in some fashion. I accept the account of those quotations at least for this purpose. Similar quotations have been adduced by Senator Mansfield from the same time period. The point about those quotations is that they can only be judged in the context of the evaluation of the situation that prevailed in Washington at that time. I don't think there's any doubt that Kennedy wanted to reduce the American role if this was possible, consistent with the survival of a non-Communist South Vietnam.

And in the spring of 1963 there was a good deal of optimism, which later proved to be quite false but which was nonetheless widely held at the top levels in Washington—held by people like Sir Robert Thompson, who reported personally to Kennedy and at just about the same month of April or early May 1963. There was a lot of feeling that things were now going well, that the Strategic Hamlet Program and the American advisory effort were on the right track, and that in another year or two it should be possible to reduce the American effort, consistent with the objective of preserving South Vietnam from being taken over by guerrilla action, subversion, and military force, from the North.

What you have to set against that is that when Kennedy came to the first crunch in the fall of 1963, from August onward, specifically when Kennedy spoke on the inaugural nightly news program of one of the television networks in early September, and was asked what he thought of the "Domino Theory" and gave the most categorical judgment that he ever gave on that particular subject, you were seeing in effect the other side of the coin. One can speculate as to whether he thought the original degree of commitment was wise or unwise, but he certainly took the Chinese threat to the whole of southeast Asia very seriously, although he never supposed that the North Vietnamese were the puppets of Peking or anything of the sort—none of those simplistic views that are sometimes used by critics without looking carefully at the record.

There's no doubt that Kennedy felt that we were by then in a situation where it was extraordinarily hard for us to pull out, and all the hindsight critics here say, "Wouldn't it have been a wonderful occasion to pull out, when Diem got into his trouble in the fall of 1963?" The fact is that except for one stray mention by Robert Kennedy at a meeting, which was not apparently followed up in any way, I can't either as participant or as a later reader of all the records find any clear evidence that anybody thought seriously of withdrawal in the face of these political difficulties.

AVERELL HARRIMAN

I know that he thought before he died—we had fifty-thousand troops there—that we had too much, too big a commitment, and I'm utterly convinced—Arthur Schlesinger agrees with me—that he never would have become as involved as President Johnson. He would have found a way to reduce our commitment because he already thought we were too much committed when we had only fifteen thousand men, so I'm quite convinced that Mr. Pearson was right on that, that never should we have become so involved.

It was unfortunate that President Johnson was told that no American president lost a war and that was a challenge to him. Historically that's hardly true but, at the same time, he didn't understand what the issues were and there were several people around him who were advising him that he ought to see it through. It was a great tragedy because President Johnson's domestic policies were very advanced and he got through more social legislation, civil rights legislation, health legislation—the unfinished business of the New Deal and some of his own—and he would have been a great president if it hadn't been for that unhappy war.

Roosevelt, you know, did not want to let the French back into Indochina, and, in fact, I was with him when he talked to Stalin about that. He wanted Stalin's agreement to establish a United Nations trusteeship, which never worked out, of course—he wanted a trusteeship for Korea and a trusteeship for Vietnam. However, the British had a separate agreement with the Japanese in the southern half of Vietnam and they wanted to turn it over to the French and they did.

Unfortunately, we helped the French. I was opposed. When I was in charge of the Marshall Plan in Paris I sent a telegram urging that they not help the French in Indochina because I felt and still believe that it was unwise for them to try to hold their position in Indochina. I didn't think they could do it. It's unfortunate that Roosevelt's wisdom in not letting the French back into Indochina was not followed with friendship. Vietnam was desperately expensive and an unhappy affair.

At no time was there any genuine consultation on Vietnam. The United States made no real effort to discuss the situation there with Britain and France, or its other NATO allies, and find out what they thought of the use of the U. S. armed forces, including the B-52 bombers, in Indochina. The American attitude seemed to be that the "free world," as it was described, should follow the United States leadership in the struggle against Communist aggression. In any case, at the beginning of the Vietnam involvement, the Americans were not looking for support from

*anyone. Lester Pearson's advice was never really sought, according to his
son Geoffrey, not even by his good friend, President Kennedy. There was
optimism in Washington, and people were told that the war would be over
next month, next year, soon.*

*It was only when the casualties started to mount, and the United States
forces got bogged down in the quagmire of Indochina, that the Americans
began to feel that they had been deserted by their friends and allies and that
they were the only ones who were upholding the principles of collective
security. And at what a cost! As a member of the Indochina Commissions,
Canada could not be expected to take sides, but this did not impress the
secretary of state, Dean Rusk, although he did not blame Canada as much
as Britain and France and the other members of SEATO, the Southeast
Asia Treaty Organization; they had really let the United States down
over Vietnam. There was a widening gap between the United States, the
acknowledged leader of the Western World, and its friends and allies; it
was a gap of understanding, credibility, and confidence.*

PAUL MARTIN

I was in continuous contact with Rusk, and there was no
mistake what our position was, and Rusk knew it. On one
occasion when he introduced me to Willy Brandt, he said, "I'd
like you to meet our satellite foreign minister, Paul Martin," and
then he laughed and said, "That'll be the day!" Well, there wasn't
any doubt about that. Canada was the only one, through me, in
the NATO Council of Foreign Ministers that expressed opposition to what was going on in Vietnam. All the other foreign
ministers, not one, not one in the whole time that I was foreign
minister, ever criticized American policy in Vietnam. We did. We
criticized in the sense that we thought it was a dangerous venture
and we wanted them to know how we felt.

DEAN RUSK

I don't want to go over this Vietnam story because this is all on
the public record. But on these matters Canada had a free ride.
Whatever happened in the Pacific, Canada wasn't going to do
anything about it, and Canada was safe on its western front
because the United States is here. So they didn't really have the

same involvement and engagement with the consequences. Now, I don't know if there are people in Canada these days who are clapping their hands over what has happened in Vietnam, Cambodia, and Laos, but these are things that we at that time anticipated and were trying to prevent.

There was another element. My generation of students came out of World War Two deeply committed to an idea that security was the key to the prevention of World War Three. We had written Article 1 of the United Nations Charter and we reinforced it with certain security treaties, NATO, and NORAD in this hemisphere, certain treaties across the Pacific.

The idea of collective security has deeply eroded since the end of World War Two. I can understand how that could be true among the American people. We have taken over six hundred thousand casualties and wounded since the end of World War Two in the name of collective security and it hasn't been very collective. We put up 90 percent of the non-Korean forces in Korea and 80 percent of the non-Vietnamese forces in Vietnam, so when my country cousins in Cherokee County say, "Well, look, if collective security is going to cost us fifty thousand dead every ten years and it's not even collective, maybe it's not a very good idea," I have profound respect for that reaction. What concerns me is that we are not addressing ourselves to the question that, if not collective security, then what? Because we still have with us the problem of how you prevent World War Three, because if that war comes, forget it. There's nothing left.

PAUL MARTIN

At the same time this [Vietnam] was going on, I was carrying on some discussions with Rusk about recognition of China. I said that we were going to move very soon to change our policy in China. We were going to move to bring China into the UN, followed by an exchange of diplomatic missions, and I urged him to do the same. He begged us not to proceed, but I told him we were going to, that this was an inevitable and desirable thing to do, and he begged us to wait until the war in Vietnam was over. And I said, "My God, the way you fellows are going now, it will go on forever." He said, no—this was in 1964, in the fall of '64—

he said this will be over very soon. That's how impractical their view of the whole concept was.

CHARLES RITCHIE

I saw Rusk regularly. He never refused to see me or anything like that. I saw Bundy every week, often twice a week, Mac Bundy who was the head of the White House Secretariat and Bill Bundy, of course, in the State Department. So there was no lack of access and no lack of friendliness. But there was no consultation. We went in to see Rusk and put certain Canadian concerns, shall I say, suggestions. He listened with great politeness, but he never picked up the suggestions really to rebut them or accept them. There was never any interchange. And this was very, very thwarting because it went with perfect politeness up to that point. Of course, I was not the only ambassador who received this treatment. There used to be meetings with other ambassadors for briefings on Vietnam, but so far as I know, their government's advice was not sought by Washington. Suggestions were allowed just to fall and that was very frustrating.

DEAN RUSK

Under the SEATO treaty we had a commitment, in the words of the treaty, "to take action to meet the common danger." Now, Britain, France, Pakistan, who were also signatories to that treaty—Canada was not—did Britain, France, Pakistan "take steps to meet the common danger" in Southeast Asia? You would have to strain the language to its utmost to pretend that they did. So we thought at the time that basic decisions were made in Vietnam that the stakes went far beyond Vietnam and far beyond Southeast Asia into the real structure of collective security in other areas. If we had done nothing to help Vietnam, President Charles de Gaulle would have been the first to say, "You see, I told you, you cannot rely upon the United States." Suppose people like Khrushchev had believed President de Gaulle when he said that— so these were much more serious issues for us than I think they looked to be in Canada at the time.

*In his memoirs Lester Pearson mentions the International Control
Commissions (ICC) for Indochina only once, and that in passing. It was
clear that he had little enthusiasm for these supervisory bodies, which were
outside the umbrella of the United Nations; he kept asking his assistant in
the Department of External Affairs, John Holmes, when they were going
to be closed down. Perhaps, this was half in jest, but it was half in
earnest, too, because he was afraid that membership in the ICC would, in
the long run, only get Canada into trouble, which it did. At first, though,
the tripartite commissions—there were three of them altogether for the
three Indochina countries of Cambodia, Laos, and Vietnam—seemed to
function well enough, and there was harmony among the Polish, Indian,
and Canadian members.*

*The ICC, was set up at the 1954 Geneva Conference to supervise the
elections that were supposed to have been held following the withdrawal
of the French forces; however, the elections were not held, at least not in
Vietnam, and when fighting broke out between the American-backed
Saigon government and the Vietcong guerrillas, who were supported by
Hanoi, the Vietnam Commission, which was the most important, could
do nothing. When the struggle turned into a full-scale war between North
and South Vietnam, and involved Cambodia and Laos, the ICC should
have been disbanded. Instead, the commissions continued an uneasy
existence, and there were charges that Canadian members were engaged in
smuggling narcotics and gold, and that they were taking sides and even
spying for the Americans.*

ARNOLD SMITH

I was a member of the Cambodia Commission for about
twelve months very early on, and I thought it was the success
story of that period. Cambodia was the one place where the
elections, which had been promised in each of the three countries,
actually took place. The Poles, Indians, and ourselves agreed that
they were fair elections, and Sihanouk became prime minister. He
had abdicated earlier in a contrived crisis because he realized that
the boss was no longer going to be the king but somebody called
a prime minister. So he created a crisis and organized a political
party and ran and became prime minister.

PAUL MARTIN

When anything involving the other side was at issue, you could never count on an objective reaction by India, and the same was true of Poland. I myself went out to Vietnam in the fall of 1956 to discuss this very matter. We had thought at that time we might pull out of the commissions. Pearson was so frustrated by the action of the two other members of the commissions that he wondered why we should continue.

And when I went to Saigon, one of the purposes was to examine whether or not the time had not come when we should pull out, and there were a lot of supporting reasons for our taking that course. One of the supporting reasons was the desire of Diem that we should. He didn't like the commissions. They stood in the way of a possible pressure on him to have the elections, which by that time in 1954 it was decided at Geneva should take place. Likewise in Laos: Souvanna Phouma, the prime minister of that little country, was anxious that the commissions should dissolve, and for one of the most ridiculous of reasons: namely that [the members were] occupying housing in Vientiane that could have been usefully used by his citizens.

And that was a contributing factor in the assessment I finally made—namely, that we shouldn't give in to Diem or to Souvanna Phouma on that point and that whether or not the commissions were really functioning, it would have been destructive to the image of an international presence developing as a satisfactory organism in international affairs. And I think that that was a very important idea to see maintained.

GEOFFREY PEARSON

I think [my father] assumed from the beginning that the commissions would act more or less as a supervisory mechanism because they were set up to oversee the withdrawal of forces from both sides and to supervise elections, and that seemed like something which they could do. It gradually became clear, when there were no elections and when the fighting didn't stop, that the commissions had no real role. I think he then sort of lost interest in them until the Americans became involved, at which point he was very skeptical of our role because he assumed also that the Poles would be acting on the part of the North and India would be more or less in between, more on the side of the North because India was an Asian country, and the South was identified with the West. Canada was left, therefore, to be labeled as the American member. He didn't like that, but he accepted it because there was really nothing one could do about it except withdraw. We could have withdrawn and that was considered from time to time, but it didn't seem to be a very useful thing to do because they would have had to find someone else who would equally have been regarded as Western. Australia they would have accepted, I think.

PAUL MARTIN

It always used to surprise me when I became minister [how many Canadians returned from Vietnam as hawks]. I would often ask them, "Well, you know, you're not expressing my point of view. I don't agree with this." They did have that opinion and I think it was largely because they spent so much of their time in the South, where the American troops were to be found in the greatest numbers, where the American authorities in Vietnam were domiciled, and I think that human nature is always susceptible to the influences immediately around it. I think for that reason they developed that particular point of view.

No one ever restricted them from having their views, but they were under the greatest compulsion to follow Canadian orders, and our External Affairs people for the most part are people who are able to subordinate their private convictions to government policy. Pearson's reactions were mine. I remember when one very valuable Foreign Service Officer returned and Pearson came and joined me at lunch with this fellow, we were quite amazed at the point of view that he expressed. He was pro-American to the hilt, thought the war was a justifiable war and he was quite sincere about it. But his own work as our man on the commissions was very outstanding.

It was alleged that some of the military personnel of the Canadian component on the commissions were engaged in spying for the Americans. Gerald Clarke of the *Montreal Star*, I think, was the first to make that charge. Well, if some individuals did that— and it's not inconceivable that they did—they couldn't have really reported on very much. But if they did that, it was wrong, and it was completely unauthorized.

From the time that Lester Pearson became prime minister in April 1963, there was a steady escalation of the Vietnam conflict with an ever-increasing American participation. On the night of August 4, 1964, Secretary of State Rusk telephoned the prime minister to say that North Vietnamese torpedo boats had again attacked American destroyers sixty-five miles off the Vietnam coast and that the United States had decided to retaliate against this "unprovoked attack," but would ensure that the retaliation was, as he put it, "relevant to the provocation and to the attack." Pearson expressed the hope that the "retaliatory action taken would not be in excess of that which the circumstances required" and that it would be "limited in scope."

At the time, about all he could do, as he said, was to urge caution and moderation on the United States. But his admonitions went unheeded, and the protests that his minister of external affairs, Paul Martin, made at NATO meetings and elsewhere were contemptuously ignored; the arrogant attitude of some of the Washington officials was becoming hard to take. Then there were the frustrations of the Indochina commissions, which should have been closed down but were trying to act as impartial observers in what amounted to a civil war, and, as might have been expected, were soon accused of taking sides; the accompanying breakdown of morale in the ICC, especially in the Vietnam Commission, led to unseemly squabbles between the Canadian and Indian commissioners.

However, none of this would have prompted Mike Pearson to break the golden rule of diplomacy that, when you're a guest or a visitor in a foreign country, you don't criticize publicly the government of that country, if it had not been for the retaliatory action of the United States in bombing North Vietnam. Pearson was appalled by the American air raids. Not only was he concerned with the awful danger of carrying the war so close to the Chinese border, but he told Escott Reid that the idea of the wealthiest, most powerful nation in the world raining bombs down on a poverty-stricken little Asian country was obscene. He decided that he would have to cast aside the gentle conventions of diplomacy and speak out against the bombing so that all could hear.

It was a deliberate, carefully considered action on his part. Bruce Hutchison said that Pearson did not tell anybody about the speech, that he certainly did not tell the Cabinet. However, drafts of the speech were flying around the East Block of the Parliament Buildings, according to an external affairs official. Geoffrey Pearson certainly saw a draft, and so did Lubor Zink, the Czech-born journalist and Ottawa columnist for The

Toronto Telegram —*at least, the part of it that dealt with the bombing. Escott Reid was another who was probably consulted because he says that he encouraged Mike to give that speech; it was quite the reverse with Paul Martin, who was so upset when he read an advance copy that he threatened to resign.*

The Temple University speech, in the form that it was delivered, was certainly no clarion call for peace and a halt to the bombing; it may have been toned down because of the reactions that Pearson got to the first drafts. It contained adequate praise for the United States: "Its motives were honorable, neither mean nor imperialistic; its sacrifices have been great and they were not made to advance any selfish American interest." At the same time there was condemnation of North Vietnam for "aggression through subversion and spurious 'wars of national liberation.'" Then came the declaratory passage that was so cautiously and carefully worded that it is difficult to understand why President Johnson should take exception to it:

"There are many factors which I am not in a position to weigh. But there does appear to be at least a possibility that a suspension of such air strikes against North Vietnam, at the right time, might provide the Hanoi authorities with an opportunity, if they wish to take it, to inject some flexibility into their policy without appearing to do so as the direct result of military pressure."

GEOFFREY PEARSON

I saw the draft and I think I may have made some suggestions. I was on the side of those who believed that the Americans were following the wrong tactics. I can't remember whether I had any influence on the speech, but I think he got advice from various sources, as he always did. He never relied on one source. He always showed things to a lot of different people. I think he got conflicting advice and that's why the speech sets out on a rather tough line and then suddenly in the middle abandons that and talks about the pause.

I think the speech reflects advice given to him over different stages of the drafting so that he stuck into the middle of it some advice he got either from me or other people he had talked to. I think that's what surprised people because he always wrote and rewrote and revised speeches. He never accepted an official draft and left it untouched. He always was tinkering and rewriting and redrafting one of his own, but that speech was written for him in the department and he rewrote it.

LUBOR ZINK

He called me to his office and said, "I want you to read this and tell me what you think." So I read—it wasn't the whole speech, it was the passage on bombing. I told him what I thought and I almost begged him not to use it. He did use it.

PAUL MARTIN

Pearson sent me a copy of that speech, and I read it, and I took violent issue with it at once. My office was right next to his on the third floor [of the east block]. I went into his office and I said, "You can't make that speech! What you're doing is calling upon the president of the United States to stop the bombing. If you publicly criticize the United States like this, you're going to discount our influence in Washington and your own forever. And you must not do that." "Well," he said, "you feel very keenly." I said, "I feel so keenly about this I would be prepared to resign if you make this speech."

He and I always got along very well in our discussions. He said, "If you feel that way, this certainly worries me." I said, "I do! No one has been more violently opposed to the war in Vietnam than I have been, and you know that. You know of my talks with Rusk. You know of the position that you and I both took when we saw Johnson last year." "Well," he said, "try this out on your fellows and see what they think."

And I did. I sent the speech over to several people in the department, and the reaction was just as violent as mine. Before he left Mike said, "I'll tell you what I'll do. I won't say that I will make that [speech], but if I feel at the last minute, as the party leader and the prime minister, that I have to do this, I will."

I said, "If you do that you know the consequences." And he said, "What does that mean?" I said, "I'm going to quit! That is a dangerous thing to do. We have a lot of problems with the United States. Vietnam is only one of our many problems. We take violent issue with them, but we're not involved in the war. And if you go down to the United States, so close to Washington, and criticize the policy of the United States, the President isn't going to thank you. I criticize the United States even more violently than that, but I do it in a way that I think is calculated to be more effective. This is not going to stop the bombing. You know perfectly well there's a good chance it's going to be stopped. Why do it, why run all this risk?"

He called me from Philadelphia and he said, "I'm going to do it." I said, "If you do it, you know what's going to happen." He said, "Paul, that's why I called. Don't do anything foolish." I said, "I'm not doing anything foolish, but this is a very serious thing."

Well, he made the speech, and I was violent. And if it had been any other man but Pearson, I would have gone through with what I really wanted to do. I'm glad I didn't because resignations are sometimes done under impulse, and they're not wise. There are occasions when you should, but this was clearly not one of them. I was really beside myself, but I had a regard for him, we got along so well, and I just felt that . . .

So we let him know in no uncertain manner the next morning. He and I had a few pretty tough words on the phone. And he said, "Well, I'm going to the president now. Pray for me." I said, "Well, I'm not going to pray for you. You brought this on yourself, and it's going to be something you won't forget." I didn't know that at the time, but it was.

The occasion for the speech was Lester Pearson's acceptance on Friday, April 2, 1965, of the Temple University World Peace Award. Dick O'Hagan, the prime minister's press secretary, informed the Parliamentary Press Gallery that it was important, and that Pearson would be dealing with the bombing, so Vic Mackie, the correspondent of the Winnipeg *Free Press, decided to go to Philadelphia in the prime minister's plane; so did Lubor Zink. It was planned as a one-day trip: fly down that morning and be back that night in time for the weekend. However, as Pearson recorded in his memoirs, he had barely finished the last sentence of the speech when he was invited to lunch with President Johnson the next day at Camp David, the presidential retreat in the Catoctin Mountains.*

So, the next day, Saturday, the prime minister's party flew to

*Washington where they transferred to a couple of helicopters that took
Pearson to Camp David and deposited the newsmen in a small community outside the gates of the presidential retreat. A press headquarters had
been set up in a school building where coffee and sandwiches were
provided. The Canadian ambassador to the United States, Charles
Ritchie, accompanied the prime minister to Camp David and was present
at the lunch. There was a telephone on the table and, as Pearson noted,
President Johnson spent almost the entire time on the telephone; he
appeared to be speaking to Secretary of Defense Robert McNamara about
the latest developments in Vietnam. During the luncheon party Ritchie
talked with McGeorge Bundy, special assistant to the president for
national security and brother of William P. Bundy.*

CHARLES RITCHIE

We knew it was going to be a rather unpleasant occasion. It
could hardly fail to be. When we arrived, we sat at the luncheon
table. Mike had come separately; I remember his discussing the
Civil War battlefields and things of that sort at lunch and Lady
Bird politely replied. The president deliberately kept on telephoning to McNamara instructions to do with the war, technical
matters, military things. He was on the telephone the whole time
so that Mike could never finish a sentence. It was a very strained
lunch.

Then after lunch Mike raised the question of his speech and
said, "Perhaps you don't like the speech," or something like that,
or "I didn't think it was very much along your lines." The
president simply exploded and I don't remember his exact
words—"terrible speech" or something—and he and Mike went
onto the terrace.

Bundy and I walked around and Bundy rehearsed all over
again: Didn't I remember how he had warned me and what an
extraordinary thing it was to come down to the United States
[and say that]? What if an American had come from the United
States to Canada [and done that]? He said the same thing over and
over again. I kept on telling him, which I thought was perfectly
true, that they were very lucky to have Mike as the prime
minister of the neighboring country, and if the Americans
couldn't get on with the Canadians and Mike Pearson as a

neighbor in this troubled world, they were really going to be in for very, very much more complicated situations than this.

In the meantime the president was laying into Mike in no uncertain fashion. I didn't hear what they were saying, but, of course, afterward Mike told me. The president hardly allowed Mike to speak. It was really very disagreeable. The strange thing is that I think I felt it more than he did. When he got back to Ottawa, I rang him rather emotionally and he kept his head much more and said, "Well, after all, you know, the president had this reason and that reason. I'm going to write him a letter," which he did, a long letter, and tried to put his speech in perspective. Although he made that joke about its being like Dollfuss [sic] at Berchtesgaden, he wasn't at all trembling or emotional nor appeared to be deeply upset, but that was his sort of optimistic, resilient [self].

The presidential tirade, according to Pearson's own account, went on for about an hour before and after the press conference, which was held in the open air just outside the Camp David gates. Vic Mackie remembered that Pearson looked somewhat chastened and woebegone, and not his old jaunty self, when he came to meet the reporters; he gave noncommittal answers to a couple of questions and Johnson really took charge, with most of the newsmen being from the White House press corps. Then, the prime minister and the president returned to Camp David to continue their one-sided talk while the correspondents wrote their stories.

On the flight back to Ottawa, Mackie asked Pearson what had happened at Camp David. The prime minister said with a grin that LBJ had picked him up by the ears and shaken him. But why had he broken with tradition and diplomatic decorum to make that Temple University speech? Pearson replied that it had to be said, or words to this effect. But he did not want to talk about it.

WILLIAM P. BUNDY

I was not present and I was not, as it happened, in town at that particular moment, but I did get the playback. I have never quite understood why Pearson made that speech at that particular moment on American soil. I think that was more than anything what really put Johnson over the boiling point. I've heard since from various Canadian sources that some people in the Senate, or possibly even in the White House, had suggested to Pearson that a word from him could make a lot of difference. I do not know who those individuals were. I am at a loss to explain why Pearson did it the way he did it.

I do understand the viewpoint and I've reread the speech, as it happens, within the last six months, and it was in fact stated in a very modest way. But coming at a time when this was the burning issue on which President Johnson felt himself under all kinds of pressures, and in a very nasty and tough time of decision, to have the Canadian prime minister give him free advice, from a public restrum in this country, sat very badly with Johnson. That's self-evident and I can only say that the repercussions were not in any sense contrived. They were at least as vehement as anything that's been said in hindsight about that episode. It did seriously impair the relationship.

DEAN RUSK

LBJ had what I would be inclined to call a "code" for political leaders. For example, he would never allow us to criticize any foreign political leader by name whether it was Khrushchev or Ho Chi Minh or Charles de Gaulle or whoever it might be, and if any apparatus in a foreign country attacked him by name, he'd have me on the phone in ten minutes with the ambassador to that country saying, "Look, this is not the way for political leaders to work things out with each other."

Another element in his code was that you do not create a political problem for the leader of another country in his own country. For example, when my very good friend, Alex Home was Prime Minister in Great Britain, he came to the White House for a visit. On the steps of the White House on his way out, he was drawn by reporters into discussing British sales of buses to Cuba. LBJ didn't like that; he said he didn't have to talk about buses to Cuba; let him talk about it in the House of Commons in London, but not on our front steps.

So it was really not what Mike Pearson said at Temple University, it was that he said it at Temple University. He said he ought to have said it in Ottawa or somewhere else, but he shouldn't come into our own country and create problems for the president within the United States. That violated that code of conduct among political leaders that LBJ had in his own mind.

GEOFFREY PEARSON

My father was certainly stamped on. He was not the man simply to listen when somebody was rude to him. He would reply but he would never shout and he never used the language that the president used. What shocked him as much as anything was the kind of language Johnson used. It was not his nature to do that. He kept himself under control; he wouldn't lose his temper. I don't remember him losing his temper on a matter of public policy. He would on little things, but not on that kind of thing. He didn't harbor resentment. Grudges were not his thing. He wouldn't look for an opportunity to get revenge. In fact, he got home and he wrote the president a very civil, courteous letter. "It was a very good visit. Thank you for your hospitality. We had our differences. This is my view of the situation. I understand your view." I'm sure that letter was well received because it didn't need to be written.

It was a long, apologetic, letter that Lester Pearson wrote President Johnson, and it is published in full in his memoirs; however, he makes no mention of how it was received. Robert Stanfield, who was to become Conservative leader and Opposition leader while Pearson was still prime minister, felt that Pearson's stance toward the United States "was not very consistent." In fact, Stanfield said that in some ways the relationship with Washington was worse under the Pearson government than it had been under the Diefenbaker government, which was an ironic comment. Stanfield hastened to say that Diefenbaker had very good relations with Eisenhower but did not get along with Kennedy; in the same way, it could be said that Pearson had good relations with Kennedy, but could not get along with Johnson.

But what did Mike Pearson hope to accomplish by resorting to open diplomacy in this way? Even Escott Reid, who strongly supported the call for an end to the bombing, felt that it was unwise to give it in the United States. There were some observers who thought that Pearson, who was much more of a politician than was popularly believed, was taking advantage of the fact that public opinion in Canada had turned against American action in Vietnam. At any rate, the lofty moral approach that he took in Philadelphia actually did more harm than good. Paul Martin asserts that, three days before the Temple University speech, he had given Prime Minister Pearson "some indications that the Americans were seriously thinking of stopping the bombing," and there was no doubt in Martin's mind that the speech had the effect of actually delaying Johnson's order to halt the air raids.

IO The American Dilemma: Economic

THE CLOSE RELATIONSHIP with the United States, which Lester Pearson warned back in the Fifties would grow closer and more difficult, applied to economic as well as political affairs. Perhaps the greatest example of the former was the Auto Pact in 1965 which amounted to an economic union of the vast American industry, with the main plants in the United States and the branch plants in Canada producing for both the United States and Canada as if they were one market. It took long negotiations to bring about this agreement and the so-called Canadian edition of Time *Magazine, about which there had been a great deal of controversy, became one of the bargaining counters. Then there was the attempt by the Rockefellers to move in on Canadian banking which was thwarted despite the best efforts of the U. S. State Department. However, the dilemma of sharing a continent with a super-power was brought to the fore by the appointment of a task force to look into the question of foreign (American) ownership of Canadian industry: the Watkins Report was tabled in the House of Commons just before Pearson resigned as prime minister.*

It seemed that every couple of years or so in the Sixties there was an exchange crisis, either of Canada's making or that of the United States. The run on Canadian currency and its devaluation in May 1962 during a federal election campaign hurt the luckless Diefenbaker government, although it was acknowledged later that the 92-1/2 cents dollar had helped to stimulate production and was responsible for much of the prosperity of

225

the Pearson period. There was an American balance-of-payments crisis in July 1965, and Washington's action in imposing an Interest Equalization Tax had a disastrous effect on Canadian markets; however, Lou Rasminsky, the governor of the Bank of Canada, was able to negotiate an exemption (this is described in Chapter 8). Another balance-of-payments problem occurred in the United States in December 1965, and in 1968, in the dying days of the Pearson government, Rasminsky had to go to Washington again to get another exemption for Canada from American efforts to defend their dollar.

However, the 1965 crisis was notable for the intervention of a provincial minister, Eric Kierans, in the affairs of the federal government. Prime Minister Pearson was furious and angrily censured the Quebec minister at a televised press conference. What happened was that the United States government, in order to correct its balance of payments, had asked American subsidiaries abroad to return as much cash as possible to their parent companies, and the Canadian government had agreed to these guidelines. But Kierans, who was by way of being an economic nationalist, told a reporter that the Canadian government should have told Washington "to stuff it," as he put it, and that became the newspaper's headline. Rasminsky was upset and pointed out to Kierans on the telephone that the government had accepted the guidelines in order to keep open access to the capital market in New York; they had quite an argument, according to Kierans, and the governor of the Bank of Canada asserted that "you people in Quebec should know that we are doing this particularly for you"—in other words, making it possible for the Quebec government and Quebec Hydro to continue borrowing in New York.

Far from satisfying Kierans, Rasminsky's explanation only seemed to make him see red: he then wrote letters to Secretary of the Treasury H. H. Fowler, and Secretary of Commerce John Connor, in which he not only denounced the guidelines as being an infringement of Canadian sovereignty but announced that he, as an economist who had always defended foreign investment in this country, was now going to oppose it. This was a flagrant violation of the way that Canadian-American relations were conducted, and Ottawa was up in arms. Kierans asserted that he had the right to make representations to Washington because, as he claimed, Canada was without a government: the incident occurred shortly after the 1965 election when Pearson had announced that he was going to shake up his Cabinet and then had gone abroad on holidays before doing so.

*Although the Auto Pact was an achievement of the Pearson govern-
ment—and much of the complex negotiations between Canadian and
American manufacturers and Canadian and American governments was
handled by Pearson's minister of industry, C. M. "Bud" Drury—it had
its genesis at an earlier date. As Diefenbaker's minister of trade of
commerce, George Hees, said, work on rationalizing the industry on the
continent had been started in his department during the last six months of
the Conservative government, and the idea of an Auto Pact had been
originally proposed by Vincent Bladen, who had been appointed by the
Diefenbaker government to look into the automobile industry.*

PAUL MARTIN

Don Fleming [Conservative finance minister] and I had been
students of Vincent Bladen at the University of Toronto. He's an
economist. And when we got wind that there was going to be
someone examining the whole business, I went to Donald and
said, "You know, it's none of my business, but a very good man
to do that would be Vincent Bladen." He said, "I agree."

Donald thought it wasn't necessary to have a big commission.
It would be wise to have a good economist who knew something
about the problems, someone who had done some work in some
aspect of this; and Vincent Bladen had. So when Vincent was
doing his work, he spent a good deal of his time in Windsor,
naturally, and I saw a good bit of him there. He would discuss a
lot of aspects, problems that I had lived with all of my political
and parliamentary life.

The idea of the U. S.-Canada Auto Pact was something that
came out in his hearing. It was a proposal that had first been made
by George Burt of the UAW [United Automobile Workers'
Union]. True, George later, for reasons best known to himself,
criticized the Pact, but the basic idea of a reciprocal arrangement
between the two countries, lowering the tariff barriers to permit
parts and automobiles to be made, came from the UAW. The idea
appealed greatly to Vincent Bladen, who clothed it up with
economic justification, and that's how it ensued. When the actual
negotiations between the companies and the governments began,
Bud Drury played a big part, as he should have because he was
the minister of industry.

After they'd worked out the agreements between the companies, then I came into the picture with Mr. Rusk. We had to get the thing through. If it had been considered a treaty, it would have had to go to the Foreign Relations Committee of the United States. If it bore the signature of the president, there was a good chance it could get through the Congress quite easily. And I was able to persuade both Rusk and the president that the latter should sign the treaty. Originally, it was going to be signed only by Dean Rusk and myself. And I was afraid that that was a dangerous thing and it ought to have as well the signatures of the president and the prime minister.

The Auto Pact grew out of the defense-production-sharing agreements, according to Bud Drury. The government had decided that it was in the country's best interest to switch from British equipment for the Canadian armed forces to American. But, in order to do this, there had to be a quid pro quo, or, as he put it, if we were going to spend large sums of money in the United States to purchase this equipment, the Americans would have to reciprocate by buying from us. That was what Drury and Robert McNamara, the U. S. secretary of defense, argued about, and finally McNamara saw the point, and agreed. However, there were assorted legislative enactments that inhibited the Americans from buying from Canada, and these had to be removed before the defense-production-sharing agreements could go into effect. The same sort of thing had to be done, Drury said, in the case of the Auto Pact. Similar artificial restrictions, the so-called "Buy American" legislation, had to be lifted in formulating that accord.

Maurice Sauvé, one of Pearson's ministers, recalled the long but "always very positive" discussions in the Cabinet on the negotiation of the Auto Pact. At the time Canada consumed 7 percent of the motor vehicle production in North American while producing only 3 or 4 percent. The entire aim was, he said, to bring consumption and production into equilibrium; it was to redress the deficit in the balance of trade with the United States, the main cause of which was the automobile- and truck-manufacturing industry. It was the finance minister, Walter Gordon, who initiated the negotiations that led up to the Auto Pact, which seemed a strange thing for Gordon to do since he was such an ardent economic nationalist.

MITCHELL SHARP

The problem arose when we were looking for some means of shifting the balance of trade in automobiles and automobile products. The minister of finance, then Walter Gordon, introduced a system of rebates for the purpose of stimulating exports of automobiles and automobile parts to the United States. The Americans reacted by saying that if we carried that through, they would take action under the provision that they have against the payment of subsidies on exports, and apply a coutervailing duty. That would have defeated the whole purpose, so there were then discussions in which I had some part involving a different approach. The result was a suggestion that perhaps we should have free trade in automobile parts, not at the consumer level but at the manufacturer's level. So the minister of finance, after these discussions, put forward this idea in which there would be certain goals and in which there would be no duties at all between manufacturers.

Those of us who were concerned at that time were surprised that Walter Gordon, who would have opposed integration of industry in this way, actually proposed it. It was worked out by his officials with American officials and proposed by him.

WALTER GORDON

We were in this position where our balance of payments was badly out of kilter. The only way to correct it was to increase our exports to the United States of manufactured goods. And Douglas Dillon, the secretary of the U. S. treasury, agreed to that. We also agreed that the only way to do this effectively was to bring our trade in automobiles and automobile parts more into line. That was the genesis of the Auto Pact. It is an [extraordinary] industry with three companies doing 95 percent of the business in both the United States and Canada. So we worked out a plan. It had to be an agreement or treaty between Canada and the United States, but also there had to be an agreement with the automobile companies, and those agreements were really the guts of it. The net result was that as far as Canada was concerned, we brought our trade in automobiles much more closely into line. It produced many, many more jobs in Canada, which was one of our problems, to create employment. I didn't like the continentalist aspects of it, but the only alternative would have been to nationalize the industry and to run it from Ottawa, and I didn't see too many people around Ottawa who were competent to run big business, or any other kind [of business], perhaps.

LOUIS RASMINSKY

The Auto Pact was a bilateral arrangement between Canada and the United States which set out to obtain for Canada assurances of a certain percentage of the market. I may not be putting that quite correctly, but to obtain assurances that would result in greater production of automobiles and automobile parts in Canada than would have been the case under either the old tariff arrangement or under straight free-trade arrangement, without any such assurance. So the Auto Pact itself, though it took the form of an international agreement, wasn't really a classic piece of international economic policy. It was a bilateral arrangement in a sense. It was protectionist for the Canadian market.

At about the same time as negotiations on the Auto Pact were going on, the Pearson government was considering the plight of the periodical press. A royal commission headed by Grattan O'Leary, the newspaper editor and later senator, found that the very existence of Canadian magazines was threatened by the fact that the so-called Canadian editions of Time *and* Reader's Digest *took half the available advertising revenue. The commission, which had been appointed by the Diefenbaker government, reported in May 1961 and proposed that tax deductions on advertising "in a foreign periodical wherever published" should be disallowed. However, the Conservatives had done nothing about this when they were defeated. There was a lot of pressure on the Liberals to act, and Walter Gordon said that the Pearson government was fearful that European interests, as he put it, were trying to get control of* La Presse, *the mass-circulation French-language daily in Montreal, "and use it to preach separatism." There was also a rumor that the then-owner of the Toronto* Globe and Mail *was thinking of selling to an American, and the finance minister was afraid that this would lead to promotion of the United States position in the Vietnam War.*

On June 28, 1965, the Canadian House of Commons passed a bill that disallowed tax deductions for advertising in non-Canadian newspapers or periodicals—a Canadian publication was defined as one in which three-quarters or more of the voting shares were owned by Canadians. However, Time and Reader's Digest were to be exempted from the legislation, largely because, as Pearson indicated in his memoirs, "they had staff and plant in Canada and had plans to broaden the basis of their Canadian editions."

There was an angry outcry in the press, not so much because of the exemptions for the American magazines, but because the restrictions on advertising were an infringement of the freedom of the press—or so the Canadian Daily Newspaper Publishers' Association said. However, Peter Newman, the well-known journalist, condemned Gordon's "surrender" to Time and the Reader's Digest, and said that it was due to pressure from the United States government. Pearson denied this in his memoirs and asserted that the exemption of the two publications was a decision "quite unrelated to our negotiation of the Auto Pact with the United States."

WALTER GORDON

I was led to believe—I don't know who told me, I don't know whether Pearson, Tom Kent, or somebody—that the Washington authorities were very nervous that if we did do anything about *Time* Henry Luce would be stirred up and that he would take it upon himself to see that the Auto Pact didn't get through Congress. He had a lot of influence, and they thought he could easily do this. Well, the Auto Pact, we thought, was vital to our economic situation at the time, so that was why *Time* and *Reader's Digest* were left out of the legislation. While the proposal came from the prime minister, it was up to me to get the legislation through. This was a very unpalatable thing to do, to exempt *Time* and *Reader's Digest*, so I went to our caucus, the Liberal caucus— I'd always told them exactly why I had to do things—and I did it again. I said, "Now I've just got to ask you fellows to back me up." Which they said they would do, and they did. I can't prove that Henry Luce would have upset the Auto Pact, but that was what we were fearful of.

PAUL MARTIN

Rusk raised the question [of *Time* Magazine]. This was an issue to which the American government attached great importance. I could do no more than tell him it was government policy, "but I'll let my colleagues know that you have spoken to me again," which I did. I think he must have spoken to me four times. Right now I would say it was four times, and he wrote to me also at the beginning. And after that he spoke to me on at least four occasions.

It was in mid-January 1965 that Prime Minister Pearson went to the LBJ Ranch, which was "deep in the heart of Texas," as he put it, to sign the Auto Pact agreement. The visit made such an impression on Pearson that he goes into it in some detail in his memoirs. After President Johnson welcomed him before a battery of television cameras—and, in the process, got his name wrong—there was a tour of the ranch by helicopter and in a cavalcade of cars. The president, the prime minister, Paul Martin, and Dean Rusk were in the first car while the second car, according to Pearson's account, was filled with security men and staff "who had the liquor as well as the guns." They made "three pit stops for drinks" and one or two to admire the dry, rocky scenery, which Pearson found strangely fascinating. The president was in constant telephone communication with the other cars, and, toward the end of the tour, rang up Governor John Connally, who was about a hundred miles away in Austin, and summoned him to dinner at the ranch. There were more drinks and then dinner of steak and catfish served on the same plate. "It was all very homey and unpresidential," Pearson noted, "Perhaps, a little too much so, even for a ranch."

Quite obviously, Pearson was amazed and amused by the goings-on at the ranch, and did not fully approve of them. As Charles Ritchie said, Mike and LBJ were never really made for each other, and that visit to the ranch did not help. The president's love of scandal—at the dinner he exchanged political yarns and gossip with Connally—and what Ritchie characterized as "his kind of coarseness" did not appeal to Pearson. When the news came on, and there were four TV sets so that every network version could be seen. Johnson appeared astonished at his gaffe about Pearson's name and apologized profusely for it.

PAUL MARTIN

I went to Washington and flew with Rusk down to the ranch, and we were there for three or four hours before Mike [came in another plane]. We had a very interesting visit on that occasion. I'll always remember when Mike arrived—television cameras were there, and all the newspeople—and Johnson said how much pleasure he had in welcoming us to the ranch and to the United States, particularly his good friend Drew Pearson. Mike has told that story, but he doesn't say Drew Pearson.[1]

It was a slip of the tongue, but in the evening after dinner, when we were sitting around in his drawing room, Johnson said, "You know, I just got a note"—we were waiting for the television news to come on very shortly—"I just got a note that I pulled an awful boner today." And Lady Bird said, "What was that?" He said, "When the prime minister arrived I welcomed him here as Drew Pearson, and I feel so embarrassed by that because in all probability this will be on the national news."

Mike laughed, you know, and made fun of it. But my God, he'd no sooner done that than the news came on. And sure enough, the first item showed the four of us there and Johnson welcoming his friend Drew Pearson. Well, he was so embarrassed, he really was. It was one of these Freudian slips that anybody can make. Now Mike, in his book, says something else. But it was Drew Pearson. I remember it very well.

The next morning, after a breakfast of hominy grits and highly spiced sausage, which was a specialty of the ranch, Pearson and Johnson signed the agreement for free trade in automobiles and auto parts. However, Dean Rusk remembered that occasion for a very different reason.

[1]Drew Pearson was a well-known Washington columnist. Mike Pearson maintains that, in welcoming him to the ranch, Johnson referred to him as "Mr. Wilson." When he saw, on the television news that night, the mistake he made, the president said that Prime Minister Wilson had paid him a visit not long before. Pearson quotes himself as retorting, "Think nothing of it, Senator Goldwater." (See *Mike*, Vol. III.)

DEAN RUSK

A visit to the ranch was a really very special business. You had to put on a big Texan hat, and you had to go on a bus to look at the deer and the cattle and things like that. I don't know that Mike Pearson thought very much of that, although I gather he comes from a country district himself.

But one very important thing that happened on that visit had to do with the great controversy about Russian and French contributions to the budget in the UN. They had refused to pay their assessed dues because of the funds that were being used for things that they had not approved of—such things as the Congo, the peace-keeping forces in the Middle East, a few dollars for the so-called UN command in Korea, things like that. By the summer of 1964 they had got in a position where they were more than two years behind in their dues and the charter says that you lose your vote in the General Assembly unless the General Assembly especially excuses you for special circumstances.

Well, we had pledged to the Congress that among the elements of security behind the hundred-million-dollar loan we had made were Articles 17 and 19 of the charter with respect to dues. So we and a great many others set out to enforce Article 19 against the Russians and the French in the Assembly of 1964.[2] They were absolutely adamant. We wouldn't let any vote come up in the year and I think somehow we elected a president by acclamation without any voting; but during the fall of 1964 the UN General Assembly was stalemated, and the situation grew to be very tense.

Mike Pearson and Paul Martin came down to the ranch. We went out to look at the deer. LBJ was driving. Mike Pearson was in the front seat with him. Paul Martin and I were in the back seat. The question of this impasse in the United Nations came up, and LBJ very quietly said, "Well, we can't break up the UN just

---

[2]Both the USSR and France were in violation of Article 19, which says that a member in arrears shall have no vote if the amount in arrears has exceeded its contributions for the preceding two years. President Johnson indicated that the United States would not continue to insist on the enforcement of Article 19, and Rusk said he was surprised that Pearson made no mention of this in his memoirs. This was probably due to the fact that the third volume was not written by him. In the secretary of state's view, it was the most important thing that happened during Pearson's visit to the ranch.

because the Russians refuse to pay fifteen million dollars," and I could almost feel Paul Martin jump in the back seat alongside of me, and there was a little more chatting on that line.

We got back to the ranchhouse and I said to the president, "Mr. President, this was a very important statement you made. Are you sure you meant it?" He said, "How much has the United States contributed to the United Nations up to this point?" I said, "About three billion dollars." He said, "Of course, I meant it. We're not going to break up the UN just because these damn Russians won't pay fifteen million dollars."

So Mike Pearson and Paul Martin headed back to New York like jet aircraft, and that instinctive on-the-spot statement of LBJ was the thing that unlocked this Article 17 and Article 19 problem in the UN.

While the Auto Pact was a success, and the finance minister, Walter Gordon, and the prime minister, Lester Pearson, had reason for satisfaction, it was a model that was never copied. That did not mean that the government did not consider adapting the agreement for other industries, such as furniture manufacturers and the companies producing chemicals and fertilizers as well as the makers of commercial aircraft, but no progress was made. Either the United States was not enthusiastic or—and this applied to most cases—there was not a sufficient measure of homogeneity within the industry. Bud Drury pointed out that, in furniture-manufacturing, there were a tremendous number of small independent firms tending to serve local markets. The automobile industry was unique with three companies doing 95 percent of the business in Canada and the United States, as Walter Gordon said, and it was relatively easy for these three companies to get together and agree among themselves. There were many more companies engaged in making auto parts, and this was a part of the agreement that was to result in difficulties.

As a result of the Auto Pact, there was a big shift in the balance of trade between Canada and the United States, according to Mitchell Sharp, who was minister of trade and commerce at the time it was negotiated. However, there was one harmful effect in that "we lost any control that we had," as Sharp pointed out: it was no longer a Canadian industry; it was a North American industry.

It could be said that the Mercantile Bank Affair—the purchase of a

Canadian bank by the First National Bank of New York City (Citi-
bank)—was the other side of the coin to the Auto Pact: whereas the latter
represented Canadian-American cooperation and economic integration, the
former was the outward manifestation of a financial invasion of Canada
and became a bone of contention between the two countries. Although the
Mercantile Bank Affair was not settled till 1967, when the newly revised
Bank Act came into effect limiting the amount of foreign ownership of
banks in Canada, it had its beginnings in 1963. It was in November of
that year that James Stillman Rockefeller, the head of Citibank, came to
Ottawa to find out the government's reaction to his bank taking over the
Dutch-owned Mercantile and making it American owned.

The Liberals had just come to power and were greatly influenced by
Walter Gordon and his nationalist outlook. As Prime Minister Pearson
said, they had come to the conclusion that there were certain institutions of
Canadian economic and financial life that must never be allowed to fall
under foreign control; he might have added "Canadian cultural life,"
because it was only a short time later that his government brought in the
restrictions on advertising that were meant to prevent Canadian publica-
tions from falling into foreign (American) hands. Thus the Mercantile
Bank Affair was related to the Time *and* Reader's Digest *case in that it*
was effected by Gordon's nationalist policy.

Before Rockefeller came to Ottawa, an executive of Citibank had
preceded him and seen Louis Rasminsky, it was Rasminsky who made the
arrangements for Rockefeller to meet with Walter Gordon.

LOUIS RASMINSKY

The National Citibank has had a great deal of experience in
foreign countries. They know the sensitivity of every country in
the world, including the United States, toward foreign control of
banking institutions. I think it was extraordinary that they should
have gone as far as they did with the Dutch owners of the
Mercantile Bank without making sure that the Canadian government had no objection to what they were doing.

My own knowledge of it, I think, came earlier than Walter's
did. I had a call in 1963—I don't remember the exact date of it—
from Bob McFadden, who was one of the senior officers of the
Citibank, probably in charge of all their international banking
operations. He wanted to come to see me. He did. He told me

that the Citibank has entered into an agreement, subject to the ratification of their directors, a tentative agreement, to buy the Mercantile Bank. I asked him first whether the minister of finance was aware of this and he said not, that I was the first person that they had spoken to. I said, "I don't think that you should proceed a step further without talking to the minister of finance." He agreed.

I remember I went to a bookcase and I got out a copy of the report of the royal commission that Walter was chairman of on Canada's economic prospects. I looked up the reference to the banking, and there is a specific reference to banking there, saying that banks should be in domestic hands. I said, "Here's what the minister of finance thinks—he's on record on this." Then McFadden asked me how I would feel about it myself. I said, "Well, I'm all in favor of competition, including competition in the banking industry, but I myself have some misgivings about it, and it wouldn't be fair to say that it would be all right so far as I'm concerned."

One of my misgivings was that one of the techniques that is open to the central bank to use to try to influence the way the banks behave is a technique that is sometimes referred to as a moral suasion. At that time, we had eight banks in Canada— well, you could get the banks around a table in a room, and the way moral suasion would be used would be on occasions when, for broad reasons of national economic policy, it became necessary to turn the screws a bit and make it more difficult for the banks to lend money. I could say to the banks, after talking to whoever the minister of the day was, "Please go easy on small businesses—go as easy as you can on small businesses," the reason for that being that small businesses really had nowhere else to go—perhaps to finance companies, but they don't have the same access to the bond market or to foreign borrowing that large businesses do. Or I might say to them, "Go easy on parts of the country that are depressed." That usually meant the Maritime Provinces.

The Canadian banks did, I think, try to cooperate, though there's really no way of establishing how effective they were in keeping up with the flow of loans to small businesses or to the provinces that were doing worse than other parts of the country.

Any American bank taking part in such an arrangement might be subject to prosecution in the United States under the anti-trust legislation. This is what I was afraid of, and I told McFadden that I was also afraid that there might on occasion be some things affecting Canadian national policy that I would feel somewhat inhibited in talking about in the presence of non-Canadians. The principal thing, so far as I was concerned, was to be sure that he realized that it would be a serious mistake for him to go ahead without the approval of the minister of finance.

WALTER GORDON

James Rockefeller and his Canadian representative—a man called McFadden—came to see me in my office in Ottawa when I was minister of finance. They said that they had a deal which would permit them to buy control of the Mercantile Bank from Dutch interests, that the deal hadn't been consummated, and they wanted to know what the Canadian government's view would be about it. So I told them that we would be against it, and they they were now on notice to that effect.

There were two officials present—[R. B.] Bryce and [C. F.] Elderkin. Elderkin said, "You know, the only charter a bank has is subject to the Bank Act and it's renewed every ten years, though it needn't be renewed." Mr. Rockefeller said, "As I interpret this, if we go ahead, we'll be doing so at our peril." I think I replied, "Well, I wouldn't have used those words." But I thought he had sized the situation up pretty accurately. Now I had asked Bryce and Elderkin to sit in on the conversation, and immediately the meeting was over I wanted them to write down a complete record of what was said by whom, which they did. They are pretty senior, responsible officials [Bryce was deputy minister of finance and Elderkin, inspector general of banks].

Despite the fact that he had been made fully aware of the government's position, James Rockefeller went ahead with the purchase of the Mercantile Bank. He chose to ignore Walter Gordon's warning; indeed, he treated it with contempt. When he appeared before the Canadian Parliament's banking committee, Rockefeller did not try to conceal the scornful disregard he had for Canadian institutions. Prime Minister Pearson believed that he was "relying on U. S. official pressure to maintain them in Canada as a purely U. S. bank"; he also added that the representations made to him by some of the officials of Citibank were "almost offensive." It was an extraordinary situation, and Citibank's arrogant and aggressive attitude might be explained by the fact that it was the spearhead for a concerted attack on this country by the Rockefeller banking interests.

There was evidence of this in the dinner that Mike Pearson had with David Rockefeller, the head of another huge American bank, the Chase Manhattan Bank, and a cousin of James Rockefeller. Pearson had known David for many years, as well as other members of the family, and had stayed at the Rockefeller estate in the Caribbean. There were just the two of them for dinner at 24 Sussex Drive that evening, and, according to Pearson's account, David Rockefeller attacked the Canadian government for following a discriminatory, shortsighted, chauvinistic policy in banking; he asserted that his bank had no trouble in any foreign country but Canada; with their best friends and closest neighbors "they could get nowhere." Pearson noted that David Rockefeller hoped to get some control and eventually total control of a Canadian bank, and "had already taken certain steps in that direction." The prime minister quoted himself as telling the head of the Chase Manhattan Bank to go no further, that there was legislation pending that would put an end to all foreign efforts to get control of Canadian banks; and he went on to say to his friend, "Forget it because neither you nor anyone else is going to get us to change our position."

Although the U. S. State Department did come to the support of James Rockefeller and Citibank, its efforts were not to be compared with the pressure that it brought to bear on behalf of Time *Magazine.*

PAUL MARTIN

Once the government decision on that was taken, I had to communicate the result, and I did to Rusk and this was another sore thing with him. But there's so many transactions between Canada and the United States that it was just one more, you know. We just overlook the fact that in any one day the number of decisions that are made by either government in respect of matters concerning the other is just legion. I don't think there's ever a day goes by when there are not two or three hundred decisions being made on major and minor issues, and that was one of them about which the Americans weren't too happy. But they likely made a hell of a lot that applied to us about which we weren't happy.

LOUIS RASMINSKY

James Rockefeller certainly made a very strong effort to get the support of the State Department, and I think the State Department did enough to get him off their back. I don't think—I never had the impression—that the U. S. administration regarded this as a really major issue in Canadian-American relations or that we were being pushed terribly hard by them. A reason for that may be that they weren't really too well placed to push us because there's a great deal of nationalism in American banking legislation. For example, at the time when these things were taking place, there was a provision in the National Bank Act, which governs the First National Citibank—it is a national bank—which prevents any non-American from becoming a director. So the Americans are quite used to countries regarding banking as something that they do want to keep under national control. There were no doubt some dispatches, but the amount of pressure was nothing like what I would judge the amount of pressure was in connection with *Time* Magazine.

It was in May 1965 that the amendments to the Bank Act were introduced in the House of Commons, but it was not until 1967 that they were adopted. The key provisions limited foreign ownership of any Canadian bank to 25 percent, and individual holdings to 10 percent; if these percentages were exceeded, the bank would not be allowed to grow. The Mercantile, now owned outright by Citibank, protested that the amendments were "discriminatory and retroactive," despite the fact that James Rockefeller and his associates had been warned against acquiring the Canadian bank. Finally, a compromise was worked out whereby the Mercantile would be granted an exemption to the Bank Act if Citibank reduced its ownership of the Canadian bank to 25 percent, instead of the 10 percent required by law for an individual holding. [3]

[3] In one of the zanier episodes of the Sixties, Bryce Mackasey, a back-bench MP, sought to act as a mediator between the government of Canada and the Rockefeller bank. Judy LaMarsh, who was a Cabinet minister, described it as "the most infuriating incident"

However, the compromise resulted in political ructions and almost a split in the Liberal government: Walter Gordon was violently opposed and insisted on the letter of the law, that Citibank's holdings of the Mercantile be reduced to 10 percent; he obviously wanted, Pearson said, "to use the situation to get the Rockefellers out of Canada once and for all." However, Mitchell Sharp, who had succeeded Gordon as finance minister, and the prime minister insisted that they had given their word to the American bank over the compromise arrangement and were not going to break it.

MITCHELL SHARP

I did accept Walter's restriction on foreign banks. I agreed with it, and I had no difficulty with this at all. Subsequently, we had real trouble over that because he [Gordon] wanted to go a step further at a later stage, and I felt that I was committed to the [Bank] Act and committed by many things that I had said to the way it would work; and, therefore, that I wasn't going to be called a liar.

I said that when a bank got to 25 percent it could expand. Well, Walter, however, was so committed to keeping the Citibank out of Canada that he wanted to go further and to apply other limitations, including a limitation on increase in capital. You see, the First National Citibank put forward a plan, which was later adopted—not in my time but in Benson's time—for a gradual expansion in the capital, all of the shares being sold off to Canadians until the bank got down to a 25 percent holding. Walter opposed that; he wanted them to be forced to sell off their existing stock. Well, there was no stipulation about that and I felt that that was to change the rules of the game, and I wouldn't have it. That was the cause of our later disagreement. But at the time, we had no disagreement about the Act as far as the Mercantile Bank was concerned, or foreign banks.

and said that the private member made a fool of himself and "grovelled" before the Americans. Although it was on his own initiative, Mackasey said that he informed Mr. Pearson, who did not object to his going to New York. There, he was royally entertained by Citibank officials and maintained that he got a written agreement from James Rockefeller saying that the American bank would sell 75 percent of its shares in the Mercantile to Canadian residents over a period of time.

WALTER GORDON

When the Mercantile charter was to be renewed, the bank was not going to be permitted to expand until the ownership of its shares was treated the same way as the ownership of every other bank in Canada. Well, there was a long, gory series of meetings [of members of the Cabinet] and nobody seemed to say the same thing two days running, but eventually it was agreed that no concessions would be made to the Mercantile. But it was at a time when the leadership race was on, and Sharp was an aspirant for the leadership, and I think he may have felt that he should win this battle with me. Whether he did or not, I don't know. I didn't think he did. But he let them [the Mercantile] continue with the 25 percent holding by Citibank for a period. And they've still got it. And when the Bank Act comes up for revision, I would hope that the Canadian government would say, "Now, no further expansion until the controlling block is cut down to not more than 10 percent." The same as for any other bank.

The Mercantile Bank Affair, and the way that the Rockefellers would go to almost any length to get control of a Canadian bank, made the government and the public more conscious than ever of the fact that so much of the country had been sold to the United States or U. S.-based multinational corporations. Almost three-quarters of Canadian mines and natural resources and fully 60 percent of the manufacturing concerns belonged to foreigners, mostly Americans. Walter Gordon had tried to remedy this alienation of the country's economy with a 30 percent take-over tax, but it proved to be impractical and unworkable, and collapsed with the rest of his first budget. A Canada Development Corporation, which would help to Canadianize industry, had been in every Speech from the Throne since 1963, but, as Prime Minister Pearson said: "Unfortunately, the difficulties over our first budget and the atmosphere of controversy surrounding it tended, quite naturally, to push the creation of this corporation down on our priority list."

After the 1965 election Walter Gordon resigned from the Cabinet. He had assured Prime Minister Pearson of a majority win if he called an early election, and, when this did not happen, the finance minister, who had been the Liberals' campaign chairman, took the blame and offered his resignation. Little or no attempt was made to get him to reconsider, and Gordon felt that he had been let down by his old friend, Mike Pearson, for whom he had done so much. Actually, the two of them had been drifting apart ever since that disastrous first budget, which had been brought down within two months of the Liberals' being returned to power in the spring of 1963.[4]

Even though he was outside the government, Gordon continued to be one of its movers and shakers: he had a strong following in the party caucus, particularly among the Toronto members, and there was no doubt that his brand of economic nationalism had a popular appeal. Soon pressure mounted to have him back in the Cabinet, but it was not until Gordon, who had become increasingly disillusioned with politics, had decided to resign his seat and become a private citizen again that Pearson acted. It was a difficult situation for the prime minister: if Gordon returned to the Cabinet, there would be trouble because he differed with Mitchell Sharp, who had succeeded him as finance minister, on some matters and certainly on the Mercantile Bank Affair. If Gordon did not return, they would lose his seat, but, what was more important, there would be a split in the party, with the left-wing Liberals leaving for the New Democratic Party. Finally Pearson decided that "it seemed better to have him back in the cabinet, with its collective responsibilities of membership, than to have him attack our financial and economic policies from without."

However, it was one thing to have decided to have Gordon back in the Cabinet, but it was another thing to persuade him to return. Once bitten, twice shy, and Walter Gordon insisted on certain conditions that really amounted to his becoming deputy prime minister in all but name. In a lengthy "letter of intent" written on January 5, 1967, Prime Minister Pearson listed the many responsibilities he would have on becoming a minister again, including the following: "A major responsibility, which we have already discussed, would be your chairmanship of a small committee (say three or five) to draft a report to the cabinet which, after consideration and approval there, would become a White Paper. It would deal with problems arising out of foreign, primarily of course American, control and ownership of our resources and our industry. This problem, as you know so well, is becoming more difficult and more dangerous to our separate national existence."

[4]For a full account of Walter Gordon's first budget and the split that developed between him and Prime Minister Pearson, see the first volume, *Lester Pearson and the Dream of Unity*. Gordon was generally credited with reviving the Liberal Party after its shattering defeat in the 1958 election and doing more than anyone else to make Pearson prime minister.

As soon as he returned to the Cabinet as the beginning of 1967, Gordon appointed a left-wing economist, Professor Melville H. Watkins, to head the task force to look into the question of foreign ownership. Gordon's concept of the whole undertaking was that it should be a small task force, which he hoped would come up with some kind of report in three months' time, six months at the outside. However, he counted without the Cabinet subcommittee with which Pearson had saddled him, and it was this subcommittee that gave Watkins directions and not the minister who had appointed him. Besides Gordon and Mitchell Sharp, the other members of the subcommittee were John Turner, the minister of consumer and corporate affairs; Jean Marchand, the manpower minister; and Roger Teillet, the minister of veterans' affairs. Sharp had an economist whom he wanted on the task force, and Marchand said there had to be two from Quebec, while Turner insisted on one from British Columbia, and someone asserted the Maritimes had to have a representative—and before Gordon could protest, there were eight members, which meant that it could not possibly report in a short time.

MEL WATKINS

He [Mr. Gordon] certainly talked to me about that [the work]. Again, his interest was to keep the inquiry as small as possible and get it done as quickly as possible and not launch it into some huge public inquiry that would hear evidence, not become a royal commission and not launch large research projects which couldn't be finished in any short period of time, which would take two or three years. Then, of course, this Cabinet subcommittee had its views. Now, beyond that—and I think this was really Mr. Pearson's idea—they struck a committee of senior officials. I've forgotten now what name they gave to it, but it included people like Mr. [Robert] Bryce, who was deputy minister of finance; Jake Warren, who was then trade and commerce; Simon Reisman, industry; Maurice Strong—a committee of senior officials, and I was supposed to keep in touch with them. It wasn't clear what authority they had over me, but I was to meet with them on a regular basis. The committee was chaired by Gerry Stoner, who was at that point running the Privy Council Office because Mr. [Gordon] Robertson was off, immersed in French, as I recall. That group tried very hard to encourage me to broaden the mandate, to go and visit all the provinces.

It's not being cynical but just realistic to say that most of those people were not at all sympathetic to Gordon's politics and they would have been delighted to see us spend two or three years on the inquiry. During that period nothing would have happened and by then Walter would have resigned and they would have killed me dead. I mean, there was no question, they didn't want this task force. Everybody knew that Gordon had exacted this as a price from Pearson [for returning to the Cabinet].

I think it's been said that Pearson wanted Gordon back because he thought that the NDP was cashing in too much on nationalist sentiment. I might say that some of my friends in the NDP, including some of the MPs, were very ambivalent when I took this job because, they said, "It's good to have someone like you doing this study, but you're just being used politically to head off the rising strength of the NDP." Well, since the rising strength of the NDP was always ephemeral—it didn't look like they were about to take office—I did not let this bother me.

This was no royal commission and Mel Watkins made no secret of the fact that he consulted Walter Gordon regularly. He did not have, nor did he ask for, independence; he worked for the Cabinet subcommittee, and Gordon was its chairman, so that he was not going over anyone's head. Watkins recalled that the officials' committee wanted him to visit all the provinces and get their views, but when he told Gordon about this, the latter said, "No, no. All they'll say is do nothing. We know what they're going to say, so don't go." However, in the case of Washington, which the committee said that he should visit, they talked it over and decided that he should go. Watkins went with a couple of members of the task force and saw an assistant secretary in the State Department.

MEL WATKINS

I remember him asking us, "What kind of things are you people thinking that you might recommend?" We'd been told, since we had little experience in these matters, that we should be fairly candid with people in saying what kind of things we were thinking about. So I remember telling him some of the things that we were worried about, in terms of extraterritoriality and some of the ways we thought that could be dealt with, some of our concerns about anti-trust laws and so on, and he said, "Oh, you guys are having a lot of fun. You don't really think your government is going to do anything about those things, do you? Now, what are you talking about? Your government doesn't even make companies disclose properly," which was true at that time; they didn't. I think the general impression that the Americans conveyed was that they were more cynical about the government of Canada than we were, more realistic about the government of Canada than we were.

By September, some eight months after it was set up, the task force was ready to write its report, which was much quicker than the advisory officials had expected or wanted. These officials were definitely out to delay it, as Mel Watkins soon realized. They knew that Walter Gordon was unhappy in the Cabinet, and becoming unhappier as time went on; he had not been given the work to do that he thought Prime Minister Pearson had promised him. And, as Watkins said, the officials believed Gordon would soon quit in disgust, and, they said to Watkins, albeit with a smile, as he put it, "If your minister goes, you go with him."

The task force discussed its proposed report with the Cabinet subcommittee as well as with the officials. All eight members of the task force, some of whom could be classified as conservative economists, concurred in the Watkins Report, and Pearson was to admit that the recommendations were not radical—these included the establishment of a watchdog agency to monitor foreign firms, encouragement of multinationals to offer shares to Canadians, and steps to be taken to prevent the application of American anti-Communist trading laws to American subsidiaries in Canada.

MEL WATKINS

I don't know whether there's any one single recommendation that means more [than any other]; the report was really not a radical document; only in Canada would it be seen that way. It simply said the multinational corporation is here to stay, which they are, and what's called foreign ownership is really big business and really companies with monopoly powers, and these companies happen in the nature of the case to be domiciled outside of Canada: they're big inside Canada, even bigger outside. They're subject to a good deal of pressure from Washington, and therefore the Canadian government should have a policy which is essentially a kind of regulatory policy.

I think we were groping really toward the kind of policy that came out in the Foreign Investment Review Agency. We were saying, "You've got to learn to live with foreign capital, but you've got to realize that you just can't trust the market to regulate it, that you've got to have a positive government presence to deal with it."

One of the analogies we tried to use was the American antitrust policy. That's how they deal with big business at home. How do we deal, as Canadians, with American big business abroad? What's the equivalent within Canada to an American antitrust policy? Well, it's a set of policies that police and regulate the companies. And we had a number of proposals that they should be encouraged to have Canadian shareholders so they would be more clearly subject to corporate law; that they should have Canadian directors; that it would also improve the operation of the Canadian stock exchanges if there were more securities available. Then we strongly endorsed a proposal that Mr. Gordon had made many, many times, which was that a Canada Development Corporation[5] be created.

LOUIS RASMINSKY

I don't think it had any affect on American investment in Canada, and I don't think that the Watkins Report was read by many Americans. I don't think it created a great stir in the United States. It is the case that in recent years—this is many years after the publication, but within the last three or four years—the amount of American investment in Canada has fallen off a great

---

[5]The Canada Development Corporation was finally set up by the Trudeau government on June 30, 1971, but it was a poor imitation of what Walter Gordon had in mind. Its objective, as spelled out in the Act, was to assist in the development of Canada, and it was to do this by investing in "any corporation owning property or carrying on business related to the economic interest of Canada." This allowed the business executives appointed to run the CDC to buy shares in American corporations having mines or other interests in this country, which they did because such investments produced the best returns. Thus, the Canada Development Corporation became just another money-making fund.

deal. On the other hand, the amount of Canadian investment in the United States has increased a great deal.

Now the reason for that, I think, has very little to do with attitudes toward investment. I think that the reason in both cases is that it has been less profitable to invest in Canada than it has been to invest in the United States. The reduced flow from the United States to Canada and the increased flow from Canada to the United States at the same time [means that] our balance-of-payments current-account deficit has swollen to enormous proportions—partly for the reason that I mentioned, that our costs have been out of line. We perhaps haven't done as good a job at controlling inflation as the United States has. This tends to suck in goods and to make it difficult for us to export as we lose our competitive position.

Of course this deficit, this huge deficit on current account, on goods and services, has to be financed. With direct investments a diminishing source of finance, much more of it has had to be financed by borrowing. So we've been borrowing, going into debt in the last few years at a prodigious rate—mainly through the issue of bonds by Canadian provinces and municipalities and corporations in the American market.

WALTER GORDON

I stayed in Cabinet to get the report because I thought if I wasn't there it would never see the light of day. I had always assumed it was a good report. The people who wrote it were chosen by the Cabinet at large. If anybody said, "Well, I don't like this man. I think things are slanted. These economists have this view," I said, "Well, if anybody wants to name any other economist, we'll add him to the task force." So that was done, and there were eight of them. They produced the unanimous report. Something, I suggest, that in the history of the world had never been accomplished before by eight economists. Now, I may be wrong, but normally they would dissent among themselves. Not in this case. They had a unanimous report.

I said to Pearson, "Now, I would presume that this report will be approved in principle, tabled in the House, and referred to a parliamentary committee." And he told me that he thought that made sense. But some of the Cabinet ministers didn't want to approve it in principle—especially some of those who were working hard for the leadership. So it was not approved in principle. As a matter of fact, they arranged with, I suppose it was the Privy Council Office, to mark the thing with a great big plaster on the front of it to the effect that this had not been approved by Cabinet. So I tabled it, and within a few days submitted my resignation. All very clear and simple.

The final irony was that the publication of the Watkins Report was held up by yet another balance-of-payments crisis in the United States with its inevitable repercussion in Canada: there was a run on the Canadian dollar. The report was finished at the end of December 1967— it had been translated into French on an ongoing basis so that there would be no hold-up—and it was just about to be released when President Johnson, in his 1968 New Year message, announced guidelines that would cut down the amount of American investment abroad: this was at a time, as Louis Rasminsky said, when Canada was very dependent on the inflows of capital.

MEL WATKINS

I was at a meeting with this advisory committee [of officials] and they said the report cannot be issued at this time until the Canadian dollar is stabilized because, while it's not an outlandish report, it's critical of the role of foreign capital, and therefore it wouldn't help and it might hurt the run against the dollar. I'm a professional economist and so I didn't have any great difficulty understanding that. I thought it was fairly ironic that we couldn't issue a report on foreign capital because of the existing vulnerability of the economy; I thought people should recognize the irony of what was involved there. But I remember Mr. Gordon being not very happy when I came back to him and said I certainly had to agree with them that we couldn't go ahead right now. We'd have to wait.

At the time the United States undertook to correct its balance-of-payments crisis, the Canadian government was running a large deficit and the budget seemed to be out of control. One of the reasons for this was the wild scramble among many of the ministers, including Mitchell Sharp, the finance minister, to succeed Lester Pearson; the prime minister had announced his retirement, which had been long expected, at the end of December 1967. Since so many of them were away from Ottawa, beating the boondocks for delegates to the Liberal Party's coming leadership convention, the government, which had always been in a minority position, was defeated in the House of Commons on a money bill. This did not increase confidence abroad in the Canadian economy: the Canadian dollar weakened, and there was some export of capital. In fact, the situation became so serious that the governor of the Bank of Canada was called on for consultations.

LOUIS RASMINSKY

There were quite frequent meetings with Pearson and other ministers. Early in February, at one of these meetings, I expressed the view that the crisis was due to a mixture of external and internal causes: the large deficit in our balance of payments, the view that the government didn't have a coherent policy. The real basic question, on the internal side, was whether the government could create the conviction that its expenditure policies were directed against continued erosion of the value of money. Pearson listened well, and his attitude was generally to sigh and to shake his head. I mean, Pearson never felt terribly at ease with these problems. I also suggested at the time that the government should make a start toward an incomes policy.

However, the run on the dollar continued, and once again Rasminsky had to make the journey to Washington to persuade those in power that Canada was so close to the United States, and the Canadian economy so inextricably intertwined with the American economy, that Ottawa had to be granted an exemption from the guidelines. This time the secretary of the treasury was not Douglas Dillon but H. H. Fowler and the Canadian ambassador was not Charles Ritchie but Ed Ritchie, who was no relation. Once again the Americans were being pressed by their European friends to do something, and Fowler (who was always called Joe), while a good friend of Canada, was afraid of charges of discrimination if he were to make an exception for this country. The argument that Rasminsky put forward was the same as the one he had used in 1963: that if the Canadian dollar was knocked off parity, which was threatened at the time, there would be immediate repercussions on the American dollar—in other words, the attention of speculators would then turn to the American dollar.

During the dinner break Rasminsky phoned Ottawa and found that there had been what he described as "enormous exchange losses that day."

LOUIS RASMINSKY

The conversations went on the morning and afternoon of March 6 [1968] and then when I found out how much exchange we had lost, I came back and started the evening discussion by recalling that I had been saying before to the Americans that one reason why they should give us the exemption was that if we got into trouble the attack would turn on them. But I now had to tell them, in all honesty, that even if we got the exemption, I wasn't at all sure that the Canadian position was viable. So they were on their own so far as that was concerned. I think that that triggered them into a pretty early action. In the end the Americans did give us a complete exemption from their direct investment guidelines and the government took some action here on the budget and we made some commitments to them, which are of a rather technical nature, that Canada shouldn't be used as a pass-through.

Mind you, this wasn't the first that Fowler had heard of it. I had some help too because I had explained the situation before going down to the chairman of the Federal Revenue Board, Bill Martin, and to the head of the Federal Reserve Bank in New York, Al Hayes, and also to [Pierre Paul] Schweizer, the head of the International Monetary Fund, and they had spoken to Fowler. As a result, Fowler had been pretty well softened up. We had an exchange of letters incorporating what they would do, and what we would do.

Meanwhile I rounded up through my Central Banking contacts, the BIS [Bank for International Settlements], the Bundbank and the Bank of Italy and the Fed, which helped to get a line of— they put together four hundred million dollars. Then the Department of Finance was concurrently negotiating a large loan from the Export-Import Bank, so we had a large package then to put in the shop window. This whole program, including the borrowings, was announced in Parliament the next day [March 7, 1968]. Then, the government declared its intention of cutting its domestic borrowing requirements in half and of appointing an Incomes Commission—that's the one that was headed by Jack Young.[6] In fact, everything settled down very quickly, and the exchange crisis was over.

On March 11, 1968, after it was obvious that nothing would be done about the Watkins Report, Walter Gordon resigned from the Cabinet for the second and last time. A month later Lester B. Pearson gave up his office, and Pierre Elliott Trudeau, who had been elected leader at the Liberal Party Convention on April 6, became prime minister.

Although the Watkins Report did not propose a Foreign Investment Review Agency, it laid the groundwork; as Mel Watkins said, it was not only part of the process but it was a symptom as well. Very reluctantly the Trudeau government gave in to the nationalist sentiment, and in the spring of 1970 appointed another group under Herb Gray, who was then minister of national revenue, to look into the problem. This inquiry had a much bigger budget and much more time—too much time in the view of the opposition. On May 2, 1972, fully two years later, Herb Gray tabled what was described as a background report, which had detailed proposals for setting up a watchdog agency, albeit a watchdog without teeth. Even at that, it took another year and a half before the FIRA Act became law, and almost two years more before the agency was fully operational. There had been a slow-down in American take-overs of Canadian enterprises during the last few years, but, as Louis Rasminsky said, this was due to the fact that Canada was no longer as attractive a place for investment; it had nothing to do with the Foreign Investment Review Agency, which rubber-stamped most applications and, for all its effectiveness, represented just another layer of bureaucracy. The ratio of American ownership remained the same, according to Watkins: the reason for this was that the quantum leap, as he put it, took place in the late Forties and early Fifties and while some movement had occurred, there had been no real change.

In the decade since the publication of his report, Mel Watkins saw no

---

[6]It was not till June 19, 1969, that a Prices and Income Commission, chaired by a professor from the University of British Columbia, Dr. John H. Young, was appointed. The commission could and did set guidelines for management and labor but had no powers of enforcement.

advance in the cause of Canadian economic independence, and blamed this on Prime Minister Trudeau; he said that Pierre Trudeau more than any other Canadian politician represented an anti-nationalist position. There was another irony in the fact that Walter Gordon had actively supported Trudeau for the leadership of the Liberal Party; he had lived to regret this. Nationalism, Watkins said, as far as Trudeau was concerned, meant national unity.

II *Vietnam War: the Missions*

IT WAS THE RESORT TO DOUBLE-TALK over the Vietnam War that really muddied Canadian-American relations during Prime Minister Pearson's years of office, particularly the later years. William P. Bundy and the others of the "brightest and best" around President Johnson could be excused for believing that Canada stood squarely beside the United States on this issue if they read only what they wanted to read. There was Paul Martin, the external affairs minister, who spoke of the infiltration of South Vietnam and the civil war there as "this insidious form of [Communist] aggression." The Canadian member of the International Control Commission issued a minority report at the time of the United States air strikes in February 1965, objecting to the Indian and Polish majority report as "an over-simplified and misleading impression of the root causes" of the war, and declaring that the "so-called South Vietnam Liberation Front, of which the Viet Cong are in effect the armed forces, is a creature of the ruling party of North Vietnam." Which could not have been better put by an American briefing officer in Saigon.

Even in his famous "stop-the-bombing" speech at Temple University in Philadelphia, Pearson said that "the government and great majority of the people of my country have supported whole-heartedly the U. S. peace-keeping and peace-making policies in Vietnam." This was the way the Americans liked to describe their conduct of the war, as a police action or peace-keeping, and they might very well have asked why, in the circum-stances, Pearson should object to the bombing of North Vietnam. Was this

254

not a logical extension of their "peace-making policies?" No wonder President Johnson was bewildered and outraged: he took the full-blooded American stand that anyone who was not for United States action in Vietnam was against it, and he had always regarded Canadians as "our good friends and neighbors," and had said so. Furthermore, he had been told by his advisers that Pearson and the Canadian government were in favor of what the Americans were doing to defeat Communist aggression in Asia. These same advisers had simply ignored the parts of the speeches or statements where the prime minister and the external affairs minister appealed for a cease-fire and negotiations—except in the case of the Temple University address, where they took his carefully worded call for a bombing halt out of context.

It was at Washington's request that the Canadian diplomat J. Blair Seaborn visited North Vietnam in 1964. This was the first of two Canadian missions to Hanoi, and it became clouded in controversy with the publication of the so-called Pentagon Papers a decade later. Seaborn was described, in this study prepared by the U. S. Department of Defense, as the "secret envoy to Hanoi for the United States govern-ment"; this was hotly denied by the Department of External Affairs, which said that he was carrying out Canadian instructions and merely delivered a message from the United States.

In the spring of 1964 the political situation in South Vietnam was so shaky that the government of General Nguyen Khanh was in danger of falling. Henry Cabot Lodge, who was the United States ambassador in Saigon, advocated an escalation of American military activity, including the bombing of the North, as a way of saving the regime. However, 1964 was a presidential election year, and Washington felt that Hanoi could be frightened into calling off the Vietcong and suing for peace; as the Pentagon Papers put it, there was an underlying confidence among decision-makers like Dean Rusk and Bill Bundy that "if this mightiest nation resolved to use its vast power, the other side would buckle." But, obviously, this information had to be conveyed somehow to the Com-munist authorities of North Vietnam, and no less a person than the secretary of state flew to Ottawa to seek the good offices of the Canadian commissioner on the ICC for Vietnam who paid regular calls on Hanoi. Paul Martin said that Rusk phoned him before coming up, but Dean Rusk doubted if he would have visited Ottawa for this purpose alone and wondered whether there had been a NATO foreign ministers' meeting at the time.[1] However, the Pentagon Papers record the fact that Rusk visited Ottawa on April 30, 1964, "to set up the Seaborn Mission [interlocutor] to Hanoi for mid-June."

The government had already appointed J. Blair Seaborn, an able and experienced foreign service officer, to be the Canadian representative on the International Control Commission for Vietnam. Seaborn said that his departure to take up this post was speeded up because of the American desire to have him deliver this message to the North Vietnamese. His first trip to Hanoi was on June 18, 1964, and the Pentagon Papers reported that he met secretly with Pham Van Dong, North Vietnam's premier, and warned him of "the greatest devastation that would result from escalation by North Vietnam." Paul Martin denied this although he acknowledged that Seaborn did tell the North Vietnamese that the Americans intended to escalate the war. Bill Bundy maintained that the Canadian employed the "carrot and stick strategy" worked out by Ambassador Lodge.

On August 13, 1964, Seaborn made his second trip to Hanoi and again saw Pham Van Dong. On August 8, just before this visit, a U. S. note was delivered to the Canadian Embassy in Washington containing a number of points that the Americans wanted Seaborn to make when he saw the Communists again. Among them were such strictures as "U. S. public and official patience with North Vietnamese aggression is growing extremely thin," and "If the DRV [the Democratic Republic of Vietnam, as North Vietnam was called] persists in its present course, it can expect to suffer the consequences." Also, Point 8 of the note read as follows:

"Mr. Seaborn can again refer to the many examples of U. S. policy in tolerance of peaceful coexistence with Communist regimes, such as Yugoslavia, Poland, etc. He can hint at the economic and other benefits which have accrued to those countries because their policy of Communism has confined itself to the development of their own national territories and has not sought to expand into other areas."

As might be expected, Seaborn prepared a detailed, almost verbatim account of his conversations with Pham Van Dong which he dispatched to Ottawa and later gave to the American authorities in Saigon; he did not return home to report on his mission, although he did fly to Tokyo, after the second trip to Hanoi, to brief the external affairs minister, who happened to be visiting Japan at the time. Altogether, Seaborn spent a year and a half as the Canadian member of the ICC for Vietnam and

[1]The North Atlantic Council met in Ottawa in May 1963.

visited Hanoi four more times although he did not see Pham Van Dong again.

PAUL MARTIN

We gave general acceptance to what Rusk wanted. Mind you, I had tremendous confidence in Rusk which was in no way misplaced. I think he is a remarkable man. I didn't agree with his point of view: he saw Communists behind every tree; I didn't, and Pearson didn't. But we agreed that he would send a man to see me and then they would convey to us a general description of their exacerbation of the war in the North. We examined it carefully and we both came to the conclusion—I came to the conclusion with my officers and then I discussed with Pearson and he agreed—we came to the conclusion that the North should know what the American ultimate intention was, so that they could decide whether the time had not come when they should sit down and try to work out a cease-fire. But we didn't pass on to Seaborn all that Rusk asked. We decided—as I clearly indicated to him what would be decided—what would be passed on.

Now, when Seaborn went, he made it clear he carried a message from Pearson to the head of state, Ho Chi Minh, to say that we had decided in the interest of peace and in the interest of the cease-fire that we should send this particular representative, Seaborn, to convey certain information that had been passed on to us and which we regarded as essential information for them to know in the hope that it might assist in the objective which we thought should be pursued. He saw everybody that counted; he saw the prime minister, he saw the foreign minister, and I think he saw the minister of defense. In any event, he had full discussions. The information that he conveyed, of course, did not alter the policy of North Vietnam.

He made a second visit, and by the way, after the first visit, the North said, "We welcome the Canadian intervention. We welcome this contact. We know you are members of the commission, and you have contacts with us, with Saigon, with Washington. You are close friends of the United States. You have influence in the United States. We welcome all this, but we don't want this to be made known. We will deny our talks with you. We are at war. We are not going to give the impression that we are weaklings looking for peace." That was their understandable argument, and that's why I was so concerned about anything like this being revealed. That's why I had to deny certain things.

He made a second visit. I insisted that he go back and report on the American reaction. Why did I insist? Because I wanted it clear that we were working in this particular matter with both sides equally. You can't hope to bring about a cease-fire if you don't treat both sides to the bargain the same way. I wanted to report on what the American reaction was, and that we did in the second visit. They [the North Vietnamese] thanked us for coming and telling them—they said that they knew that already because the war was exacerbating all the time. But we were reporting to them our report to the Americans after our visit to them. Some of our people didn't want Seaborn to go back a second time. I said, "He must go back. He must report to the North what the American reaction is [to expand the war]."

WILLIAM P. BUNDY

There was the very important Seaborn episode, which is so fully covered in the Pentagon Papers that I really don't have much new. However, beginning as early as June 1964 Pearson had, as far as I could tell, willingly and fully cooperated in having Seaborn convey these messages that were a combination of the carrot and the stick. One could argue about the proportions. They were distinctly "at some point we may have to act" messages, and I think that had given Johnson the feeling that Canada was not unsympathetic to our standing firm, if it came down to the kind of crunch where we felt we had to engage in some level of bombing of the North and so on.

I'm not sure of this, but my impression is that in December 1964, when we were at the stage of clearly laying out plans for a graduated and measured program of bombing of the North, we told the Canadians that this was very much on our minds, and that we were conceivably quite close to a point of decision on it, and didn't pick up any marked objections.

I think even then there may have been a desire to be sure that we didn't plan, in the first instance at any rate, attacks on the major urban centers, that this would be aimed at the communication lines and military targets. I wouldn't say that there was any note of approval and "high time" and so on, which there certainly was from the Australians, but there seemed to be at least a benevolent attitude on it. Of course, this goes back into the reports of Canadian members of the ICC and things of that sort.

PAUL MARTIN

Seaborn was not an agent for the United States, and there were no threats in the message carried. I am not saying there was no element of threat in the original documents shown to us, but we decided what would go and there were no threats in what was passed on.

What did he pass on? Just their intention to exacerbate the war. And we pointed that out that there would be no limit in it, that that was what the Americans were going to do, according to the best information we had, and that is all we passed on.

DEAN RUSK

There were all sorts of intermediaries all through this period: governments, organizations, private citizens, direct contacts between us and Hanoi—and it looked as though there was a great race on to win the Nobel Peace Prize. We had tried in almost every conceivable way to engage the North Vietnamese in discussions, comparable to the discussions that occurred in Korea, but we also had a chance with some of the different kinds of communications to check one out against the other and we really never got any indication that Hanoi wanted to make peace except on the basis of taking over the entire country. I have no doubt that Mr. Seaborn tried on some ideas to see what their reaction would be, but it would be quite incorrect to say that he was an agent of ours or that he was having plenipotentiary powers to negotiate for the United States. But it would have been normal for him, I think, given his role in the ICC, to explore the possibilities. The Polish representative tried to do so; why shouldn't he?

One reason why the Seaborn mission was so sensitive was that the second meeting with Pham Van Dong occurred after the Tonkin Gulf incidents. In fact, the U. S. note of August 8 on points for the Canadian envoy to relay to Hanoi contained lengthy arguments that the attacks on two American destroyers by North Vietnamese torpedo boats were "obviously deliberate, planned and ordered in advance" and that, since the scene of the action was at least sixty miles from the nearest land, "there could have been no question about territorial waters."

Whatever the validity of the American claims, the Tonkin Gulf incidents were used to get the U. S. Congress to adopt a resolution supporting American action "to oppose firmly, by all necessary means, DRV efforts to subvert and conquer South Vietnam." It was pointed out in the note that this blank-check resolution was passed with near-unanimity. This was one of the "sticks" of the "carrot-and-stick combination" that Bill Bundy mentioned, that Seaborn was supposed to have used. It was little wonder, therefore, that Americans should have asserted that Seaborn had an "intelligence role," according to the Pentagon Papers, although it would have been wrong to interpret this, as some Canadians did, to mean that he was engaged in espionage.

At the end of May 1964 Pandit Nehru died; he had been an influential and virulent critic of American policy in Vietnam. Nehru had been such a dominant figure in India—he had been prime minister since independence—that there were fears that his death might lead to an upheaval, if not the break-up of the country. Because of them, Prime Minister Pearson wanted the Canadian high commissioner to India to have political experience; that is what he told his old friend, Roland Michener, the former speaker of the House of Commons, when he offered him the job. However, Pearson had another motive: he wanted to give Michener some diplomatic experience in preparation for his succeeding General Georges Vanier as governor-general of Canada; it was the possibility of this appointment as head of state that made Michener, who was enjoying private life, agree to return to public service as high commissioner to India.

The Commonwealth, with the exception of Australia and New Zealand, was opposed to the Vietnam War. Most members considered the American policy there very dangerous and ugly, Arnold Smith said; they attributed it to American imperialism and aggressiveness, which he did not think was right. In his view it was based on a genuine fear of communism, which was a result of a misreading of history. Smith could speak for the Commonwealth because he became its first secretary-general. In 1964, at the heads-of-government meeting in London, Kwame Nkrumah, the president of Ghana, proposed that there be an independent secretariat for the organization; this would mean taking away control of the administration of the Commonwealth and the Commonwealth conferences from Britain. At first the Canadians were opposed to such a move.

ARNOLD SMITH

I started out with the traditional Canadian line that most of the things that a secretary could do could be done equally well by our diplomatic services. I was given hell by the Kenyan and one or two other senior officials who said Canada is a rich country and could afford missions but most countries couldn't and they needed a secretariat. I came to the conclusion that it made quite a lot of sense and so did Gordon Robertson, and we wrote a telegram to Ottawa for Pearson saying that we thought we ought to reverse the Canadian traditional opposition to the idea.

Pearson was away for the weekend, at Checkers with all the other heads of government. And when he came back Sunday afternoon we showed him this telegram, and we discussed it a bit and he signed it and sent it, and the Cabinet met on Monday morning and by Tuesday morning we got agreement on Pearson's recommendation that we should support this idea. Each head of government was to authorize or to nominate people to be secretary-general and it was agreed that senior officials of each Commonwealth government would meet at the call of the British to draft terms of reference for the secretary, and the latter meeting took place, I guess, in January of 1965, and I was the Canadian representative. It took about ten days.

In the meantime a couple of Commonwealth governments, heads of government, had asked Pearson to nominate me, and I had said I didn't want it. I promised my wife; we had been abroad so much, and I was thinking of getting out and going into Canadian politics. But the next two or three months proved to be quite interesting in world politics and I realized it was not less important and quite exciting. So I told Mike that I changed my mind and would be prepared to be nominated. He did nominate me, and at the '65 meeting I guess there were eight or nine candidates nominated, but I was elected, and I have never regretted that. It was a fascinating job.

Among the important international events that may have prompted Arnold Smith to agree to becoming secretary-general of the Commonwealth was Cyprus, where the Greek and Turkish populations were at each others' throats. The situation on this Mediterranean island had deteriorated so much since it gained independence from Britain that there was a danger of war breaking out between Greece and Turkey. Finally the United Nations acted and in March 1964 established a peace-keeping force for Cyprus. Canada had agreed to contribute to this force, and, within twenty-four hours of the necessary UN resolutions being adopted, Canadian troops were on their way. In fact they had set out, as Lester Pearson noted in his memoirs, even before Parliament had authorized their dispatch, although he hastily added, "we could and would have brought them back if we had not been given authorization that night."

One reason why Canada moved so quickly over Cyprus was that President Johnson had telephoned Prime Minister Pearson and told him of his great anxiety about the possibility of Greece and Turkey becoming involved; they were both NATO allies and he was afraid that a conflict between them would have serious consequences for the North Atlantic Alliance. The president was therefore amazed and delighted at the speed with which Canada acted, and Pearson wrote in his memoirs, "He phoned me again the night we began the airlift to say, 'You'll never know what this has meant having those Canadians off to Cyprus and being there tomorrow. You'll never know what this may have prevented.' Having praised us for our action, he concluded, 'Now what can I do for you?' I replied, 'Nothing at the moment, Mr. President.' But I had some credit in the bank."

For some time there had been rumblings that the white minority in Rhodesia would go it alone, and on November 11, 1965, —Ian Smith had deliberately picked Armistice Day—a unilateral declaration of independence, or UDI, was made. By this time Arnold Smith was secretary-general of the Commonwealth, and UDI presented him with his greatest crisis. The Commonwealth could have broken up over this issue, and, according to the testimony of Smith and Malcolm MacDonald, who attended the crucial 1966 conference, Mike Pearson was largely responsible for saving the multi-national association. MacDonald, who sat behind Prime Minister Wilson at the conference, said he was thrilled with Mike's behavior and conduct and wisdom.

ARNOLD SMITH

Pearson played a major role in preventing a breakdown of contact and dialogue between the Africans and their Asian allies and the British and their Australian and New Zealand allies. That was in the January 1966 Commonwealth heads-of-government meeting in Lagos and the September 1966 meeting in London where we got the British committed at last—but only after a very dangerous three-month truce period—to the principle of "no Independence before majority" rule. Mike was very important in helping to get this agreement.

I remember calling on Harold Wilson before the September 1966 meeting began and saying, "You've got to agree to no independence before majority rule." He said, "This has never been our policy and I won't agree." Well, I said, "your country made two big mistakes giving independence to South Africans before majority rule and giving it to Zanzibar before majority rule,[2] and you had good reason to regret both of those. Now, for heaven's sake, don't make the same error in Rhodesia." Well, Wilson wouldn't promise me that he would agree to the principle of NIBMR, as it was called—No Independence Before Majority Rule—but by the end of September 1966 at the heads of government conference, he did agree to it. This was one of my goals for that conference. I always tried to plan what I wanted to come out of a Commonwealth meeting before I organized it.

MALCOLM MACDONALD

The Rhodesia crisis had arisen from the moment when [Ian] Smith's regime illegally declared independence. At the conference the African representatives of those several nations were tremen-

---

[2]The British granted independence to Zanzibar, an island off the east coast of Africa, under a minority Arab regime, which was essentially the heirs of the slave-trading Arab aristocracy. This government lasted only a few months before it was overthrown by left-wing African nationalists representing the black majority. The British did not recognize this coup for a long time and urged their friends in other Western countries not to, which Arnold Smith described as a very silly policy. The Communists established relations immediately and tried to turn Zanzibar into a naval base. In the end Zanzibar joined Tanganyika to become Tanzania, and Smith felt that it was a very venturesome, courageous initiative on the part of Nyerere in organizing this merger: the president of Zanzibar was called Mr. President in Zanzibar although he was vice-president in Tanzania.

dously critical of the British government for not using force to defeat the rebellion in Rhodesia and for also being in favor of negotiating an agreement with Smith's illegal regime which would have given Rhodesia independence under minority rule, but, of course, on condition that there was a steady progress to majority rule, a condition which a lot of us thought Smith would not carry out. He might sign an agreement, but it would be broken.

The African nations, which is what matters, were sure Smith would break any such agreement and therefore thought the British government were absolutely wrong in being prepared to make such an agreement. Now, they were supported at the Commonwealth conference by most if not all of the Asian independent nations and the Caribbean independent nations. The British government's attitude on selling arms to South Africa to some extent and on this sort of settlement with Rhodesia was supported by Australia and by New Zealand and partially by one or two other independent nations in the Commonwealth like Malta, if I remember rightly, under the previous prime minister.

It was Canada who was the only white nation that disagreed with the British policy and was critical of it without going the whole way to the African attitude. Mike was not only skilled but wise, which is even more important, and his delegation helped to keep the Africans and the other non-whites feeling, "Well, this isn't a Commonwealth where the whites are on one side and the non-whites on another."

So the discussions went on, they went on for days and days on Rhodesia, and the other items on the agenda were hardly dealt with until the last twenty-four hours. But, in the end, I would say almost entirely because of Mike and his delegation's policy and their handling of the discussions inside and outside the conference, there was an agreed communiqué phrased in a way which enabled everybody to keep together and agree. That was only one example of the way in which Canada at that moment under Mike's leadership saved this international partnership.[3]

---

[3]Malcolm MacDonald was present at an earlier heads-of-government conference at which another Canadian prime minister, John Diefenbaker, was instrumental in saving the Commonwealth. South Africa had become a republic and, since it no longer recognized the sovereignty of the Queen, had to apply for continued membership in

If I remember rightly, the compromise was that Wilson and his government would make one more attempt to get the sort of settlement which they thought would be expedient, and that if they did not succeed in that attempt, then they would abandon the plan for independence before majority rule, and from then on the British government policy would be no independence for Rhodesia except after majority rule. There were indications then that this final attempt by Harold Wilson would not succeed, that Smith and his chaps would not accept it.

ARNOLD SMITH

I think Mike Pearson saw the Commonwealth as an enormously important instrument for consultation and exchange of views. Gradually we built up a lot of functional cooperation among a fair cross-section of the world; countries in Africa, big ones, small ones; countries in Asia, big ones like India and small ones like Singapore; little islands in the Mediterranean and Caribbean and Pacific; rich countries like Britain and very rich ones like Australia and Canada; in the Pacific and in North America. I think Mike saw it straight as an exceedingly important instrument to help shape the thinking of leaders and peoples and thereby shape the future, and this, of course, is the right way to see it.

On March 29, 1966, the French government, in a series of aide-mémoires, *announced the withdrawal of all French forces from the NATO Command, to be completed by July 1 of that year; it also requested that the headquarters' establishments of the alliance should leave France within the next twelve months, by April 1, 1967, and that most U. S. and Canadian installations be removed in the same time. The abruptness of the order to "get out" came as a shock to Lester Pearson; in*

the Commonwealth. The application came up at the 1961 meeting in London and was quickly changed from the question of admitting another republic to that of extending membership to a country governed by white supremacists who maintained a color bar as official policy. MacDonald said that Diefenbaker, who sided with the six Asian and African prime ministers, made an excellent statement, calm, not emotional, but effective. Partly because it was a white head of government who had spoken out against apartheid, the issue was resolved without creating a crisis. South Africa withdrew its application. It was yet another example, as MacDonald said, of the way that Canada played such an important part in Commonwealth survival.

fact, Paul Martin said there was nothing that upset him more. As a diplomat, Pearson was an advocate of consultations and negotiations, and a fait-accompli *such as this was anathema to him. He had pressed for full and free discussions within NATO of all major international questions, but, as Dean Rusk noted, there was a reluctance on the part of many members to deal with matters that were outside the scope of the North Atlantic Treaty. Thus, NATO never became the forum for the exchange of ideas and information like the Commonwealth; the reason for this was that it was a military alliance and, as such, was much more rigid and inflexible. Despite the best efforts of the Canadians, Article 2, which would have given the organization an economic role, had never been accepted.*

Then, there was General de Gaulle and his politics of grandeur. He regarded the presence of NATO in Paris and of American and other foreign troops on French soil as a gross infringement of France's sovereignty; he was prepared to cooperate with the alliance but he would not have French troops integrated in the NATO Command. Although de Gaulle did not hide his views, nobody apparently believed that he would insist on the allies getting out of France and the French withdrawing from the alliance.

PAUL MARTIN

The first official visit Pearson [as prime minister] made to any country [aside from Britain and U. S. A.] was to France. He and I went there in January 1964. We were received by de Gaulle and we had talks with him and other members of the government. We had a long discussion about NATO. Pearson knew of the reservations that the general had and kept emphasizing his support for the alliance. De Gaulle was opposed to the integrated-force command and the integrated force itself, and Pearson understood that.

Then we had developed a policy of, I won't say rapprochement, but of close understanding with France. I was very anxious that our foreign policy should reflect our bilingual policy, and this, of course, was Pearson's view as well. And for that reason, without sacrificing our own convictions and beliefs, whenever the occasion arose in the NATO Prime Ministers' Council, we tried to support the French. We tried to explain their position. We didn't agree in their not being a member of the integrated force, but with the idea of getting them to come back in, we sought to explain their reasons, and to befriend them, in other words. And so we felt that we had built up a pretty good reserve of good will; we had a lot of money in the French bank, so we were rather disheartened at the way in which de Gaulle said, "Get out."

The Americans were, too, and the negotiations are still under way for compensation because we had a big bit of real estate, and, of course, the Americans much, much more. We had invested a lot of money in the permanent physical infrastructure of NATO. De Gaulle kept insisting, of course, all along when we saw him in '64 that that was his view of NATO. He had great support and belief in the alliance, but he did not want to see an erosion of French sovereignty, and he felt the joint military command or an integrated-force command structure was a violation of French sovereignty and that he would not and did not want to tolerate. Cooperation in military matters, yes. That was his view and we knew it, but we never anticipated that he would give effect to it in the way that he did when he asked us to get out.

DEAN RUSK

President de Gaulle did not want to be in any forum where smaller countries were present. He had proposed to President Eisenhower the directoire of three nations, France, UK, US, to be the executive committee of the free world. President Eisenhower turned that down for the simple reason that President de Gaulle never really understood, and that is that the United States was not prepared to nominate itself to be a member of any such directoire because there were other countries—Germany, Italy, Canada, Brazil, and Japan and so forth—that would not have accepted any such role. President de Gaulle repeated that to President Kennedy and President Kennedy for the same reasons also turned it down. So France's view about consultation in the NATO community I think was very special, especially President de Gaulle.

But there are also some other problems about consultation in NATO, some of them being of a technical sort relating to communications intelligence. You pretty much have to assume that what is said in NATO goes to Moscow. But more importantly, at least during the Sixties, it was very difficult to get NATO to discuss matters that were outside the geographical limits of the NATO Treaty area—matters such as the Middle East and North Africa or China or questions of that sort. When I once suggested to my fellow NATO foreign ministers that it would be appropriate to have some discussions about China in NATO because the NATO territory went to the Bering Sea separating Alaska from Siberia, they looked at me as though I was some man from Mars. To them NATO meant the central front in Europe. So there was a bit of reluctance on the part of NATO to talk about these things.

They don't even caucus about things that are on the agenda of the United Nations; they won't even do that. If there are internal political problems, it's very difficult to get a point of view out of NATO. And the question of initiative is extremely interesting. One would think that the way to consult is to consult. When you compare the initiatives taken by the United States to bring questions to NATO with the initiatives of any other members of NATO to bring questions to NATO, it's astonishing. Up through the Sixties almost never did any other government bring anything up in NATO.

PAUL MARTIN

The French are a wonderful people, they are a very civilized people, they have got great experience, but they have developed, in my judgment, in the last twenty years a posture and an arrogance and an assertion of infallibility that does France great harm. The people of France are not an arrogant people, but their military hierarchy, their governmental hierarchy, assumes that they have all the answers, that God has given them a knowledge of how to comport themselves and conduct government policy as no other people can. And it's done France a great deal of harm. I am a great admirer of de Gaulle. I always respected de Gaulle, so much so that I explained his " *Vive Québec Libre*" speech in a little different terms.

It was in March 1966 that Chester Ronning embarked on the second Canadian mission to Hanoi in as many years: his task was to try to find if there were any way of starting negotiations that would lead to the end of the Vietnam War. Some time before, President Johnson had called on all countries to do whatever they could to get some kind of accommodation that would result in a cease-fire, and this had prompted the Canadian external affairs minister, Paul Martin, to act, although he said that it did not require such an appeal to convince Prime Minister Pearson and himself that something had to be done. The secretary-general of the United Nations was also seeking a settlement at the time, as were Prime Minister Harold Wilson of Britain and Aleksei Kosygin of the Soviet Union. Martin said that U Thant had told him about his own peace moves and had urged him to continue the Canadian efforts.

Blair Seaborn had returned from his tour of duty as the Canadian member of the International Control Commission for Vietnam, and Martin discussed with him and with other officers of the department the plans for another mission. They decided that the best person to send would be Chester Ronning, who had recently retired from the foreign service. Ronning, who spoke Chinese fluently, had taken part in the 1962 Geneva Conference on Laos and knew Chou En-lai and Ho Chi Minh.

Furthermore, the external affairs minister had been considering the next step to be taken with regard to the recognition of Communist China, and felt that it might be a good thing for Ronning to see Chou En-lai on his way to North Vietnam to discuss with him the development of this policy. It would be a way of killing two birds with one stone. Bill Bundy recalled that the Ronning mission was supposed to have run counterpoint, as he put it, to the question of Chinese representation at the United Nations. So Ronning went to Hong Kong, but Martin said that when he rang Chou En-lai, he was told that the Chinese regretted very much that it would not be possible to receive him at this time in China. However, that was not what happened according to the principal: Chester Ronning said that he never rang Chou En-lai, that he knew there were differences even then between the North Vietnamese and the Chinese, and that he never intended to go to Hanoi via China.

This was one example of the sort of misunderstanding there was over this mission, the wishful thinking that went on, and the way that people interpreted events to suit their own particular prejudices. It was clear to the Canadians—to Chester Ronning as well as Paul Martin and Lester Pearson—that the Communists had moved and had made a concession, but to the Americans—to Dean Rusk and Bill Bundy, as well as Henry Cabot Lodge—there was nothing new in the report that Ronning brought back from Hanoi. In fact, the Americans felt that the Canadians did not know how to deal with the Communists. The misunderstanding and the lack of communication reached such a point that there were disagreements over what was said at the time. Martin asserted that Rusk considered Ronning to be a Communist and that the U. S. secretary of state said that he was not the kind of man that the Americans would send as a mediator. However, Rusk categorically denied this when interviewed years later.

PAUL MARTIN

Rusk had told me, as I fully knew he would, what the disabilities of Chester [Ronning] were. But I wanted to tell him what we had in mind, and I did. I also went and saw Harriman. Harriman knew Chester Ronning. Harriman had been the beneficiary of Chester's intervention in the 1962 conference on Laos; Ronning had played a very important role in that conference, a role that was appreciated by Harriman. I went and saw Harriman and I said, "Now, this is what we are going to do. Rusk isn't overly happy about this and I suspect on the basis of what he will tell the president and others, they won't be happy. But this is what we're going to do." Harriman said, "Well, I know Ronning; I think this is a great idea, and you couldn't have picked a better man and I will help in every way," and I'm sure that Harriman did play a part in finally getting American approval—not that I had sought that as a condition to action.

AVERELL HARRIMAN

I had a great respect for Chester Ronning. I was satisfied that he would look after the interests of this country and play fair, which he did and proved himself. Some people in the department who were quite reactionary felt that he was a Communist, but that was nonsense. President Johnson had asked me to see what possibly could be done to start negotiations for ending the war, and I remember that Chester Ronning undertook to do that. I encouraged him to do it, but unfortunately he was not successful.

CHARLES RITCHIE

Ronning came to Washington and expounded his views, which were very coldly received by the State Department. The only person who understood what he was talking about was Harriman. That was my impression of his conversations. They were entirely prejudiced against Ronning. Ronning had a rather emotional and missionary manner of delivery which didn't suit at all with the tone of the State Department, and which was part of the trouble, I think. He was vehement; he spoke of the peasant masses and all this sort of thing, and was the ex-missionary son from China.

There was total noncommunication, and Ronning was very general and impressionistic in his presentation, which really was based on the inevitable triumph of peasant risings, you know, rather reminiscent of Mao Tse-tung—"the fish in the water" and all that sort of thing—and this didn't go down naturally at all well. But, of course, his knowledge of the situation and his experience and his sincerity were very valuable and should have been given an objective assessment without prejudice and taken into account, but I don't think they were.

WILLIAM P. BUNDY

We were totally convinced at the time—and I may say I am as totally convinced today as I was then—that Hanoi was not then ready to enter into serious talks, that they were quite relentless about pursuing their objective. Quite possibly they had weighed this very heavily. There were indications even of some debate within the Politbureau in Hanoi. But the outcome was clearly and categorically negative, and when Ho Chi Minh spoke on January 28, 1966, he was expressing the viewpoint that for that time was absolutely negative.

If that was the reading as of the end of January and early February, when Ronning came to us in early March, with Paul Martin's good offices and blessing, we had to start with the feeling that it was most unlikely that any Communist government, or any other kind of government, would change its position very rapidly and that therefore this wasn't much of a time to be exploring new gambits. We weren't prepared to make our position any more liberal and in fact we were by then saying that whereas during the long pause we had given a kind of open-ended invitation to Hanoi to respond in any fashion, they had declined even that gambit.

We were now saying—Rusk was saying, we were saying on all diplomatic frequencies—"We've got to have some indication of what military restraint Hanoi would apply." That was the position we were taking. We didn't think the timing was good in any circumstances. We also knew that the political situation in the South was quite shaky. It seemed as though Hanoi could hardly be anything but *more* hopeful than it had been during the period of the pause. So that the timing was just plain not propitious.

I explained this to Ronning and to Ritchie. I went through it. I said we obviously were always anxious to get firsthand readings from Hanoi, but unless and until we saw more willingness to exchange views seriously than we were able to unearth by the exhaustive effort of December and January, we were very skeptical. I had to say it frankly. This is our position. It was our public position; it was our position to everybody who asked us." Try it on them and see what they say, we can't lose by this."

PAUL MARTIN

We drafted a letter for Chester [Ronning] to carry to the authorities in the North saying that he was an official representative of the Canadian government and that he was there for only one purpose and that was to see whether or not he could help to provide a basis for a cease-fire. Mike was doubtful about going to the North via China, and particularly for the reasons that I had in mind. He was all for a change in our China policy at some point, but he had some preoccupations as prime minister that I didn't have as foreign minister. I knew what they were, and they were mostly political, but I thought that we should take advantage of it. He said, "Well, if you think you want to do that, I won't stand in the way."

So Chester went directly to Hong Kong and from Hong Kong he communicated with Chou En-lai and also with Chen Yi and from both he got a communication, a friendly one, saying that they regretted very much that it would not be possible to receive him in China at this time. This was a rather surprising reaction because a group of Canadian businessmen under Senator [Donald] Cameron of Alberta had got into China at that very time, and why would they refuse a man with the well-known political inclinations of Chester Ronning and accept a Canadian businessmen's group? And, particularly, why would Chou En-lai, who had known Chester so long—although it was clear from the letter that Chou En-lai wrote to Chester that he had nothing but friendly feelings toward him.

But it may be that Chester being a sophisticated visitor, as he would be, he would have an understanding of the Cultural Revolution that was well under way, and that possibly might not be the best knowledge for someone not living in China to have, particularly when he had contacts with the West. Whatever it was, he didn't get in. He communicated with me and then we had to make other arrangements to send him in from Saigon in a plane, and we wanted that kept secret and that was a very difficult thing to do with so many newspaper people in Saigon. However, he got into Saigon; nobody knew he was there except Cabot Lodge, who was then U. S. ambassador there.

WILLIAM P. BUNDY

I never was quite sure to what extent this [the Ronning Mission] was really Mike Pearson personally, or to what extent it was Paul Martin. I had the impression that Paul was a little out front on his own, but I may be wrong. Mike had participated but not very actively in the previous year [1965] in various Commonwealth discussions and initiatives, but I can't single out anything that Canada had done particularly during 1965; he seemed, as it were, to have decided to go slow after the experience of the Temple University speech. But in March of 1966, Ronning appeared on the horizon from our standpoint as the suggested emissary to Hanoi. I didn't know Ronning. He came to Washington and I was asked to come to the embassy to understand what he wanted to do. He was going to Peking first and then he had the opportunity to go on to Hanoi and so on.

CHESTER RONNING

I did not make any request to go there [to China]. You see, this was a Canadian proposal altogether. I knew that, while China supported North Vietnam wholeheartedly, in opposition to the Americans, there were differences in opinion between the Vietnamese and the Chinese which were traditional. I did not intend ever to go via China to Vietnam. If there were any suggestion that I should do that, I knew nothing about that whatever. I did not phone Chou En-lai from Hong Kong. I didn't have any conversation with the Chinese. None whatever.

One of the first persons whom Chester Ronning saw when he reached Saigon was Henry Cabot Lodge who was the American viceroy in Indochina. They had known each other at the United Nations, where they had both been delegates, and Lodge was very frank with the Canadian envoy. Although he said that he did not approve or disapprove of the mission to Hanoi, Ronning got the impression that he was not in favor of it, because he said that there was no question that they could win the war. The trouble was that everything for Vietnam was being funneled through Saigon, and Lodge went over to a large map and raised the curtain covering it and pointed to various places on the narrow waist of South Vietnam, which was much closer to the border with the North. The American ambassador said that U. S. reinforcements and ammunition and other supplies would be sent in the future to these places. Not only would they avoid the bottleneck of Saigon but they would be much closer to the action. Ronning said that Lodge had him convinced that this was a very wise tactic. However, he did not mention it to the North Vietnamese because he felt that the information had been given him in trust, which may not have been exactly what Ambassador Lodge wanted.

Before setting off for Hanoi, Chester Ronning also called on the South Vietnamese foreign minister and the head of government who happened to be, at the time, General Nguyen Van Thieu. It was one of the ironies of the Vietnam War that most of the Saigon leadership, the military officers of the ruling junta, were from the North and were homesick for Hanoi. General Thieu, who was resplendent in uniform and medals when he received Ronning, practically begged him to convey greetings to individuals in Hanoi.

CHESTER RONNING

General Thieu said, "You know it is most unfair, I can't go from here to my home, to my residence except in, in a bullet-proof car, accompanied by troops. And there, that man, Ho Chi Minh walks with his hat on, up and down the streets of Hanoi." That revealed to me the difference in acceptance by the people of the heads of these two governments. You see, Ho Chi Minh was called Uncle Ho by the South Vietnamese as well as by the North Vietnamese. He was very, very popular throughout Vietnam. But Thieu was merely a puppet of the United States.

When Chester Ronning flew to Hanoi in the ICC's plane—the route taken was via the Cambodian capital of Phnom Penh and Vientiane in Laos—he noted that parts of North Vietnam looked like the surface of the moon. There were great craters in the fields and large patches of the jungle had been burned out by napalm bombs. It was a scene of utter devastation. Paul Martin said that Ronning was received by the Communists almost with presidential honors. A government delegation met him at the airport, and a teen-aged girl presented him with a large bouquet of chrysanthemums which, Ronning said, was very significant. Then they insisted on his staying in the best suite in the government hotel instead of at the Canadian headquarters.

Actually, Chester Ronning saw the same people that Blair Seaborn had seen, but the difference was that he knew them all personally and had a much better rapport. He recalled that he used to go out for walks with Pham Van Dong, the North Vietnamese premier, in the parks of Geneva during the 1954 Indochina and Korean Conferences, which went on for so long. Pham Van Dong could not speak much English, although he understood quite a lot, but they were able to converse in Chinese. Now, in wartorn Hanoi, Ronning talked to the North Vietnamese premier; he shared the latter's fury and indignation at the death and destruction being heaped on his country by American bombers, and at first wondered whether he would get anywhere. The discussion went on, and Ronning asserted that he had never worked harder or used more arguments to put the United States intervention in the Vietnam Civil War in the best possible light and to advance the cause of negotiations. Finally the break came when Pham Van Dong said that the North Vietnamese would agree to begin talks with the Americans once they stopped the bombing.

CHESTER RONNING

All of a sudden [Pham Van Dong] changed and he said to me— and I couldn't believe my ears—"We will come to the conference table to talk peace with the United States if the United States will stop bombing North Vietnam." I said, "How about the war in South Vietnam, will you continue that war?" "The war in South Vietnam is an issue that is entirely separate from this. If the Americans will stop bombing North Vietnam, we'll come to the conference table to discuss all the issues, including the issue of South Vietnam." And I said, "Does that mean that the Americans must stop fighting in South Vietnam?" He said, "No, it does not mean that. It means only that if the Americans will stop bombing North Vietnam, we'll come to the conference table immediately to settle all the issues, including North Vietnam and including South Vietnam."

So that it was not a proposal to end the war in South Vietnam; it was only a proposal to end the war as far as North Vietnam was concerned and particularly in regards to the bombing of North Vietnam.

The Canadian envoy, his mission accomplished, returned home and reported to the prime minister and the secretary of state for external affairs. Ronning claimed that Mike Pearson was most interested in the proposal that he had brought back and approved of it wholeheartedly. Paul Martin appeared to be less enthusiastic but nevertheless felt that there had been some movement on the part of the North Vietnamese and that Ronning had met President Johnson's conditions that he would sit down and talk with the Communists if they showed some movement. However, the American policy-makers like Dean Rusk and Bill Bundy belittled the Ronning mission, which they had never wanted and only reluctantly approved, and did not consider that he had brought back any worthwhile assurances. This so incensed Martin that he charged that President Johnson was playing games and that the Americans did not really want a cease-fire.

PAUL MARTIN

Chester was able to get some slight movement on that [the North Vietnam position]; not much, but some slight movement. President Johnson had said, "I will sit down and talk to the North if they will show but some movement." Those were his words. Some inclination that they were prepared to engage in serious peace discussions. Now we know that they weren't, but that was the picture at that time. Chester was very pleased with that modicum of achievement and his instructions were to come right to us after seeing Cabot Lodge. He was to report to Cabot Lodge on what he got, that one point, and that was to be conveyed at once by Lodge to his principals in Washington. We were given the information that Lodge got about two hours before it was given to Lodge. In other words, the Americans didn't get something from their man that hadn't first reached us.

Now Bill Bundy played an important part in all this. Bill Bundy was a friend of Mike's. He was the man in the State Department who lived nothing else but Vietnam, and he was the closest adviser on the subject to Rusk. He deprecated right from the beginning what Chester had conveyed. He didn't regard it as substantial. He didn't regard it as movement at all. I had some strong words with him about this at the time, but it was clear, as I told him only the other day: "You people didn't intend at that time to seek a peace unless you got a tremendous concession and you made a military advance. That is clear." But it wasn't clear at the time. And that is not what President Johnson had said.

I don't like to say that they were playing games with us. They were engaged in a big military venture. They were playing games with all of us, including Wilson, including Kosygin, including the secretary-general [U Thant], including the Poles. And I can understand that even though I regretted that was the case.

DEAN RUSK

Well, what kind of assurances? Because we had a lot of people who went to Hanoi who didn't really understand what they were hearing and they would come back seven months pregnant with peace, but when we would check those things out again with Hanoi, there was nothing to it. There were a lot of people who talked with North Vietnamese here and there who didn't know how to understand the words they listened to. We had ways to check these things out with North Vietnam, and so the idea that we rejected peace was absurd. We might have rejected the particular phraseology that Ronning might have brought back because it might heave meant something very different to us and the North Vietnamese than it meant to Ronning.

No, that's fundamentally wrong; utterly wrong [that the U. S. were playing games]. We were looking for peace; we weren't looking for something else. Remember, in those days we were trying to prevent the overrunning of Southeast Asia by Hanoi. We were not looking for some sort of face-saving formula by which we could get out and turn South Vietnam, Cambodia, and Laos over to them. That wasn't our purpose. A good many people in those days were more anxious to find a face-saving formula than they were in saving South Vietnam, Cambodia, and Laos, but we weren't interested in anything like that.

American attitudes changed. At the grass roots here in this country in 1968–69 many of our people decided if we couldn't tell them when the war was going to be over, we had better chuck it. That's the thing that made the difference. But if we could have gotten peace in 1961, we would have grabbed it. After all, in the Laos accords of 1962 we had flat commitments from the North Vietnamese, Russia, and China that Laos would not be used as a path of infiltration into South Vietnam, that all foreign troops would be withdrawn. But the North Vietnamese never did withdraw. They kept using Laos as infiltration routes. They wouldn't let the ICC operate in those areas of Laos held by the Communists.

WILLIAM P. BUNDY

At the end of March the political situation boiled over in the South [South Vietnam], and Ronning went on that first trip in March and brought us back a reading that just didn't seem different from any other reading. The possibility of his going again was raised. And he did return. There was an acute political crisis in South Vietnam all through April and May which was only resolved toward the end of May when the government was able to re-establish its control over the northern cities where the Buddhists, in effect, had taken over.

Then the skies were clear as far as the domestic political situation in South Vietnam was concerned; it wasn't about to come apart any more, but the episode had weakened the government. At that stage the suggestion was renewed that Ronning could go

off again and try out and see what response he could get. We said,
"We don't want to stand in the way of this; our position, however, remains that we'd be very interested in any indication of
what Hanoi would do in the military restraint area if we were to
stop bombing. Unless you could bring back something on that
score, we're afraid we wouldn't regard the situation as basically
changed from the January-February reading."

As was evident perhaps more to others than to Ronning, it was
just impossible to believe that Hanoi could be depressed or ready
to offer anything in May or June, or indeed in March, if it had
been firm in January and February. So we certainly didn't think
the omens were good, but we were very correct about it. We said,
"This is our position; if you bring back something of this sort we
will take it very seriously."

Concurrently, we were getting proposals at that stage for
bombing of the oil refineries near Hanoi and Haiphong. These
were always shorthanded as the "Hanoi and Haiphong oil
refineries," but they were in fact, and I think we measured this at
the time, as far from the metropolitan built-up areas as the
refineries in Bayway are from New York City. But we knew that
this was kind of daring; we weren't dismissing this factor, but we
did not anticipate that there would be significant civilian casualties
in these attacks and they were, by any World War Two thinking
and most thinking of any kind, military-related targets. So that
plan existed. We didn't discuss it specifically with the Canadian
government, but it was being rumored in the Washington papers,
it was in the air. The Canadian government can hardly have been
unaware of it at any time along the way, that the possibility
existed. It was at that stage that Ronning went out again.

*Chester Ronning saw the same people in Washington that he had seen
before he set off on his Hanoi mission, and his instructions were to get
their reaction so that he could return to North Vietnam and inform the
Communists about how their proposal had been received. Paul Martin
said, "He's going back. He has to go back," and added that the Americans
were less than pleased at this. They kept delaying Ronning's departure for
his return trip to Hanoi, and this angered the external affairs minister.
Finally, in June 1966, they let Ronning go.*

PAUL MARTIN

The Americans kept asking us to wait and wait and wait and this annoyed me very much, because when he finally did get back, it coincided with a very heavy program of bombing in the North. I can't prove that the two were related but they certainly did take place at the same time. Chester went back, was well received again, saw the same people, and gave a report, which was a negative report. He asked, "Well, now this is it. Is there anything more we wish to do?" Of course, by this time there was nothing. They weren't going to—Hanoi was being pounded, you see. You'd almost think it was done deliberately. I can't deny that it was not done [deliberately]. My impression is that it was part of the [U. S.] strategy.

When Ronning came back from the second trip to Hanoi, the Canadian government decided that this time the Americans should come to Ottawa to be briefed. So, on a hot summer day, Bill Bundy was flown to Canada's capital, where he spent an afternoon and evening before flying back to Washington. Aside from cocktails with Prime Minister Pearson before the working dinner party in the Chateau Laurier, the time was spent almost exclusively on Vietnam and the results of the mission. Bundy kept on saying that he did not see anything significantly new in what Ronning had brought back and, according to his own account, would look around the room and ask if Paul Martin or anyone else saw anything in the terms of the United States position, as he put it. He did not say what the Canadian reaction to his appeals was or whether there was anything but an embarrassed silence.

It was a dialogue not so much of the deaf as of those who could hear but could not comprehend. Aside from the fact that the Canadians were afraid that the bombing of the North so close to the Chinese border might lead to World War Three, there were other reasons why they wanted a cease-fire, if not a peace settlement. Most Canadians were opposed to the war and Martin said that he knew of only one Cabinet colleague who favored the American position. However, the worst issue for the government was the fact that Canada was making hundreds of millions of dollars out of the war; this was as a result of the joint military production arrangements with the United States. It was difficult to say what amount went to Vietnam, and, in any case, if the agreement were abrogated, it would have been a repudiation of NATO obligations. The external affairs minister, rather than the prime minister, bore the brunt of the criticism over this "hypocritical" situation. Whenever a new man like Pierre Trudeau entered the Cabinet, he would want to know about the military arrangement, and Martin said that they would have to go over the whole thing again. On their side, the Americans were not ready for negotiations— they would not reach that stage for a couple of years—and Bundy's job was to protect the U. S. interests in South Vietnam.

WILLIAM P. BUNDY

If Paul is saying that when I visited Ottawa any conspicuous bombing was going on, I must say I recall none and certainly no bombing in the Hanoi–Haiphong areas. The general pace of the bombing moved up and down. This or that incident might catch a headline, but as Hanoi would have seen it there had not at that point been any marked step-up, or change in targetting. So that's the story in a nutshell.

There were some side parts of the conversation over dinner about this, in which Ronning was describing seeing shelters built in downtown Hanoi. I made some remark, as I recall, to the effect that "That's not something that they need to worry about," and this was indeed correct. We had no plan at that time to hit anything that either was aimed at or seemed likely to involve the dropping of any bombs in the area he was describing, which as I say was quite far removed geographically from the refineries that were being considered for attack.

Well, I think Ronning, in his rather simplified way of looking at things, made a confusion in that he's since written something in his book about being misled by me on this point. I don't think the professionals could have been misled because they knew the geography. He didn't know the geography. It was one of those cases where my brief was not to discuss what we might next do on the bombing; that remained to be decided. It hadn't been decided at that point.

I knew that if I brought back a negative report the issue would be moved to the presidential level for decision. I didn't, as it were, go with the bombing plan in one pocket and the request to know what was happening in the diplomatic channel in the other. You couldn't anticipate what Ronning would have brought back. He might have brought back nothing substantive, but a suggestion of another meeting in another place. It would have been something which we'd have had to weigh very carefully.

What I'm saying is it unfolded in a reasonably straightforward manner as governments deal with each other. We needed to get the best possible reading of what Ronning had found. We got it, in the presence of Canadians, hearing the same words from the same man's mouth that Canadian listeners were hearing. We invited them to say if they thought they could see any light in this. They couldn't see any. We so reported and the president went ahead from there with the proposals to bomb the oil refineries.

It must be said that about all that came out of the Ronning mission was misunderstanding and disagreement. Paul Martin felt that he had been double-crossed. He asserted that not only had he been misled by President Johnson but so had Wilson and Kosygin, who had the conditions for their peace efforts changed while they were in the process of negotiation. Martin concluded that the motives of the United States government were quite different from what they should have been.

Chester Ronning suffered pangs of conscience, as he was to say later. After reporting to Washington on the results of his first trip to Hanoi, he began to wonder whether he had not encouraged the Americans into thinking that the North Vietnamese had made these concessions because the bombing was really hurting them, and that the United States therefore became all the more determined that bombing should be pursued relentlessly until North Vietnam was crushed. In his memoirs Ronning wrote that at that dinner party in Ottawa Bundy had given his assurance that there would be no escalation of the bombing of North Vietnam. This was where he claimed to have been misled, and not over the location of the bombing, and thus the confusion was not Ronning's but Bundy's. However, confusion was widespread. The Americans had agreed to the Ronning mission reluctantly anyway, and they felt that they were being chivvied around by people who, as Dean Rusk scornfully said, were in a race to win the Nobel Peace Prize.

Then, there was the counterpoint, as Bundy called it, of the Chinese representation issue, and, in this case, the Americans felt that they had been let down by their good friends and neighbors. Was it deliberate, a diplomatic tit-for-tat? At any rate, in March 1966, at the time of Ronning's first trip to Hanoi, the U. S. State Department took stock of

*the situation at the United Nations and came to the conclusion that the
United States would lose if it continued to press for a moratorium on the
question of Chinese representation—there had been a tie vote on this
matter at the 1965 Assembly. In May 1966 Bundy said that Mike
Pearson was told that if Canada wanted to suggest a two-China solution,
such a move would be favorably regarded by the United States.*

WILLIAM P. BUNDY

In June of 1966, on a swing around Asia, Dean Rusk looked the
Chinese right in the eye on Taiwan and said, "We don't think the
position can be held and therefore there may be initiatives by
other nations, and this is not something we can oppose." It was a
very important encounter in June—late June 1966. He said the
same thing to Shiina, the foreign minister in Japan. In short, we
did prepare the way for a Canadian initiative, and when Paul
Martin came to Washington in late July, at some point we thought
he might say, "This is what we propose to do." However, he
rather surprised us by not having a plan in his pocket and saying,
"This is what we're doing." We were puzzled but we thought,
"Well, in their good time, they'll come forward with it."

Then in August the Chinese Cultural Revolution, which had
got under way in June, boiled over, and there were attacks on
newspaper people and various nasty incidents. By the time the
United Nations met in mid-September, all our soundings were
that there was much less sympathy than there had been the
previous year. When Martin came to Washington in late September, Dean Rusk said, "It's all off in effect," or so we interpreted the
conversation. "We now think that sentiment is clear. Even the
Russians clearly oppose really moving on this, at least privately.
With the Chinese so totally irresponsible and unpredictable, nobody now thinks that this is the time to move." Then we went off
on the trip all around Asia that included the Manila Conference;
that is President Johnson, Rusk, myself, we were all off on this.
We came back on the first of November, to find, lo and behold,
the Canadians had launched an initiative. We were absolutely
dumbfounded.

All the diplomacy of that November was an immensely preoc-
cupying and distracting experience that we could have lived

without because we'd much rather have followed up the Manila Conference with a much more thoughtful set of diplomatic set of moves on Vietnam. Instead, Rusk and I had to spend the bulk of our time on the Chinese representation thing, dealing with this belated and rather scatter-shot Canadian initiative. I must say I found it a simply unhelpful contribution.

GEORGE IGNATIEFF

We worked out a formula which, in effect, proposed that the seat of China on the Security Council should be given to mainland China, but both Chinas would be regarded as members of the General Assembly pending the resolution of the problem of Taiwan. Now this was called a Two China Policy, but in international law and logic it was a perfectly legitimate thing to suggest. It so happened that both Chinas refused to entertain that view, but it was one of the options which we felt should be considered. However, it required a great deal of consultation, and for reasons that I didn't understand [at the time], there was dilly-dallying in Ottawa.

I was in charge of the Canadian mission in New York, and I asked for instructions some three weeks before the Chinese issue was to come up in the General Assembly [at the beginning of November]. Paul Martin was in Ottawa and only came down a couple of weeks before that occurred and asked me to make a quick assessment. I went to see Arthur Goldberg [U. S. representative at the UN], with whom I always kept in close touch— we were good friends—and apparently he had not been kept better informed about the reassessment due to the Cultural Revolution than I had. At any rate, I said to Arthur Goldberg that I wanted to consult with the Pacific Rim Powers on the [two-China] proposition, rather than wait to have Taiwan thrown out of the UN, and that we work together on this and conjointly advise others that this was the best situation in fairness and justice. Arthur Goldberg said to me that morning, "We're in business, George." It was agreed that we would meet at the U.S. Mission at five o'clock.

When I arrived at the mission, there were the delegates of Japan, Australia, Philippines, and New Zealand there, and, instead of saying that this was a joint proposition of the United States and Canada, Goldberg said, "Our Canadian friends have been thinking about Chinese representation and want to tell us something about their conclusions." I did, and then came an avalanche of opposition. It was all due to lack of consultation and communication.

Although the results of the Ronning mission proved to be disappointing, there was no let-up in Canadian efforts to bring about a cease-fire in Vietnam. Paul Martin, with Prime Minister Pearson's encouragement, talked to the Russians and the Poles and tried to enlist their support in his peace efforts. He visited Moscow and Warsaw and had long conversations with Gromyko, Kosygin, and Brezhnev, as well as with the Polish statesman, Rapacki, whom Martin considered the most brilliant foreign minister of the postwar period. Their reply was always the same: "You're a great friend of the United States. The Americans are the aggressors. Get them to stop the war."

Martin was also in constant contact with the Americans at the United Nations, and, as he said, after all these frustrations, he decided to do what Pearson had done in the Temple University speech: call upon the United States to stop the bombing, but he did it, as he was careful to point out, from the podium of the General Assembly. The external affairs minister said there was no guarantee that if the Americans did stop the bombing North Vietnam would agree to unconditional discussions, but there was no other method open. As might be expected, the Americans did not like this.

In May 1967 Walter Gordon entered the fray with a concerted attack on United States policy in Vietnam. As president of the Privy Council, he had been given little to do, and it was frustration as much as pent-up emotion that drove him to make this speech. It upset the prime minister, who did not like anyone other than himself and the external affairs minister making statements on foreign policy. Gordon claimed that Pearson told him privately that he agreed with what he had said. Paul Martin was furious, but more over a speech that Gordon had made the day before when he criticized NATO and said that Canada should opt out of NORAD, the North American Defense Alliance. There were demands for his resignation, and Pearson told a press conference that the president of the Privy Council had not been expressing government policy.

Then President Johnson paid a courtesy call on Expo 67 in Montreal, as did many other heads of state and heads of government, and, after a brief tour of the World Fair, took off in a helicopter for Harrington Lake, the prime minister's summer residence. Pearson was appalled at the amount of security surrounding the president's short visit; there seemed to be secret servicemen everywhere, in the house, on the grounds, and on the lake. He told Bryce Mackasey that when he went upstairs, he found his passage blocked by an agent who said, "Where are you going, little fellow?" The prime minister said, "To my own bloody bathroom." However, the opportunity for negotiations on Vietnam came to naught.

PAUL MARTIN

I suppose the final effort was when I went to Montreal and saw President Johnson, and accompanied him to Harrington Lake where Pearson and I had a two-hour chat with him. It was the same old story. We mentioned the desirability of bringing the war to an end. Pearson was particularly good on that occasion. But always looming in the background was the fact that we had antagonized Johnson earlier and the president never got over that. Johnson's responses, however, I thought, were—I won't say infantile but they certainly weren't very convincing. He said, "I am not going to jeopardize the safety of my boys." That's what he kept saying. He was doing that very thing. He was jeopardizing their safety by carrying on the war.

GEOFFREY PEARSON

I was at Harrington Lake when the president visited us. He landed on the lawn in a helicopter; he was there for three hours in which there was some lunch but at least three-quarters of the time was spent by the president talking about Vietnam and nothing else. Talking is not the right word: it was shouting or lecturing or gesticulating. He used very emotional and colorful language. He talked about his son-in-law: "Surely Mr. Pearson would understand if he had a son-in-law involved in Vietnam, surely he would take a different view." It's hard to argue, hard to discuss something when it's expressed like that. I came away with the impression that this man simply would not, on that subject anyway—and this was 1967—listen to any other point of view.

DEAN RUSK

Except for those who carried the battle flags and their families, no one agonized over the Vietnam war more than Lyndon Johnson. There was so much that he wanted to do, as represented by his astonishing legislation covering the Great Society that he put through after 1964, so much that he wanted to do, and this wretched Vietnam thing had come to him with deep roots in the past, and he invested a lot of agony in it trying to find a way to bring it to a conclusion. That was his biggest disappointment in office, that he was not able to wind that thing up while he was still in office.

But, you see, LBJ also was a man in a great hurry. I think that was partly because he never really knew from one day to the next whether he was going to be alive. He had had a massive heart attack back in the Fifties. And so he was driving hard; he was a very hard taskmaster for the rest of us, but we all accepted it in high spirits because he was hardest of all on himself. We could never get him to slow down. That desire to move, to get things done, sometimes was a bit hard to understand for other governments because governments normally live a more leisurely pace than LBJ wanted them to have.

On March 31, 1968, President Lyndon B. Johnson made a nationwide television broadcast in which he announced that he would not be seeking re-election to a second full term; he indicated that he had removed himself from partisan politics in order to devote all his energies to the task of finding a peaceful settlement of the Vietnam War. At the same time he said he had ordered a halt to the bombing of the northern part of North Vietnam, which the Canadians considered to be the most dangerous area because of its proximity to the Chinese border.

Thus, as Chester Ronning was to point out, the president had partially accepted the offer that he had brought back from Hanoi two years before and which the Americans had then spurned. The broadcast brought a reaction from the Communists, and Premier Pham Van Dong said that they were ready to come to a conference table and talk directly with the United States. After some argument, Paris was chosen as the site of the conference, but the Americans had reckoned without the South Vietnamese, who wanted no part of these talks. The first Paris meetings were a fiasco, and nothing was achieved that was of any help to Hubert Humphrey, the Democratic candidate, and Richard Nixon was elected president.

12 Trudeau and Neutralism

ON DECEMBER 14, 1967, toward the end of Canada's centennial, Lester B. Pearson announced that he would be retiring as prime minister and leader of the Liberal Party. The news was not unexpected because Pearson had been bitterly disappointed over his failure to win a majority in the 1965 election and had threatened to resign then: the fact that he had to head another minority government with all its tensions and uncertainties was an appalling prospect for him. He would have liked to have retired on April 23, 1967, which was his seventieth birthday, only he had to remain in office during the centennial year, and he realized this. As might be expected, the prime minister's desire to quit became known and gave rise to the unseemly spectacle of several of his ministers engaged in a struggle for the succession. Now that he had made it official, the leadership race was out in the open, and by the end of January 1968 there were seven declared candidates, six of them Cabinet ministers, although the convention was not due to begin till April 4. Pierre Trudeau, the exciting newcomer to Parliament, was one of the last to enter the fray.

From the beginning, Prime Minister Pearson had let it be known that he favored a French-speaking candidate to succeed him; this was in the Liberal Party's tradition of alternating English-speaking and French-speaking leaders. At first, as he said, he looked on Jean Marchand, who had been his Quebec lieutenant and was generally accepted as the Liberal leader in Quebec, as a possible successor. However, Marchand told him that he had decided not to run—there were various reasons, not the least of which was that he felt that his English was not good enough—but he had a French Canadian candidate in mind, Pierre Trudeau, and wanted the prime minister to see him and persuade him to stand. Pearson did so and wrote, in his memoirs, "We met in January, and I let Mr. Trudeau know that if he were chosen [leader] it would meet with my whole-hearted approval." Although Pearson insisted that he did not support any candidate for the leadership, there were others involved like Paul Hellyer who felt that he did everything, short of public endorsement, to help the Quebec candidate. Certainly, he persuaded or, as he said, encouraged Mitchell Sharp to withdraw from the race and throw his support to Trudeau, which proved to be a crucial move.

After Pierre Elliott Trudeau was elected leader, Pearson had several briefing sessions with him before turning over the prime ministership. He was impressed by Trudeau's cool approach—he called it "tough, resilient and realistic"—to the problems ahead, and noted at the time, "The choice is a gamble, of course, but a good one and worth taking. It is a case of a new man for a new era." Pearson seemed to be obsessed by the popular view, largely created by television, of his successor as "the man to match the times," "the new image for the new era," and wrote in his memoirs that Canadians saw Pierre Trudeau "as a man for this season, uncontaminated and uninhibited." Mike Pearson was so much taken with his personality and style that he seemed to have paid little attention to his policies and attitudes. Although Trudeau was his parliamentary secretary for a time, there is no evidence that Pearson had any heart-to-heart talks with him or got to know him very well; and Trudeau was not the kind to reveal any of his plans or thoughts. At any rate, it came as a painful surprise to Mike Pearson to find his successor not only denigrating what he had done on the international stage but out to scuttle NATO and lead the country down the path of neutralism.

However, there was no doubt that, at first, Pearson was pleased with his party's choice of a new leader, and happy and delighted at his successful retirement. Above all, he was relieved that it was all over, that he would no longer be subject to the strains of the prime minister's office, but he did not intend to be inactive. He did not retire in order to write memoirs, his son Geoffrey said: he retired because he felt he had done his duty and because he did not regard politics as his life work. There were other things that he wanted to do, including international jobs, and he was only *seventy-one when he stepped down and, according to his son, expected to have many years ahead.*

Mitchell Sharp, who had been appointed external affairs minister by Prime Minister Trudeau, was asked if Pearson would look into the Irish problem.

MITCHELL SHARP

I was in London at a conference of some kind, and I was at a party at the [Canadian] High Commission. Terence O'Neill [Prime Minister of Northern Ireland] sought me out, and he was anticipating the problems that were going to arise and he asked me whether Mr. Pearson would be willing to come to Ireland and to form a commission of inquiry into the problems of Northern Ireland. I took the liberty of saying that I was quite sure he wouldn't, that he could not be persuaded to undertake anything of that kind now. I saw Mr. Pearson later, and I told him the conversation. He said, "You were quite right."

When it became known that Lester Pearson was really retiring, there was a scramble by various institutions and international organizations to obtain his services. However, while still prime minister he had apparently decided on Carleton University, and Professor Peyton Lyon recalled his speaking at the university in June 1967 and saying that he was looking forward to becoming again "a learned authority instead of merely a Cabinet leak." There was no doubt that Pearson was looking forward to teaching but Davidson Dunton, the president of Carleton, wanted him not only to conduct a graduate course in Canadian foreign policy but to be chancellor of the university as well, a position that he accepted with some reluctance. But before he could take up his dual academic role, the World Bank came along with the request that he head the Commission on International Development, and he had to beg off his university commitments, at least temporarily.

For some time there had been concern that the steam was going out of development, as William Clark put it. The rich countries were getting richer and the poor poorer, and the gap between the developed and the developing world was widening at an alarming rate. Something drastic had to be done if the Second Development Decade (1961-71) was not to be a failure, and Barbara Ward and others who were worried about the situation felt that there should be nothing less than a Marshall Plan for the Third World. They interested George Woods, then president of the World Bank, in the venture, and they agreed that Sir Oliver Frank should be in charge of a commission to ascertain what ought to be done. Sir Oliver had played a major part in the great aid program that had revived Europe after the war; however, he was not available. When Robert McNamara became head of the World Bank on April 1, 1968, he felt that it was a worthwhile project and wanted to go ahead, and William Clark, who had joined the bank at the same time as vice-president for external relations, put forward the name of Mike Pearson, who had just stepped down as prime minister.

WILLIAM CLARK

We drafted a letter from McNamara to Mike Pearson. It so happened that Norman Robertson had just died and his funeral was to be in Ottawa, and I decided that he was such a close personal friend that I should go up representing myself and also the bank. There was a typical mail strike in Canada at the time, so I took the letter up and handed it to him [Pearson] myself. He said to me, "It's interesting, and I'm beginning to feel that perhaps I'm not wholly content getting my own breakfast . . ." Then, about a fortnight later, Mike rang me and I gathered that he was likely to take this on. We asked him to come down here [to Washington].

We had dinner with McNamara at Tracy Place [where McNamara lived] and he agreed to go ahead. I remember McNamara greeting him by saying, "Mr. Prime Minister, how nice to see you again." And I remember Pearson saying afterward that it was a great deal nicer than the last time he had met McNamara, when he had been called back by LBJ after making a speech slightly critical of the Vietnamese war and had been given a talking to by the president. The next day he came into the bank and formally agreed and there was an exchange of letters.

I rang up a young man in the White House, Ed Hamilton, the brightest young man—he was twenty-nine at the time—and asked him to lunch with Mike Pearson and myself. I said to Mike that I thought this was the man who might be the head of his secretariat and, in fact, they agreed to this at lunch. Hamilton went back to the White House and told his superiors, and eventually LBJ, that he was going to leave. LBJ was in a terrible rage. He rang up McNamara and said, "What are you taking my people away for? I never did anything like that to you." "Yes, you did," said McNamara. "You took Joe Califano from me." And they had a blazing riot.

Mike Pearson's first task, once he had agreed to this international undertaking, was to select the members of the commission. William Clark would have liked it called a "grand assize," but Robert McNamara insisted on its being known as the Pearson Commission and actually wrote the original press release so describing it, largely because Americans did not know what an assize was. Sir Edward Boyle was the British representative; he had been minister of education and had an abiding interest in development. He was to tell Arnold Smith that he thought that Pearson was perhaps the best chairman that he had ever known in his life, and he had had a lot of experience. McNamara put forward the names of several people who might be the American representative, and Douglas Dillon, a former secretary of the treasury under both Presidents Kennedy and Johnson, was picked. Pearson himself chose the German representative, Wilfried Guth, a banker who had written Capital Exports to the Less Developed Countries. *The commissioners included a Frenchman, a Japanese, a Brazilian, and the Caribbean economist Sir Arthur Lewis.*

Before he could go any further, Pearson realized that he would have to be relieved of some of his teaching duties at Carleton University; he put the problem to Davidson Dunton, who got him a partial leave of absence on a reduced honorarium from September 1, 1968 to December 31, 1969. It could be said that Pearson was the only professor to be granted a sabbatical before he really started to work.

While the International Bank for Reconstruction and Development, to give the World Bank its full name, financed the Commission on International Development, it did not want to have any further involvement. McNamara told Pearson, "Don't feel that you have any obligation to us. None of us will attend your meetings. We will not interfere in any way. You're completely independent." Clark kept in fairly constant contact with the chairman and the commission, for administrative purposes, and he asserted that while the secretariat was housed by the bank and made good use of its services, Ed Hamilton and his group did not seem to be influenced in any way by their parent body.

Among those whom the commission consulted was Arnold Smith, the secretary-general of the Commonwealth. He emphasized the importance of development as a major issue in world politics and as a major interest of the West. Malcolm Macdonald saw it as one of the two great problems facing mankind, the first being the racial one, which, as he said, could blow up and cause another world war, and the second, and equally important in his view, the question of aid and of narrowing the gap between the developed nations and the developing nations. The over-whelming majority of the developing nations were non-white; and if the developed white nations did not do all they could to narrow this gap, then, Macdonald warned, the racial problem would be greatly exacerbated. Smith expressed the view that the commission should propose a target of a certain percentage of the Gross National Product (GNP) for aid.

That is what was done. The report of the commission, entitled Partners in Development, *puts a time limit on countries reaching the target percentages of their GNP for aid. Actually, two different figures are given in the report's two main recommendations:*

"1. Each developed country should increase its resource transfers to developing countries to a minimum of 1 percent of its Gross National Product as rapidly as possible, and in no case later than 1975.

"2. Each developed country should increase its commitments of official development assistance to the level necessary for net disbursements to reach 0.70 percent of its Gross National Product by 1975 or shortly thereafter, but in no case later than 1980."

However, the report explains that the 1 percent figure is not, strictly speaking, an aid target at all, as it does not differentiate between commercial transactions and what it calls concessional aid. In other words, it is the figure for trade and aid. Furthermore, the report says that the first recommendation is to set a floor, not a ceiling. The second recommendation is for development assistance provided by governments, and the 0.70 percent is a real target figure.

It took a little more than a year for the World Bank Commission to bring out Partners in Development, *which is a four-hundred-page book; Pearson's letter of transmittal is dated September 15, 1969. Perhaps, the former prime minister was out to show Canadian royal commissions, of which he had appointed so many, how quickly things could be done.*

The report was generally well received, particularly in the developing countries. The key phrase was Mike Pearson's, that poverty is "lickable." It was not a pioneering report; it was a conservative one that, according to

William Clark, said two things: first, that we are going along the right lines and have had some successes, and second, that we need to do more, to continue, and not to fall back. For the first time there was the suggestion that aid might have to be continued until the end of the century.

Pearson was well aware that, if it was to do the most good, the report should have its greatest impact on the United States, but it failed to do so. Congress was unmoved. Partners in Development *did not lay the groundwork for a Marshall Plan type of program.*

WILLIAM CLARK

I think that we felt that the report was very useful. MacNamara took every reference to the bank in the report out and had it analyzed and the Bank Board considered the recommendations and, generally speaking, accepted them, with some exceptions. Possibly one opportunity missed was the suggestion that there should be a world development authority set up, in the last paragraph of the report. We turned that down on the grounds that we really weren't in a position to take the leadership of this in the World Bank. I sometimes think if we had done so at that time we would have been resented but we might have been in a firmer position today. I don't know.

What I am certain of is that Mike did understand the continuing problem of extreme poverty; he did understand that development was not fully taking care of that; but he didn't go on, as MacNamara did three or four years later—'72, '73—to say we must adapt our development program to deal with the poorest. In a way, the Pearson report is a summing-up of the experience of the first twenty years, from '47 onward, of political independence and economic development, and it laid the foundation on which the second development decade was built, both intellectually, I think, and in terms of trying to encourage the donor nations to continue with their aid.

ARNOLD SMITH

I think the developing countries felt that it was a very good report. I think the disappointment came from people like Bob McNamara and his colleagues in the World Bank who were hoping to really make an impact on the thinking of American senators and top officials and leading congressmen and so on. That's a hard job to do. Look at Africa until quite recently. Kissinger wouldn't pay attention to African problems and the problems of race discrimination in South Africa until they got Cuban troops there. Once there were Cuban troops there, he started taking it seriously. It was a serious problem before; it was an invitation to Cuban troops. This is a reflection, I guess, on the Western prescience, typical democratic Western prescience rather than a reflection on Mike. The reception in the Third World including the Commonwealth, which is a pretty representative cross-section of Third World countries, was very good, and I think rightly.

WILLIAM CLARK

I must say one thing, it was very much intended to be influential with the Americans, and it was here that it probably had its least success. We have never succeeded in tapping the American sense of interest, obligation, and generosity toward development that existed toward Western Europe in the Marshall Plan.

What Bob [McNamara], Edward [Boyle], and I were hoping for, let's put it that way, was that the dollar overhang, as it was known in those days, would be plowed into the Third World. The overhang is a mixture of currencies and is partly owned by America and partly owned by the owners of Euro-dollars and partly owned by the OPEC countries, but the problem of how to use the simplest capital of the developed world to develop the poorer parts of the world remains today. It was analyzed fairly carefully in the Pearson report but the necessary leap forward never came, and it is a question of whether it could.

ARNOLD SMITH

Aid isn't the main thing; the main thing is [trade], helping them earn more for themselves by encouraging their capacity and ability to produce exports and to export them to industrialized markets, to have more international purchasing power and thereby increase Canadian exports. We could all gain from this. I don't think men as a whole—except of course the saints—react adequately to moral imperatives; they react to a perception of a relatively short-run interest and calculations of prudence. Now, in the case of the Marshall Plan we had short-run calculations of prudence. We had every reason to fear Soviet expansion into Western Europe, so we came to rely on the economies of Western Europe.

If you took a longer view—I talk about Soviet expansion but totalitarian expansion of one sort or another—it's very much in the interest of the industrialized countries to help the development in the Third World. But there's not the immediate strategic fear, you see; there ought to be; maybe Cuban troops may help develop this.

But I think the explanation for the disappointment on the part of the World Bank leadership is a disappointment with the lethargy of human nature. I don't think it's a criticism of Mike Pearson or his analysis. It was a very good report that he wrote, that was written by the commission which he chaired. But you see, the problem of development, of helping the poor countries move to growth, is an enormously difficult one, far more difficult than in Western Europe, and I think at the time people didn't realize how hard it was going to be.

LORD HOME

I saw Pearson when he came to London at that time. I thought he was very much the right fellow for this, absolutely. And I think he got a lot of cooperation out of the World Bank people. He was the 1 percent fellow, of course, wasn't he? I mean 1 percent GNP, which broadly we accepted. Everybody accepted the target but nobody reached it; still, it was the right idea. And he was very good, I thought, with the developing countries. He was very persuasive with politicians and very sensible with them too.

WILLIAM CLARK

I went up to see him after he had had his eye removed[1] and he asked me whether I had noticed, which I hadn't. We had lunch—I

[1] In 1970 Pearson lost the sight in his right eye and, in July of that year, he underwent an operation in an Ottawa hospital and the eye was removed. That was the first sign of cancer.

think he was in his office at the university— and we talked about the results of the commission and about what the commissioners had done since. I certainly got the feeling— though part of Mike's charm was that he always did do this to you—that the commission was in a sense a very happy culmination to his career. He said something to the effect of how grateful he was to MacNamara, and to a lesser extent to myself, for having brought him into this, which had been one of the most enjoyable experiences.

Although he had been granted leave of absence while undertaking the World Bank study, Lester Pearson did appear occasionally on the Carleton University campus and, according to Dunton, even gave the odd lecture. Quite clearly, he could not be expected to conduct a course on Canadian foreign policy until he had completed the commission's report. Once that was done, however, he set about teaching with a will and used the first of the seminars as a sounding board for Partners in Development. *The graduate students taking his course were interested in the plight of the developing nations of the Third World. They were critical of the way the report concentrated on economics, on means of boosting the GNPs, rather than on social reform, according to Professor Lyon, who attended many of the seminars. While the whole purpose of the study was to increase aid, Pearson conceded that there was some justice in the criticism. There was no doubt that he saw international poverty, the growing gap between the developed and the developing nations, as a threat to world peace, and his class sensed this and wondered whether this was not the reason for his becoming such an ardent proponent of aid.*

The former prime minister gave a weekly seminar at Carleton, lasting some three hours in the morning. As might be expected, he had a tremendous rapport with young people, who were charmed, as Peyton Lyon said, by his informality, his frankness, his apparent detachment, his deprecation of many of his decisions, and his fund of political anecdotes. There was never a more popular course. However, as a teacher, Pearson left something to be desired, according to Lyon. He gave very little guidance to his class, and, while he was tough in marking papers, he made very few comments. And then there was his excessive tolerance of long-winded students reading dull essays, and of academic discussion generally.

In the summer of 1970 the government brought out a White Paper on Foreign Policy for Canadians, *actually the title of the first of a series of six pamphlets. Their publication came as a nasty surprise to Mike*

Pearson, who had just finished his first full year of teaching. He might have known that this was going to happen because Pierre Trudeau had made it plain from the beginning that he wanted a new and fresh approach, as he put it, to the whole problem of external affairs. He must have known of Trudeau's neutralist leanings and read reports of his opposition to the NATO alliance, but evidently Pearson had not paid much attention to all of this, nor had some of his ministers who were serving with the new government. If they had, they did not expect that there would be much change, and certainly not this calling into question all that Pearson had done and held dear.

There were those who said that Trudeau had campaigned for the leadership on the basis of bringing the boys back home (from Europe where they were serving with NATO) but Paul Hellyer, who was a leading candidate at the Liberal convention, did not recall anything as specific as that. He spoke of rumors of Trudeau's leftist and neutralist leanings but said that most people dismissed them as nothing but gossip. Mitchell Sharp was unaware of Trudeau's views on foreign policy when he was appointed external affairs minister, and he also asserted that this was not a matter of great importance during the leadership campaign.

However, on Sunday, April 7, 1968, the day after he was elected leader, Pierre Trudeau gave a press conference during which he made it clear that he wanted a complete reassessment of foreign policy. He explained that "most of our foreign policy today is based on either prewar premises or immediate postwar premises, when Canada was a very important country in relative terms—we had the strongest currency in the world and we were the fourth, I think, or third trading nation in the world." He seemed to favor a "concentration on continental defence rather than trying to play a big role in Europe" and asserted that "our participation in NATO is one aspect of" the reassessment. The same thing was true of Canada's peace-keeping role, and he said that "we can't go along there being the policemen of the whole globe."

It was not long after this that the new prime minister met Parliament only to have it dissolved and an election called. Mitchell Sharp drafted most of the party's platform on foreign policy; he said that he worked with somebody in the prime minister's office.

MITCHELL SHARP

The two principal planks in the platform were recognition of the People's Republic of China and, secondly, a review of our

NATO commitments. On the first, if it hadn't been suggested, I would have suggested it myself because I felt very strongly [about this]; on the second, I don't know that I would have suggested it. I went along with it, however, because I believed that it was desirable that our NATO alliance should be reviewed. However, my reasons for wanting the review probably were somewhat different to Mr. Trudeau's and certainly different from those of some other members of the Cabinet. I believed that the review would support Canada's continuing membership in NATO. I believed it was a useful thing to do from that point of view. There were others in the Cabinet who probably interpreted it as meaning that there was going to be a reconsideration of our membership in the alliance and some of them hoped that we would drop out. That was not my view.

There were other ministers besides Sharp who felt that the review of the NATO commitments in the party's platform was merely a sop for the left wing and would mean no change; these included such Liberal stalwarts as George McIlraith, Arthur Laing, Bud Drury, and John Turner. It is probable that Paul Hellyer and Léo Cadieux, who had insisted on remaining defense minister, suffered from no such illusion. Cadieux, the senior French Canadian Cabinet minister at the time, said that he had no misunderstanding of Trudeau's attitude toward the armed forces, and recalled his opposition to nuclear warheads during the 1963 election, and the way that he scarified Lester Pearson as "the unfrocked prince of peace" in an article which he wrote at the time. Trudeau had supported the socialist New Democratic Party then, and Cadieux was sure that he accepted that party's anti-NATO neutralist stand.

Almost the first thing the new Trudeau government did was to honor its pledge to review the NATO commitments and, as might be expected, this turned out to be a review of foreign policy generally. Actually, Mitchell Sharp maintained that the new prime minister wanted a review of all department policies and asked every Cabinet minister to do so, and to submit papers. The external affairs minister said that he was the only one who did. However, Hellyer, who was minister of transport then, had never heard of this; he said that Trudeau might have spoken about this, but there was no written directive to look at the policies of all departments. In any case, the only review that counted as far as Prime Minister

Trudeau was concerned was the review of foreign policy.

It was proclaimed as an impartial review to find an appropriate foreign policy for Canada, but by the time it got under way in the fall of 1968, Hellyer felt that it was just a charade. He said that Trudeau knew what result he wanted, and the whole discussion in the Cabinet and in the country was to get the Liberal Party and the Canadian people on the prime minister's side and to agree with his views. Hellyer called it an exercise in the manipulation of public opinion. There were discussions both inside and outside the Cabinet on neutralism, and Léo Cadieux had to point out that a neutralist policy, whether of the Swedish or the Swiss model, could be very expensive.

LÉO CADIEUX

I think the difficulty was ideological between him and me. I claimed and I still claim that peace is indivisible, particularly so in the case of Canada in the context of NORAD, for instance. Also, if you really want to trade, which was evidently our vocation, you must accept the responsibilities of a military organization and, therefore, you could not get away, for whatever ideological or practical reason, from your obligations. In our case, I claimed and I still say that we are doing the minimum that can be done, although it may be a very expensive form of contribution because it is professional force.

But, when all is said and done, if you dream of being neutral, you first have to spell out what kind of neutrality you want; you also have to state right away that you consider everyone to be a potential enemy and therefore you have to guide yourself accordingly. In the case of Canada, that implies twenty-seven thousand miles of coasts plus the frontier with the United States. You know, to me it was crystal clear that the kind of formula we have—that is, to belong to alliances—was the only way that we could deal with the problem of national security.

PAUL HELLYER

I personally didn't take part in the discussion in Cabinet because I had already decided to resign on other issues. Consequently, I just sat quietly and listened and it was most fascinating. The two men who carried the ball for the status quo, as it were—in other words, for strong Canadian involvement in NATO and in Europe—were Sharp and Cadieux. Most of the rest didn't say anything; they weren't that directly involved. I think it was [Jean-Pierre] Goyer who started the opposition but that's something that should be checked because my memory is fallible.

In the early stages of the Cabinet debates certainly the preponderant point of view was the status quo: why change, we've got our troops there, they're doing a good job, they're in the front line, that's where they should be and it's been reviewed before and we've always come to the same conclusion, so why bother going through this exercise now.

Little by little, however, opinion changed, or at least it appeared to change, as the prime minister's views became privately known to more and more ministers. Donald MacDonald, who was, of course, close to the prime minister and had been one of his great promoters in the leadership campaign, was used as a spokesman in Cabinet and a very effective one. Kierans, of course, was an outspoken critic of large Canadian involvement in Europe and, as a matter of fact, made a speech in Victoria which was absolutely contrary to government policy at the time. I suspected then and still suspect, that Kierans was put up to it by the prime minister, that this was floating a kite, that it was done deliberately. Now, I don't know but it just seemed so out of character for one minister to be publicly espousing a view which was directly contrary to the official view that I felt he must have done it either at the bidding of the prime minister or at least with his knowledge and consent. Especially as he was just the postmaster general.

But in any event, as the days went by, you could see more and more of the leaners in Cabinet lining up on the side of change and this was, in my opinion, the purpose of the whole exercise. It was merely to shift the balance of discussion in favor of change so that the prime minister, when the decision was ultimately made, could point to the process and the higher degree of support for a reduction in Canadian troops abroad than had been evident at the beginning of the debate. And to conclude naturally, of course, that this had been accomplished on the merits of the discussion.

LÉO CADIEUX

When we started to talk about neutrality, I personally asked those very specific questions. Please give us a description of the kind of neutrality that you are talking about. So we started to study the problems and there were so many formulas. Since I suspect that part of the exercise was also to save money, it was out of the question because neutrality is a much more expensive proposition than active participation. You only have to look at what it cost the Swedes to be neutral—if you can call that neutral—or the real neutrality like you have it in Switzerland, for instance. I don't know how many times more expensive that is: there is the contribution of the citizens, up to fifty-five years of age and they have to train every year, they have to keep their guns at home. And so, you know, it's almost irrelevant to talk about that in Canada when you have a system that is so flexible with the militia and with the active forces.

PAUL HELLYER

The discussion was taking place, and it wasn't complete before I left, as I recall, so that, although I got most of the evolution, I wasn't there for the final count, as it were, to really be able to see who had ultimately succumbed to the new prevailing wind. But I was there long enough to see the process in action. Donald MacDonald, for example, met with a number of academics in Toronto. Well, I was there, but I noticed the choice of academics and they were ones who with one or two major exceptions— people like John Holmes who had been in External Affairs and who knew what the score was and consequently weren't going to be pushed around easily on the subject of this sort—they were selected to provide majority support for change. At least that would be my interpretation.

I suppose that's an accusation of sorts but I had the clear impression, when I walked into the meeting, that it wasn't in the composition of the group so much to seek out some great new policy, because most of the people there weren't well informed enough to really know what the score was. This became obvious during the discussion—but rather people who had expressed views publicly, people like Stephen Clarkson and Louis Hertzman and others who were known for more neutralist views and who would be more naturally in accord with what the prime minister wanted to come up, with the policy that he wanted to evolve. While this process was going on simultaneously—because the press had been told it was a national debate and that it was made to appear that the government was really seeking out the enlightened views of the community—I think, in that regard, it was nothing but a hoax.

LÉO CADIEUX

I believe that he had no particular detailed plan but I really believe that the object of the exercise—whether it was his own or the majority, the plan of the majority in the Cabinet—was to get out of NATO. That's very clear to me. So, as far as the ideology, whether you should be neutral or not, I think it flows from the discussion itself, once you start, if you want to be thorough, you have to examine every aspect. There [were] all sorts of arguments that were popular in those days; for instance, one that said that if you handle a very sophisticated defensive system and detective system, you sort of provoke the enemy into refining his own attack. You know, where do you end?

MITCHELL SHARP

I'm not certain, even today, what Mr. Trudeau really thought at that time. As I have said on other occasions, Mr. Trudeau very strongly supports the principle of collegiality in government decisions and he generally went with the consensus of Cabinet, and my impression is that when the NATO review was finished and the decisions were made, he was seeking a consensus that would carry the Cabinet generally without any serious breaks. In other words, he was looking for a formula that would keep everyone happy and the formula that he struck upon was, or at least that emerged that he accepted, was that we confirm our partnership in the alliance. We rejected all other alternatives, we confirmed the importance of having Canadian troops in Europe but we were going to reduce our contribution.

Now, at that time, this was partly influenced by the feeling that the Europeans were in a much better position to take a larger share of the burden. This was a view held not only in Canada but in the United States very strongly. I was inclined to share that view, too, and I think the minister of defense probably was. Our problem [was] not really with the decision, it was with the implementation of it. We felt that in the interest of the alliance we should have gone to the Europeans and the Americans and said, "Now these are the circumstances that we find ourselves in; you will understand that we have to make reductions in our troops in Europe. How can we bring this about?"

In the spring of 1969, while the review was still in process, Prime Minister Trudeau let the Alberta Liberal Association know what he thought, and quite clearly he did not think much of Canada's involvement in NATO. He said: "We had no defense policy, so to speak, except that of NATO. And our defense policy had determined all of our foreign policy. And we had no foreign policy of any importance except that which flowed from NATO. And this is a false perspective for any country." Mr. Trudeau told the dinner meeting in Calgary that the first priority in Canada's defense policy was not NATO but "the protection of Canadian sovereignty in all the dimensions that it means."

The outcome of the review was the series of six pamphlets or booklets, the first being Foreign Policy for Canadians. *The others dealt with various areas such as Europe, international development, Latin America, the Pacific, and the United Nations. There was none on the United States: Sharp's explanation of this omission was that Canadian-American relations permeated all six booklets, that they were central to Canadian policy and were just as much a domestic as a foreign issue. However, the government was embarrassed by this lacuna and, some time later, did try to define economic relations with the United States in a separate report.*

Foreign Policy for Canadians found a public disenchantment with Canada's foreign policy, and spoke of a changing outlook in a changing world. It made statements such as: "The world powers could no longer be grouped in clearly identifiable ideological camps, groupings which had conditioned political and military thinking since the war." It went on to say that "Canada's 'traditional' middle power role in the world seemed doomed to disappear after the United Nations ordeal in the Congo, in the face of peace-keeping frustrations in Vietnam, following the collapse of the

UN Emergency Force (UNEF) in 1967. Western Europe had not only fully recovered from the war but was taking steps toward integration that put strain on transatlantic ties and, combined with changes in the Communist world, called into question the need for continuing Canadian participation in NATO."

Perhaps, the main criticism of Canadian foreign policy, such as it was then, was that Canada was cast in the role of the "helpful fixer" in international affairs. This was a reactive rather than an active concern with world events, and the White Paper came forward with the admonition that "To be liked and to be regarded as good fellows are not ends in themselves; they are a reflection but not a substitute for policy." It said that "Canada must in future develop its external policies in a coherent way, and in line with closely defined national objectives, as set by the government." The booklet declared that foreign policy was the extension abroad of national policies and asserted that this had to take into account what it described as the renaissance of French Canada.

The White Paper on foreign policy was not tabled in the House of Commons by Mitchell Sharp until June 25, 1970. Months of discussions and arguments, of writing and rewriting, had gone into the production of the six booklets, especially the first one, and the final version bore the imprint of Prime Minister Trudeau's political philosophy and his peculiar English phraseology.

LÉO CADIEUX

I recall that there were extensive, very extensive discussions at the Cabinet committee meetings which lasted for months. We worked on texts that had already been prepared by the department and the Privy Council—they were direction papers. Then we— what do you call it?—we took them apart and drafted and redrafted them. I remember many, many meetings on which every page was discussed and in many cases probably rewritten. Yes, I think that would be a good description of the process.

PAUL HELLYER

It seems to me that two people—it could have been Geoff Murray [a senior External Affairs official] and [Robert] Ford [Canadian ambassador in Moscow]—prepared something for the department. But it was so similar to the previous review [done by Norman Robertson at the request of the Pearson government] that it was rejected. It was rather interesting that the departmental view was just once again tossed aside, and it was after that, or, at least, in so far as discussion was concerned, it was after that the [Ivan] Head version, probably prepared in cooperation with the prime minister, was brought into the discussion. [Ivan Head was Trudeau's adviser on foreign affairs]. But it's an interesting technique. Normally, the person who writes a Cabinet document has a 90 percent edge over anyone else, and the way they got around it on two or three occasions—and it was an entirely new technique of the Trudeau government—was just to have someone else write a paper; then they would switch gently from one paper to the other.

The one from the department was in effect rejected and the one written to be more coincident with the prime minister's views was the one that was ultimately incorporated into the policy decision. I don't know enough of the details to be able to document precisely how it was done, but I suspect it was a matter of strategy too, that if Mitchell Sharp insisted that the department do a paper, then it probably was the prime minister's strategy to have that one introduced first and cut to pieces a little bit before introducing the other one. That would be a sensible way of manipulating the final result.

MITCHELL SHARP

It went into several drafts, of course, and the Cabinet read it, discussed it, and also read and discussed each of the accompanying pamphlets on specialized subjects. I don't know that everybody in Cabinet read it as carefully, of course, as I did because in a Cabinet government one is inclined to leave ministers to discharge their own responsibilities and I wouldn't look too critically at a paper put out by the minister of trade or the minister of finance. I would assume that they knew their business and I wasn't going to second-guess them. But as such things go, it received fairly careful consideration.

Did Mr. Trudeau have a hand in editing it [the White Paper]? Not substantially to my recollection. I think he probably read it

more carefully than he would have read other documents, but I
don't remember him taking exception to it in Cabinet any more
than any other minister. But of course the paper was prepared, as I
say, very much on an interdepartmental basis and the prime
minister's office and the Privy Council office were particularly
concerned with it, more than any other department would have
been. Most departments didn't care very much but that wasn't
true, of course, of the offices that he was responsible for.

The publication of Foreign Policy for Canadians *not only upset
Lester Pearson but came as a distinct shock. Mitchell Sharp maintained
that, when Prime Minister Pearson had urged him to come out in favor of
Trudeau for the Liberal leadership, they had discussed his views, and they
were puzzled by him because he was out of the ordinary. Pearson was
worried, Sharp said, that Trudeau might reach conclusions that went at
the roots of what the prime minister had determined, from his great
experience, to be the necessary foundations of Canadian foreign policy. If
this is true, then it seems strange that Pearson made no note of it at the
time; his memoirs would lead one to believe that he was so overcome with
his protégé's dazzling image as the man for the times that he had no
reservations.*

*However, Mike Pearson soon became disenchanted. Tom Kent, who
was his executive assistant when he was prime minister, recalled his
saying, not without pleasure, as Kent put it, "Pierre's finding that this
'Look, no hands business' doesn't really work out that well." Geoffrey
Pearson acknowledged that he did not know what his father thought about
Trudeau, but that was not exceptional because he did not know what his
father thought about a lot of things. Latterly, Pearson was to complain
that Trudeau had only consulted him twice: the first occasion was to get
his agreement to lowering the time limit on keeping government documents secret from fifty years to thirty years, and the second was during the
October 1970 Quebec Crisis when Trudeau told him that he was imple-
menting the War Measures Act.*

*Although Pearson was not a man to show much emotion, he was
infuriated, according to Bruce Hutchison, by Trudeau's charge that his
foreign policy was dominated by the military. Hutchison, who was an old
friend, said that this was the only time he had ever seen Mike really
angry. He had read the text of the speech—it was probably the Calgary
speech, made some time before the White Paper was tabled—while flying*

*back from Japan, and Hutchison had met him at the Vancouver airport
and described him as "howling mad." It was outrageous, Pearson said,
and he would have it out with Trudeau when he got back to Ottawa. But
Hutchison said he never did. Douglas Fisher, who had become a newspaper columnist, said that the thing that really hurt and burned Pearson was
the way that Trudeau disowned his international and diplomatic contributions, and treated him as "an incompetent dunderhead."*

*With the publication of the White Paper, Pearson decided to devote the
first term of his 1970-71 Carleton course to replying to the criticism of
himself implicit in* Foreign Policy for Canadians. *He was particularly
indignant about the description of Canada's role in international affairs as
that of the "helpful fixer," which, ironically enough, was the brain child
of his son. At least, Pearson told Alex Inglis, who worked on his
memoirs, that he thought that Geoffrey was responsible for the offending
phrase. Geoffrey Pearson had had a hand in helping Norman Robertson
with the review of foreign policy that his father had ordered while prime
minister, and "helpful fixer" had appeared originally in that review.*

*In the university seminars Mike Pearson expressed himself as greatly
disturbed that young Canadians should be encouraged to look inward and
reject internationalism, which, he felt, had not only served the world but
was entirely consistent with the national interest. He asserted that it was
the height of folly, according to Peyton Lyon, to proclaim anything other
than peace and security as the nation's main foreign policy objectives. And
Professor Lyon quoted him as telling the students, "Economic growth will
be our last words when the first atomic bombs fall." He argued that
Canada, as one of the wealthy and relatively secure countries in the
world, had a moral responsibility to play a prominent part in international affairs. He could see nothing wrong with Canada being "reactive"
since he believed that smaller countries, and even larger ones most of the
time, were inevitably put in the position of having to react to world
events. As for Trudeau's quip that diplomats were no more relevant than
reporters now, Pearson felt that this was demoralizing for the Canadian
foreign service, an organization in which he took great pride.*

*But, above all, Pearson was concerned with the way that the White
Paper called into question the continuing Canadian participation in
NATO, and it was because of this that he asked to see Prime Minister
Trudeau and External Affairs Minister Sharp. The meeting was held in
Pearson's home in the Ottawa suburb of Rockcliffe and Sharp's recollec-
tion was that it lasted for half an hour.*

MITCHELL SHARP

Mr. Pearson felt that what Mr. Trudeau was saying and what these various reviews were saying were critical of his policy, and he was disappointed. This became quite clear, I remember, when we visited Mr. Pearson. He felt that the whole basis of his approach to Canadian foreign policy was being criticized. Then, there was that reference to the "helpful fixer," and Mr. Pearson resented that. He said that he was not the helpful fixer, that was not the purpose of his policy, and he looked upon that as a personal criticism.

Mr. Trudeau listened and there was some exchange of views. I don't think he was very much affected by it. Mr. Trudeau is not a person who is affected so much by relationships with people as he is by ideas, and he took the view that it was time that we should have a good look at the foundations of foreign policy as of all other policies, which was done. It was a rather extraordinary thing to do. I remember talking to some diplomats at the time who said that Canada must be one of the few countries in the world that ever attempted to express their foreign policy in a paper.

Indeed, at the time that we began the exercise, when I took over as foreign minister, there [was] virtually no literature available on Canadian foreign policy except ministers' speeches. And if you look now at the volume of papers and all the rest of it that has been produced, it all begins from about 1968. I remember we called in the academic community during the NATO review and we said, "Now, here is an opportunity for you to express your views in advance of the government decision. What do you think we should do?" And they were absolutely bewildered by such a request. They said, "Well, you tell us what you're going to do and we'll criticize it." We said, "No, here's an opportunity for you to make an input," and it was quite abortive. We never got anywhere, not until we published the paper; then they were very happy to criticize it.

It was because both Pierre Trudeau and Mitchell Sharp were self-confessed amateurs in the field of foreign policy that the extraordinary review was undertaken and the half-dozen booklets produced. The old professional, Lester B. Pearson, would never have done that and, in fact, *questioned the wisdom of attempts to articulate a comprehensive approach to foreign policy, as Professor Lyon put it. Pearson told his class at Carleton University that few if any countries could have a definite long-range policy because of the sheer unpredictability of future events.*

The review went on much longer than was expected, and if it had not been for the stubborn opposition of Mitchell Sharp and Léo Cadieux, particularly the latter, Prime Minister Trudeau might have had his way and Canadian troops would have been withdrawn from NATO forces in Europe, and Canada would have left the alliance. There would have been opposition from the United States, but such were the delusions of the times that the Trudeau government seemed to believe that it could follow a neutralist course without repercussions from Washington. However, the prime minister and his clique of supporters realized that they could not very well opt out of NORAD, and so they went to the opposite extreme and expressed the view that there should be greater Canadian participation, and almost exclusively Canadian participation over Canadian territory, despite their insistence on cutting back on defense spending.[2] At the same time, Léo Cadieux said, they proposed a time limit on the North American Air Defense pact, as they did not want to be bound to this agreement for too long a period.

Many of Trudeau's ministers disliked NORAD because of its reliance on nuclear weapons; always, at the back of their minds, according to Cadieux, there was this dirty business of nuclear weapons, which was embarrassing for them since they were ideologically opposed to them. The defense minister did not appreciate this attitude and told the Cabinet that he could not see the difference between someone being killed by an ordinary bullet or someone being killed by an atomic bullet. However, he fully understood that this was a very important consideration, and said that "what we managed to salvage in Europe was at the expense of atomic participation." Canadian planes became conventional, Cadieux asserted, and the Honest John rocket launcher was done away with, as were the self-propelled howitzers that could have used atomic shells. Fifty-five of the latter had just been bought and they were taken out of the arsenal.

It was largely due to Cadieux's adamant stand that Canada continued

---

[2]Pacifism was popular at the time and was not confined to the more radical ministers. Léo Cadieux complained that there were people in the Cabinet like James Richardson, the Winnipeg tycoon, who wanted to cut the defense budget in half. Richardson was to become defense minister and showed a proclivity for increased spending on the armed forces. He was later to split with Trudeau and the Liberals over bilingualism and cross the floor of the House.

as an active member of NATO. He would not allow Eric Kierans to get away with flying a neutralist kite and replied immediately in an address to the Rotary Club in Ottawa. For obvious reasons, Prime Minister Trudeau could not afford to have his French Canadian defense minister resign, and, shortly afterward, made the conciliatory speech in Winnipeg that ended the crisis: he said that Canada would remain in NATO but that there would be a planned and phased reduction of Canadian forces in Europe. It was taken for granted that there would have to be such a reduction because, as Sharp said, the budgetary restraints at the time made it impossible to arm them properly. The only question now was how big would the cut be and how would it be done.

LÉO CADIEUX

I did not resign. I said there were things that I could accept and things that I could not accept, and I would not have stayed in the Cabinet if we had decided to leave NATO. As minister of defense, I could not accept that. I honestly believed that the interest of Canada was that we stay in NATO. And you know, it's not the end of the world, one man who doesn't agree. Although I was very deeply, very emotionally involved in the armed services—I had been there for five years and I was there for four years during the war and I sort of really felt that I belonged—outside of that, I felt that the problem was simply intellectual honesty. In my case, I believed we should stay in NATO. So, as long as we stay in NATO, I'm willing to accept modifications. If we're committed, I don't care. I care to a great degree what form it takes, but you know you can always just cut back, but there are things that are practical and things that are not practical. And finally, in the final analysis, it's the practical things that prevail.

PAUL HELLYER

His [Cadieux's] threat to resign came after I left Cabinet and only after the government's proposal, or the prime minister's proposal, was on the table. By objecting to it and threatening to resign, he moved the ball a few yards back the other way and, and kept the NATO contingent several thousand stronger than it would have been otherwise. He didn't get what he wanted but I guess he felt [what he got] at the time was sufficient to justify his continued participation as a member of the government.

MITCHELL SHARP

We came out in favor of a continuation of the status quo insofar as the principles of our membership in the [NATO] alliance were concerned. Where we ran into difficulty eventually was not so much over the size of the Canadian contingent in Europe as how it was to be reduced. I knew from my previous experience as minister of finance that it was virtually impossible to have gone to Parliament and to have obtained a very large increase in the expenditures on defense, as it was a time of great budgetary restraint. So I knew that we would have to reduce our troops in Europe because we couldn't at that time re-equip them to per-form the role they were supposed to be performing. So I knew then, well, there had to be some change.

Where the problem arose was how was it to be done and I was very strongly opposed to what did happen, namely that we announced unilaterally first that we were staying in NATO; second, that we were continuing with troops in Europe but we were reducing the number by half. I felt we should have gone to our allies and said, "This is our position. How can we effect the change with the least damage to the alliance?" This was objected to by those who wanted to go further on the grounds that, you mean to say we go through all this exercise and we come up with the same answer. We must give evidence of change. So that was the basis upon which the unilateral declaration was made of the reduction in the number of troops.

PAUL HELLYER

I think Mitchell may have changed his views a little bit over the years and perhaps has forgotten the extent to which he was opposed at the time. It was a case of really changing, by the so-called collegial method, his policy and he didn't want it changed then. I suspect that when he suggested that it be done by negotia-tion with NATO, he would have known that NATO would have strongly objected to any cuts whatsoever and that this would have been a debating device on his part.

Certainly if the NATO Council had been consulted, there was no way that they were going to voluntarily agree to a unilateral reduction in the contribution made by one of the member countries. Once they have no choice, they have to accommodate themselves to it. So, sure, he proposed that it be done in consultation or that any changes be done in consultation, but he would have known full well that, when he made that suggestion, consultation would have resulted in very strong pressure from other members of NATO, not to make any reduction whatsoever. Changes within the existing level of forces, yes, but certainly no reduction in the over-all strength of the component.

It fell to Léo Cadieux's lot, as defense minister, to have to tell the partners in the North Atlantic Treaty Organisation of the planned and phased reduction of the Canadian forces under NATO command in Europe. He was well aware of Mitchell Sharp's view that they should have discussed the matter first with the Allies before making it a fait-accompli, *but felt there were practical difficulties in the way of taking such action. It would have been easy enough if the government was engaged in restructuring and adapting them to a new situation, but not when it was cutting them in half. However, the defense minister admitted that "restructuring" was often a euphemism for reducing commitments, and every time a NATO member wanted to cut down on over-all expenses, the case was presented to the alliance as one of restructuring.*

There were no consultations over the planned and phased reduction of the Canadian forces in NATO, and Léo Cadieux's only task was to inform the members of the alliance of the government's decision to cut its commitment in half. He expected a confrontation and knew there would be resentment when he went to Brussels for the defense ministers' meeting in the spring of 1970.

LÉO CADIEUX

The planned and phased reduction didn't please our colleagues in NATO but, you know, one has to be quite hard-boiled in these negotiations because everybody is doing the same thing, trying to reduce his contribution a little bit but dress it up so that it doesn't show too much. The British have been very adept at this, so have the Germans, even the Germans; not to mention the Belgians and the Dutch, and everybody.

When it was a case of Canada, of course, we had to produce an explanation, too, so we decided that the best way was to have an informal meeting before the NATO defense ministers' meeting. It took the form of a luncheon at the residence of the Canadian NATO ambassador, Ross Campbell, in which I spelled out what we were planning to do. We had a gentleman's agreement that in the afternoon at the general meeting, that matter would not be raised, but I willingly gave them a description of what we were planning to do for their private information. Everybody, of course, really jumped on me and, you know, the American ambassador who was present and later wrote in *Reader's Digest* that in his experience this was the toughest meeting that he ever attended.

It *was* tough, I can tell you. I stood firm and I said this is the way it is, but I explained. I gave them the rationale for the transformation of the brigade group—we were trying to keep in military balance the same kind of structure and calling it a battle group.

Everybody played the game very nicely. You see, we didn't want the subject to be raised at the General Meeting because it did concern only the people who were contributing forces. It didn't concern the Portuguese, it didn't concern the Turks, it didn't concern the Italians. We didn't want them to get involved in the discussion in which, you know, what the hell can they say and what the hell, why should they blame you for reducing when they haven't got [any NATO forces]?

It was by mutual consent that Léo Cadieux left the government. Prime Minister Trudeau did not want this prickly French Canadian around and offered him the post of Canadian ambassador to France. However, Léo Cadieux, who had no intention or desire to stay in the Cabinet, refused to go until he had closed the NATO bases: under the planned and phased reduction, the Canadian forces were to be concentrated at Lahr, West Germany, and the bases at Szolst and at Werl given up. It was a painful thing to have to do, but Cadieux felt that he owed it to the armed forces with whom he had been so deeply and emotionally involved. The closing ceremony was at Werl in July 1970, and Cadieux said that the weather was right because it rained. However, the parade went off beautifully, and there was a mess dinner that night which was a memorable occasion. Finally, some six months after his appointment, Léo Cadieux left Canada to take up his ambassadorial post in Paris.

When he was back in Ottawa on home leave, Lester Pearson invited him to lunch and thanked him for his defense of Canada's NATO policy. Cadieux recalled Pearson saying to him, "You know, you're one of my successes; I've had so few." That was probably in the summer of 1972, as it was the last time Cadieux saw Pearson.

MITCHELL SHARP

When I think back on that period, what is really extraordinary about it is that after all the studies and inquiries and discussions, the pattern of Canadian foreign policy was not changed in any vital way. We remained in NATO, Mr. Trudeau became one of its strongest supporters in due course. On foreign aid, we increased it but that was only a reinforcement of policy that had been followed in the previous administration. We did, however, make one change of emphasis which was very significant and for which I was about as responsible as Mr. Trudeau—namely, to shift the emphasis away from Canada's *role* in the world to Canada's *purpose* in the world—its objectives or its interests. Indeed, I invented a phrase at the Harrison Hot Springs Conference when we were considering this question of foreign policy when I said that foreign policy was a continuation of domestic policy by other means. In other words, what we emphasized was the continuity of domestic and foreign policy, that foreign policy was not something that was done in order to establish Canada's place in the world, the purpose of Canadian foreign policy, like the foreign policy of Britain, the United States, France, was to promote Canada's interests and objectives. That may not have been a change from what Mr. Pearson thought, but it certainly was a change from the way that Canadian foreign policy was thought of during his regime.

After his first angry reaction to the White Paper, Lester Pearson came to realize that Trudeau's bark was a good deal worse than his bite, and that the substance of the new government's foreign policy would not be much different from the one that he had practiced for so long. In 1971, the year following the issue of Foreign Policy for Canadians, *he told the students taking his course at Carleton University that he had changed his mind to some extent. He said that he was delighted to read accounts in the papers of how Prime Minister Trudeau had saved the day during the Commonwealth Conference in Singapore when the question of arms sales to South Africa threatened disruption. And he suggested that he was going to write a letter to the editor complaining about all this "helpful fixing."*

The controversy over the Canadian contribution to NATO and the direction of Canadian foreign policy generally went unnoticed outside the country, and to most people, Mike Pearson, in retirement, continued to be the world statesman.

WILLIAM CLARK

After he had ceased to be prime minister and when he was more reflective, he began to see clearly what a narrow base the whole of the rich north developed world had to stand in, as "an island of prosperity in a sea of poverty," which I think was one of his phrases. In his final days he was more of a world statesman than he had ever been in his premiership and his foreign secretary- ship—he was a world statesman who had emerged into the really modern world, which is not just an East–West struggle, a balanc- ing of NATO versus the Warsaw Pact, a united Europe versus a North Atlantic Market. It was, it is a world divided between a small number of relatively satisfied powers and a large number, something like four-fifths of the world population, which is in need of assistance to move upward on the economic, social, and consequently political scale. In our final conversations, which occurred after the Pearson report, this was what he was really concerned with, and, I know that, in talking to his successor, [Trudeau] he made a point of saying that this was really the problem of our times.

Aside from this increased interest in the developing world—which was evident in the first seminars that he conducted at Carleton University— Lester Pearson's international outlook had not changed much since he was prime minister and external affairs minister and first represented Canada abroad. To him, peace and security were the all-important aims of diplomacy, and the United Nations was the great hope of mankind, despite its weaknesses, which he understood all too well. It was as a result of the UN's "lack of teeth" that he helped to establish NATO and he insisted on calling the latter a collective security organization rather than a military alliance. While he objected to certain statements in the White Paper, and was annoyed at the way it seemed to denigrate his past efforts, Pearson lived to see that there was no fundamental change in Canadian foreign policy.

In fact, Paul Martin noted, with what he described as great satisfaction, that, ten years later, Canada had come back to the same NATO policy that the Pearson government was pursuing in 1963-68. Martin, who had been Pearson's external affairs minister, was a member of the Trudeau Cabinet at the time of the foreign policy review. He maintained that it did not matter what leaders said; there were few instances in contemporary history of any real shift in the foreign policy of a country. Foreign policy, Martin said, was not something that one turned on and off like a tap. When all the hue and cry over NATO and being a "helpful fixer" had subsided, the Trudeau government carried on the same foreign policy as its predecessors; the only difference was that it had seemed a lot more polished, a lot more authoritative, under Mike Pearson.

Epilogue

IT WAS ONLY WHEN he was close to death that Lester Pearson realized that he was terminally ill. He had always been an optimist, and had never suffered a reverse from which he had been unable to recover: the only major defeat was the 1958 election when the Liberals, under his leadership, were reduced to a rump of fewer than fifty members by the Diefenbaker landslide, but in five years he was able to bring them back to power. So that, in the view of his son Geoffrey, he thought that he could conquer cancer, and that the malignancy had been removed with the removal of his eye in July 1970. There was no need to hurry, and that was why, when he finally got down to his memoirs, he began at the beginning, and did not deal with the most important part of his life, when he was prime minister, until it was too late.

When Pearson asked his old associate, Escott Reid, to review a couple of chapters that he had drafted on the formation of the North Atlantic Alliance (for the second volume of his memoirs), Reid visited him at his office in downtown Ottawa. This would have been in late October or the beginning of November 1972, some two weeks after the publication of the first volume of his memoirs, and he found the former prime minister in a warm and happy mood, "bubbling over with happiness," at the reception of his book. He looked ten years younger, Escott Reid said, and

319

added that it was only a couple of weeks later he learned that he was going to die very soon.

On November 28, 1972, Walter Gordon went to Ottawa and saw Mike Pearson at his Rockcliffe home. They had been the greatest of friends and allies, but had fallen out over politics and the conduct of public affairs, and, by his own account, Walter had not seen Mike in four years, and now, on this last visit, he found him better than he expected, "clear in his head, witty, and quite reconciled to whatever may be in store." Gordon congratulated him on the first volume of his memoirs, and Pearson said that someone else would have to complete the remaining two volumes; he had been trying to put down his recollections of certain events and individuals but would not have time to do the necessary checking. In a way the visit served as a confessional, with the dying man saying that one of the things that troubled him most was the way, as he put it, they had drifted apart.

Early in December Jack Pickersgill had been told by Paul Martin that if he wanted to see Pearson again, he had better go right away, rather than wait till after the Christmas holidays. So Pickersgill visited him in his Rockcliffe home on the day before setting off for the Caribbean. He found him working on the third volume of his memoirs. "I'd like to read you some of the stuff I've been writing," Pearson said. He seemed to be just the same as he had always been. When Pickersgill left, they shook hands as if they would be meeting again, although both knew that this was very unlikely. Toward the end Pearson concentrated as much as he could on his memoirs, and Geoffrey said that they had pages written by him two weeks before he died.

Lester Pearson faced death in the same lighthearted manner that he had faced life. In late October he attended the Liberal Party's closing rally of the 1972 election campaign at Toronto's Maple Leaf Gardens, and, according to Jim Coutts, who had been his appointments secretary when he was prime minister and was accompanying him to the meeting, he said to his wife, "Well, Maryon, this is the last hurrah. This is the last big rally. You'll soon be playing bridge with the widows of Rockcliffe."

A couple of weeks before his death, Keith Davey, who had directed his election campaigns, went to see him. They were both avid fans of the Toronto Maple Leaf hockey team. "You know,

Keith," he said, "you probably haven't had time to look, but the Leafs aren't going to make the play-offs this year." When Davey expressed disbelief, Pearson went on to say, "It's a little worse than that: it's a crisis you're going to have to face alone."

On December 27, 1972, Mike Pearson died. He was given a state funeral and was buried in a small private cemetery in the province of Quebec. Many years before, he and a couple of his oldest and closest associates in the Department of External Affairs, Hume Wrong and Norman Robertson, had bought plots in this cemetery, which overlooked the Gatineau River. Hume Wrong was the originator of the scheme, according to Geoffrey, and his father had gone along with it, more or less as a lark, and because he liked the area where the Pearsons have had a summer cottage for a long time. Thus, Lester B. Pearson lies buried with his diplomatic colleagues and away from all the political turmoil of Ottawa.

His greatest achievements were, as Christopher Young said, in diplomacy, and few would disagree with the Ottawa editor and commentator who also happened to be his nephew, that Lester Pearson's greatest contribution to history and the welfare of mankind would be in the period from 1948 to 1957 when he was foreign minister.

Even such a virulent Conservative critic as Gordon Churchill felt that he was "superlatively good in external affairs" and that he would have been happier to have continued as minister rather than become prime minister. Malcolm MacDonald regretted in a way that he had become prime minister and had not stayed on as foreign minister. The British statesman said that he had the same view about his father, Ramsay MacDonald; his father had been foreign minister as well as prime minister in the first Labour government, and he wished that someone else had become prime minister in the next Labour government and allowed his father to be foreign minister. Lord Home would have liked to have seen Lester Pearson become secretary-general of the United Nations.

To Arnold Smith he was one of the greatest men he had ever known, and, as the first secretary-general of the Commonwealth, he had got to know most of the world leaders. Pearson was charming, intelligent, humorous, cheerful, morally courageous, patient, creative with a wide vision, to quote some of the diplomats who knew him. Dean Rusk described him as "a man of the new era," in that he hoped that organizations like the United Nations would really come to rule the world. He was not always a wisecracking good fellow; he could be moody and irritable like anyone else. There was a tough side to him, and he seemed coldblooded and aloof on occasion. To some politicians he was devious and tricky, indecisive and even cowardly. As Walter Gordon said, Mike Pearson was a much more complex character than the general public realized.

At the end, he was worried about the possibility of a third world war, and, as Charles Ritchie said, he was saddened and disappointed by the developments at the United Nations and in the Third World. There was the continuing agony of Vietnam: he had broken the cardinal rule of diplomacy when he called for a halt to the bombing while he was a guest in the United States, and it had had no effect. He tried to influence American policy, but always bowed to American leadership. At times his attitude toward the United States appeared tentative, if not ambiguous, and he had never resolved the conflict between Canadian nationalism and continentalism in terms of developing a consistent policy. Yet, in a sense, his fumbling in this regard was an expression of the dilemma that Canadians have in dealing with the United States.

However, as Escott Reid said, he did provide this country with a golden decade in foreign policy. Lester B. Pearson was the great myth-maker of international affairs, and part of the myth was a willingness to be the helpful fixer, and it is the absence of the myth that makes Canada a lesser place.

Biographies
of Contributors*

BUNDY, William Putnam: b. Sept. 24, 1917, Washington, D.C. Lawyer. CIA 1951–61. Asst. Sec. of State for East Asian and Pacific Affairs, 1964–69. Editor, *Foreign Affairs*, 1972.

BURNS, Lieut. Gen. E. L. M. "Tommy": b. June 17, 1897, Westmount, Que. Soldier. Served W.W. I, 1914–19; won MC. Permanent forces, 1919–39; held various commands W.W. II, 1939–45, including command 1st Can. Corps, Italy, 1944. Dep. Min. of Veteran Affairs, 1950–54. Chief of Staff, UNTSO, 1954–56. Commander, UNEF, 1956–59. Adviser on disarmament, 1960–68.

CADIEUX, Joseph Alphonse Léo: b. May 28, 1908, St. Jerome, Que. Newspaperman. War correspondent, *La Presse*, Montreal, 1944. Elec. to H. of C. for Terrebonne, g.e. 1962; re-elec. 1963, 1965, 1968. Assoc. Min. of National Defence, Feb. 15, 1965. Min. of National Defence 1967–70.

CLARK, William Donaldson: b. July 28, 1916, Haltwhistle, Northumberland. Journalist. British Information Service in U.S., 1938–46. Diplomatic correspondent, *Observer*, 1950–55. Public Relations Adviser to Prime Minister, 1955–56. Dir. of Overseas Development Inst., 1960–68. Dir. of Information and Vice-Pres., World Bank, 1968.

COTÉ, Ernest A.: b. June 12, 1913, Edmonton, Alta. Lawyer. Served overseas W.W. II, 1939–44. Joined External Affairs, 1945. First Sec., Canada House, London, 1949–52. Asst. Dep. Min. of Northern Af-

*Up to 1968.

323

fairs, 1955–63. Dep. Min. of Northern Affairs, 1963–68. Amb. to Finland, 1972–75.

FEAVER, Herbert Frederick Brooks-Hill "Temp": b. June 18, 1907, Glace Bay, N.S. Diplomat. Joined External Affairs 1930. Second Sec., Can. Legation, Tokyo, 1939–41. Chief of Protocol, 1950–54. Amb. to Denmark, Switzerland, Mexico, Greece, 1958–70.

FOURNIER, Jean: b. July 18, 1914, Montreal, Que. Lawyer. Served overseas during W.W. II. Joined External Affairs, 1944. Consul Gen., Boston, 1954–57. Chairman, Quebec Civil Service Comm., 1964–71. Agent Gen., Quebec, in London, 1971–77.

GORDON, Walter Lockhart: b. Jan. 27, 1906, Toronto, Ont. Chartered accountant. Elec. to H. of C. for Davenport (Toronto), g.e. 1962; re-elec. 1963, 1965. Min. of Finance, 1963–65. Pres. of Privy Council, 1967–68.

GREEN, Howard Charles: b. Nov. 25, 1895, Kaslo, B.C. Barrister. Served overseas in W.W. I. Elec. to H. of C. for Vancouver South, g.e. 1935; re-elec. 1940, 1945; re-elec. for Vancouver Quadra 1949, 1953, 1957, 1958, 1962. Sec. of State for External Affairs, 1959–63.

HARRIMAN, William Averell: b. Nov. 15, 1891. N.R.A., 1934–35. Special envoy to UK and USSR, 1941–42. Ambassador to Moscow, 1943–46. U.S. Sec. of Commerce, 1946–48. Gov. of N.Y., 1955–58. Asst. Sec. of State for Far Eastern Affairs, 1961–63. Amb.-at-large, 1965–68.

HELLYER, Paul Theodore: b. Aug. 6, 1923, Waterford, Ont. Business-man. Elec. to H. of C. for Davenport (Toronto), g.e. 1949; re-elec. 1953; def. 1957; re-elec. for Trinity (Toronto), b.e. Dec. 15, 1958; re-elec. 1962, 1963, 1965. Assoc. Defence Min., 1957. Min. of National Defence, 1963–67.

HOLMES, John Wendell: b. June 18, 1910, London, Ont. Professor. Sec. Can. Inst. of Int. Affairs, Toronto, 1940–43. Joined External Affairs, 1943. Chargé d'Affaires, Moscow, 1947–48. Asst. Under-sec., 1953–60. Dir. Gen., CIIA, 1960–73.

HOME OF THE HIRSEL, Baron (Life Peer), Alexander Frederick Douglas-Home: b. July 2, 1903. M.P., South Lanark, 1931–45. M.P. Lanark Div. 1950–51. Sec. of State for Commonwealth Relations, 1955–60. Foreign Sec., 1960–63. Disclaimed peerage for life, 1963. Prime Minister, 1963–64. Foreign Sec., 1970–74.

IGNATIEFF, George: b. Dec. 16, 1913, St. Petersburg, Russia. Rhodes Scholar, Oxford U., 1935. Diplomat. Third Sec. Canada House, London, 1940–44. Adviser at UN, 1946–49. Amb. to Yugoslavia, 1956–58. Can. rep. at UN, 1966–68.

LODGE, Henry Cabot: b. July 5, 1902, Nahant, Mass. Senator for Massachusetts, 1936–43, 1946–53. U.S. rep. at UN, 1953–60. U.S. Amb. to Vietnam, 1963–64, 1965–67. U. S. del. to Vietnam Peace Talks, Paris, 1969.

MACDONALD, Malcolm John: b. 1901, Lossiemouth, Morayshire, Scotland. Son of Ramsay MacDonald. M.P., Bassetlaw Div., 1929–35; Ross and Cromarty, 1936–45. Sec. of State for Dominion Affairs, 1935–38. U.K. High Comm., Canada, 1941–46. Gov. of Malaya, 1946–48. Comm. Gen., S.E. Asia, 1948–55. U.K. High Comm., India, 1955–60. Gov. of Kenya, 1963–64. Br. special rep., Africa, 1966–69.

MARTIN, Paul Joseph James: b. June 23, 1903, Ottawa, Ont. Barrister. Del. to both League of Nations (Geneva), and UN (N.Y.). Elec. to H. of C. for Essex East (Ont.), g.e. 1935; re-elec. 1940, 1945, 1953, 1957, 1958, 1962, 1963, 1965. Sec. of State for External Affairs, 1963–68.

MATHESON, John Ross: b. Nov. 14, 1917, Arundel, Que. Barrister. Wounded in Italy in W.W. II. Elec. to H. of C. for Leeds (Ont.), b.e. May 29, 1961; re-elec. 1962, 1963, 1965.

O'HAGAN, Richard: b. March 23, 1928, Woodstock, N.B. Communicator. Special Asst. to Leader of Opposition, 1961–63. Press sec. to Prime Minister, 1963–66.

PEARSON, Geoffrey Arthur Holland: b. Dec. 25, 1927, Toronto, Ont. Son of Lester B. Pearson. Joined External Affairs, 1952. Seconded to NATO Secretariat, 1958–61. First Sec., Can. Embassy, Mexico, 1961–64. Counsellor, Can. High Comm. India, 1969–72.

PICKERSGILL, John W.: b. June 23, 1905, Wyecombe, Ont. Sec. to Prime Minister, 1937–52. Elec. to H. of C. for Bonavista-Twillingate (Nfld.), g.e. 1953; re-elec. 1957, 1958, 1962, 1963, 1965. Cabinet Minister St. Laurent and Pearson governments. Pres. of Canadian Transport Commission, 1967–72.

PIERCE, Sidney David: b. March 30, 1901, Montreal, Que. On 1924 Canadian Olympic team. Businessman. Canadian mission, Washington, 1940–44. Joined External Affairs, 1944. Amb. to Mexico, Paris, Brazil, etc. Can. negotiator, Kennedy Round, Geneva, 1965–67.

RASMINSKY, Louis: b. Feb. 1, 1908, Montreal, Que. Economist, banker. Staff, League of Nations (Geneva), 1930–39. Joined Bank of Canada, 1940. Foreign Exchange Control Board, 1940–42. Dep. Gov. of Bank of Canada, 1955–61. Gov. of Bank of Canada, 1961–73.

REID, Escott Meredith: b. Jan. 21, 1905, Campbellford, Ont. Rhodes Scholar, Oxford U., 1927. Diplomat. Sec., Can. Inst. of Int. Affairs, 1932–38. Second Sec., Can. Legation, Washington, 1939–41. Dep. Under-sec., External Affairs, 1948–52. High Comm., India, 1952–57. Dir. of Int. Bank for Reconstruction and Development, 1962–65.

RITCHIE, Charles Stewart Almon: b. Sept. 23, 1906, Halifax, N.S. Diplomat. Joined External Affairs, 1934. Second, First Sec., Canada House, London, 1939–45. Amb. to West Germany, 1954–58. Can. rep. UN 1958–62. Amb. U.S., 1962–66. High Comm. UK 1967–70.

RONNING, Chester: b. Dec. 13, 1894, Fancheng, China. Served with RAF, 1918. Lutheran missionary, China, 1923–27. RCAF Intelligence, 1942–45. Can. envoy, China, 1945–51. High Comm., India, 1957–64. Mission to North Vietnam, 1966.

RUSK, Dean: b. Feb. 9, 1909, Cherokee County, Ga. Rhodes Scholar, Oxford U., 1933. Educator. Official, U.S. Dept. of State, 1947–51. Pres. Rockefeller Foundation, 1952–60. Sec. of State, 1961–69. Prof., int. law, U. of Georgia, Athens, Ga., 1970.

SHARP, Mitchell William: b. May 11, 1911, Winnipeg, Man. Economist. Assoc. Dep. Min. of Trade and Commerce, 1951–58. Elec. to H. of C. for Eglinton (Toronto), g.e. 1963; re-elec. 1965, 1968, 1972, 1974. Min. of Finance, 1965–68. Min. of External Affairs, 1968–74.

SMITH, Arnold Cantwell: b. Jan. 18, 1915, Toronto, Ont. Rhodes Scholar, Oxford U., 1935. Diplomat. Editor, *The Baltic Times*, British Council rep. Tallinn, Estonia, 1939–40. Attaché, Brit. Embassy, Cairo, 1940–43. Sec. Can. Legation, USSR, 1943–45. Amb. to Egypt, 1958–61; to USSR 1961–63. Sec.-Gen. of Commonwealth, 1965–75.

WATKINS, Melville H.: b. May 15, 1932, McKellar, Ont. Economist. Prof. U. of Toronto. Headed Task Force on Foreign Investment in Canada, 1967–68.

WERSHOF, Max: b. Oct. 6, 1909, Ottawa, Ont. Diplomat. Joined External Affairs, 1937. Second Sec., Can. Legation, Washington, 1942–44. Counsellor, Canada House, 1948–50. Amb. to UN (Geneva), 1956–62. Amb. to Denmark, Czechoslovakia, 1967–74.

ZINK, Lubor: b. Sept. 20, 1920, Klapy, Czechoslovakia. Journalist. Fled from Nazis, 1939. Served with Czech forces in W.W. II. Press Officer to Czech Foreign Min. Jan Masaryk. Fled from Communists, 1948. Ottawa columnist 1962 on.

INDEX
(Excerpts from contributors are in italics.)